Finding Your Groove

Finding Your Groove is an inspiring guide that challenges you to rediscover your innate rhythm amid today's disjointed, fast-paced world. Drawing on the timeless language of music and the universal patterns of nature, this book reframes everyday challenges as opportunities for creative transformation and genuine connection.

Author Barry van Zyl, a veteran drummer and creative thinker from South Africa, and his co-author, UK business school academic Dr Chris Dalton, invite you to explore the profound impact of aligning your personal and professional lives with natural rhythms. Their insights blend personal narrative with practical reflection, offering a fresh perspective on leadership, collaboration, and self-awareness. By embracing the principles of Groove – from the beat of an individual's heart to the synchrony of a well-led team – you can foster resilience, spark innovation, and build more harmonious relationships at work and beyond. Whether you are seeking to enhance your creative potential or to inspire collective change in your organisation, this book provides a compelling, entertaining, and thought-provoking realignment with the pulse of life.

Finding Your Groove is a call to reclaim the joy of connection, balance, and mindful presence. It invites you to lead with authenticity in an increasingly complex world.

Barry van Zyl is a world-renowned musician with over 30 years of experience in the creative sector, from performance and production to education, strategy, and business development. Having toured the world for 21 years with South Africa's most famous export, Johnny Clegg, and while working with artists such as Annie Lennox, Ladysmith Black Mambazo, Peter Gabriel, and Die Antwoord, Barry completed an Executive MBA at Henley Business School and is now focused on executive education in the areas of personal development, entrepreneurship, and innovation.

Chris Dalton is Associate Professor of Management Learning and module convener for Personal Development (PD) at Henley Business School. A creative tutor, he was recognised with a University Teaching Fellowship (2022) from Reading University. His research is focused on the use of reflection in personal development in post-experience management education. Chris has over 29 years of experience in management education and training. He is a certified coach and online tutor and has trained as a systemic constellations facilitator, regularly working with the public and private sector.

"How do you:

- Hack your Flow?
- Get into The Zone?
- Move with The Force?

Written by Barry van Zyl (my favorite drummer on the planet) and Dr Chris Dalton, *Finding Your Groove* explains how."

NINJA (Die Antwoord), *Multi-platinum international recording artist, South Africa*

"Barry van Zyl is one of those rare individuals who has managed to balance the magic of the heart with the logic of the head. By merging his deep musical experience gained from years of touring as an internationally acclaimed drummer, with his and Chris Dalton's combined passion for the harmonic development of human beings within a volatile and uncertain corporate world, they have found a unique insight into how leaders and teams can find their groove."

Pepe Marais, *Co-Founder and Group Chief Creative Officer at Joe Public*

"In *Finding Your Groove*, celebrated rock/jazz drummer Barry van Zyl and business educator/scholar Chris Dalton explore the power of rhythm in leadership and life. Part memoir, part jam session, this inspirational yet practical book introduces the notion of groove as a metaphor for the practice of effective leadership. The roles that discipline, narrative-building, and resonance play – combined with the aptitudes of reflection and adaptability – are central themes that drive this joyful, innovative book. It is all about leadership with swing, soul, and – at the risk of sounding playful – the art of not missing a beat!"

Anant K. Sundaram, *Clinical Professor of Business Administration, Tuck School of Business at Dartmouth*

"*Finding Your Groove* is a riff session between a world-class musician and a world-class business mind, the two of them jamming on notes universal to music and organizational theory. It's an improvisation—their minds leaping across keys and chords to explore the connecting patterns within us, between us, and all around us. Contrary to the popular idea that the world is disconnected, van Zyl and Dalton illuminate a world that is whole; a world from which we have fallen out of relationship. We find our way back to connection by finding our own unique pulsating groove that resonates in harmony with others and that world. Like the conversations that make up this book, we discover ourselves in the back-and-forth of dialogue."

Jim Ferrell, *bestselling author of* You and We: A Relational Rethinking of Work, Life, and Leadership

Finding Your Groove

Resonant Leadership in a Disconnected World

Barry van Zyl
and Chris Dalton

Routledge
Taylor & Francis Group
LONDON AND NEW YORK

Designed cover image: PLAINVIEW – Getty Images

First published 2026
by Routledge
4 Park Square, Milton Park, Abingdon, Oxon OX14 4RN

and by Routledge
605 Third Avenue, New York, NY 10158

Routledge is an imprint of the Taylor & Francis Group, an informa business

British Library Cataloguing-in-Publication Data
A catalogue record for this book is available from the British Library

ISBN: 978-1-032-76969-1 (hbk)
ISBN: 978-1-032-74409-4 (pbk)
ISBN: 978-1-003-48065-5 (ebk)

DOI: 10.4324/9781003480655

Typeset in Adobe Garamond Pro
by KnowledgeWorks Global Ltd.

Contents

Foreword by Paul Lindley .... **vii**
Preface (Finding *My* Groove) .... **ix**

1 Foundations of Groove **1**
1.1 Introduction 2
1.2 One Question, Two Approaches 8
1.3 The Essentials for Finding Your Groove 13
References 19

2 Notes on Individual Groove **21**
2.1 Just Turn Up. And Start. 23
2.2 Say Yes and Figure It Out 27
2.3 The Art of Practice 31
2.4 Multi-Level Groove 37
2.5 If You Can Sing It, You Can Play It 43
2.6 The Power of Words 48
2.7 The Groove of Physicality 53
2.8 The Theory of Reassembly 58
2.9 The Balance 64
References 68

3 Notes on Group Groove **71**
3.1 From Big Band to Genuine Brand 73
3.2 Forming the Band 78
3.3 The Pain of Failure (When the Student Is Ready, the Teacher Appears) 83
3.4 The Rehearsal Trap 87
3.5 A Freelancer's Medley: Talent + Hard Work + Authenticity 92
3.6 Tempo of Leadership 96
3.7 Voice(s) 101

3.8 Vibes Don't Lie: Find Your People, Find Your Edge 107
3.9 The Super Groove 111
References 114

4 Notes on Universal Groove 115
4.1 Breath and Beat: the Universal Groove 117
4.2 Finding and Feeling Groove 123
4.3 Change Pain 128
4.4 The Frequency of Resonance 133
4.5 Cultural Authenticity 140
4.6 The Beatles, Bieber, and a Tree 145
4.7 Shaking Things Up 150
4.8 What Moves You (On)? 154
4.9 Disconnected Leadership in a Resonant World? 159
References 163

Epilogue – the Coda 165

Appendix: Universal Values Questionnaire 167

Index 179

Foreword

Paul Lindley OBE

Leadership is about harmony. It's about finding a way to unite people behind a goal and make it meaningful for us all so that we are in step together. It's also about resonating with the world around us, aligning our actions with our values, and creating conditions where people and ideas can thrive. At its best, leadership is not a solitary endeavour but a shared rhythm – a groove – that draws on the creativity, resilience, and humanity of individuals and communities. This book, *Finding Your Groove: Resonant Leadership in a Disconnected World*, is a timely exploration of how we can all seek and sustain that harmony in today's complex and fragmented times.

My journey, from growing up in Zambia to founding Ella's Kitchen, the UK's biggest baby food brand and, now, as a social campaigner and Chancellor of the University of Reading, has taught me the power of connection, the importance of purpose and how vital authentic, trusted, leadership is to create change. The rhythms of my life have been shaped by values instilled early on: curiosity, bravery, and a deep commitment to creating opportunities for others, especially children. This book resonates with those values, offering a framework for understanding how individuals, groups, and organisations can work together to create something greater than the sum of their parts.

The authors, Barry van Zyl and Chris Dalton, bring a unique perspective to this task. Drawing on their experiences in music and management education, they weave insights from two seemingly disparate worlds to illuminate what it means to lead with resonance. Their partnership epitomises a core belief in my personal approach to leadership in recognising that everything is connected, so it's for leaders to show how we can join the dots and also recognise the power of connecting diverse and different experiences – especially needed in a disconnected world. Their exploration of groove as a metaphor, as a dynamic balance of upbeats and downbeats, individuality and collective alignment, feels especially poignant in our fast-changing, unpredictable world.

One of the ideas in this book that particularly struck me is its call to rethink how we align our personal and professional lives with the broader rhythms of nature and society. This aligns closely with the work I've dedicated my life to: creating environments where children can thrive, where their well-being is prioritised, and where they have the tools to find their own groove. As Nelson Mandela famously said, "There can be no keener revelation of a society's soul than the way in which it treats its children."[1] Our ability to nurture and support the next generation depends on leaders who can listen, adapt, and inspire.

This book also challenges us to think critically about how we make sense of the world and how we create meaning. It's a call to embrace emergence and complexity, to look for the patterns that connect rather than divide. These are lessons that go beyond leadership; they are lessons for life. Whether we're leading a global organisation, a community initiative, or a family, finding our groove means staying attuned to the ever-changing dynamics of the world around us while remaining rooted in our values.

In *Finding Your Groove*, Barry and Chris have crafted a guide that is as thoughtful as it is practical, as reflective as it is inspiring. It reminds us that leadership is not about control or certainty but trust, rhythm, and resonance. It's about finding the courage to lead in harmony with others and with the world.

I hope this book inspires you to find your groove and to lead in a way that brings people together, strengthens communities, and leaves the world better than you found it. It's a journey well worth taking.

Keep Smiling

Paul Lindley
Oxfordshire, England
June 2025

Note

1. Address by President Nelson Mandela at the launch of the Nelson Mandela Children's Fund, Pretoria, 8 May 1995.

Preface (Finding *My* Groove)

This book represents the culmination of my learning, passions, experiences, and belief in the power of connection and flow.

Its genesis was directly linked to note-taking. Different kinds of notes have always held a special place in my life. First, as a drummer, musical notation can leapfrog over hours that might be needed to memorise a piece of music, getting me to the creative and fulfilling action far more quickly. Next, the performed notes, the sounds that come from the instrument, form the foundation of rhythm, are the building blocks of music and the portal to the elusive state of groove. Finally, as a thinker, my own notes are the fleeting ideas I scribble down, often without knowing their full significance until much later. In my writing, I started making sense of who I was, a former drummer showing up as an MBA student, by writing my thoughts down.

In this book, the various short sections called "Notes" are expanded versions of my original reflections and represent my search for identity. What emerged from this process was a new level of self-awareness and being better equipped to answer the question we must all ask: Who am I?

To complete the circle, who better to have as my co-writer than the person who triggered this transition and guided my personal development? Chris Dalton provides rigour and critical thinking, unpacking my reflections into language and coherence that helps me understand myself better. This means that the reader may have the same experience.

Notes are the beginning of everything – the spark of connection, the seed of creation, the rhythm of thought.

Barry van Zyl
Cape Town, South Africa

Chapter 1

Foundations of Groove

"Groove"
From the OED (2024):
groove, v
UK/gruːv/, U.S./gruv/
Forms: *Middle English groof, 1700s gruve.*
Etymology: < groove n. Compare Flemish groeven 'cælare, sculpere, cauare' (Kilian).

1. (passive and intransitive) To fit or be fitted as into a groove.
2. (figurative) To settle or be settled into (or in) a routine of work, habit, etc.
3. (intransitive) To play jazz or similar music with "swing"; to be "in the groove"; to dance or listen to such music with great pleasure; hence, to make good progress or co-operate; to get on well with someone; to make love. Also transitive, to play (music) swingingly; to give pleasure to (a person). slang (originally U.S.).

This book uses the third of the above meanings as its starting point for learning, leading, and living well in complex and disconnected times.

The term "groove" became culturally popular in the 1950s and 1960s, primarily linked to music genres like jazz, rhythm and blues, and rock 'n' roll. Originally, it referred to the physical grooves on vinyl records that played music. In jazz, it described steady and syncopated rhythms that supported improvisation, over the structure of a song. The 1950s introduced bebop and cool jazz, with "grooving" signifying being in sync with the music. In the 1960s, it extended to rock 'n' roll and soul, symbolising a relaxed alignment with cultural vibes. "Groovy" became slang for something cool or fashionable, representing the 1960s counterculture's focus on

DOI: 10.4324/9781003480655-1

spontaneity and creativity. Groove reflected the intersection of music technology and cultural movements during a transformative period in history.

We are at another important transformative moment that will influence our political, economic, social and technological decisions. What is required is a profound, underlying shift in our relationship with our environment (our ecology). The future of management and leadership will be defined by its response to these challenges here and now. That response must have two aspects: our awareness of our sense-making, or how we know what we know, and mastery of a relational view of society and nature, or how in tune with reality our thinking is.

1.1 Introduction

Can You Fix the World?

This book is about using the business of rhythm to understand the rhythm of business. You will find that a big part of this question is understanding the rhythm of you.

Commerce, business, and organisational life all have a beat. The basic goal of management and leadership has always been to ensure that "the beat goes on." Recently, this goal has increasingly included the injunction that it does so sustainably. The 21st century calls for coherent and integrated leadership like no other period in human history. With every rotation around the sun, the scale and scope of human achievement and invention expand our horizons and ambitions. We understand so much about how the world works yet still find ourselves locked into a messy, existential reckoning with reality. A growing body of evidence suggests that our modern lifestyle is at odds with what the environment will support. Our rhythm is off. These disparities can be observed in individual, organisational, and societal trends. Here are some examples:

1. For an Individual

According to the World Bank (2025), we are living longer. In 2022, the average global aggregated life expectancy was 72 years, up from 68 in 2000 and 56 in the early 1960s when the authors of this book were born. Lower infant mortality explains some of this, as does the improved chances of surviving the most typical threats adults face from disease. But are we seeing a corresponding improving trend in quality of life?

Poor sleep patterns, for example, are affecting our health. Technology at work and home encroaches on us; excessive screen time, scrolling, and emails at all hours impact basic human biology. We require a certain amount of quality sleep for optimal physical and mental health, and our increasingly sedentary lifestyle is creating mental conflicts and physical consequences, such as obesity, cardiovascular conditions, allergies, and musculoskeletal problems. These consequences limit our freedom to make intelligent and informed choices.

Humans have been affecting their environment through agriculture and industry for millennia. However, people are still increasingly likely to live in urban areas, cut off from anything like true wilderness. Thus, it should be no surprise that our examples and metaphors for self-understanding and well-being are mechanistic and systematic.

2. For an Organisation

Organisations are systems with one set of internal relationships within their boundaries and another set beyond which governs context. Internally, cultural imbalances increasingly produce norms of overwork to meet short-term productivity priorities. This is stressful, bringing long working hours and burnout. Hierarchical structures often perpetuate power imbalances and hinder the free flow of information needed to ensure long-term productivity. This short-term focus misaligns and weakens an organisation's resilience and adaptability, hindering its ability to navigate change and innovate. Faced with a challenge to their individuality and autonomy, staff disengage and, eventually, do not stay where they are not fulfilled. Organisations that do not understand and adapt to this context become rigid and brittle.

3. For a Society

Most of us recognise that we live in societies that promote consumerism and materialism. Until now, we haven't questioned it. Our search for novelty in our material possessions has become a validation of success via external markers. This emphasis on material wealth can disconnect societal values from sustainable individual health and well-being. A celebrity culture, for example, promotes social comparison, which can quickly become a toxic spiral. Meanwhile, rampant consumerism will, unless designed not to, deliver unsustainable resource consumption alongside temporary profits. The environmental impact of our modern lifestyle, resulting from resource-intensive practices and overconsumption, is at odds with the Earth's ecological limits.

Eventually, this misalignment with environmental realities has severe consequences now visible in climate change, loss of biodiversity, and ecological imbalance. Until now, this has been possible to put out of mind with the hope that someone further up the decision tree will put in place a plan to minimise the impact on future generations while not damaging the chances of having it all in the current generation. This is now looking increasingly unlikely.

Every individual has a unique story to tell and life to lead. The health and well-being of the human collective, subjected to rapid urbanisation, technological advancements, and changing social dynamics, demands we all stop and think. The accompanying crises of mental health and social cohesion are no longer over the horizon as a theoretical future consequence.

In sum, if you are living in harmony with yourself, employed with purpose on an activity bringing value to the world without damaging it, and contributing to the stewardship of whatever future generations will need to have available to make the choices to do the same, then congratulations. You are very much an outlier. For the rest of us, things feel disconnected and, frankly, we are having difficulty making sense of it all.

Our response to all this is a word: **Groove**.

What Is Groove?

As mentioned, Groove originates from the North American jazz tradition in the early 1900s, describing a rhythm that "swings," directly referencing West African (Yoruba) traditional rhythms. The feel of these rhythms is a harmonic mix of two pulses, counted as groups of 2 and groups of 3 at the same time (harmonic rhythm). This gave the sense of a swinging or circular motion, which was very different from the rigid linear feel of popular music of the time. This was also counted in groups of 2 or 3 but not at the same time (linear rhythm). Think of English or Dutch popular music in the 20s and 30s, and dance styles like the foxtrot or waltz, compared to the blues, stride piano, or early forms of rock 'n' roll, and the dance styles made famous by Elvis.

Groove progressed to be the term used by musicians across multiple genres to describe the experience of finding resonance with one another, deeply connected by the language of rhythm, not words. Groove was also borrowed by listeners when experiencing a performance that was "grooving." Here's how Barry recalls it:

> As a young music student in California in the 1990s, I quickly absorbed the lingo and would say things like the band was "grooving" or that a drummer had a "massive groove." This was an attempt to articulate the gravity-defying experience of what I later understood as the rhythm of nature and the interconnectivity of all things. I still use groove as a quality filter to describe situations of flow and resonant frequencies, which could range from the activities during a workday (I was in the groove today!) to the flow of a long run on a perfect morning (what a groove!).

It's interesting to note that in the same way that education and intelligence are not terms for the same thing, technically schooled musicians and musicians who understand Groove are not interchangeable realities. Many musicians with doctorates have never experienced groove in performance, and many natural musicians with no formal education create groove with every performance.

The central insight of Groove is that, when looked at correctly, our messy life is a polyrhythm, an emergent pattern of two or more different rhythms running simultaneously. Life is a nested system of organic rhythms, flows, and complimentary *upbeats* and *downbeats*. In our attempts to control things, we tend to swim against the stream, at odds with ourselves, our collectives, and nature. Featuring deep lessons and truths from a lifetime spent in the creative world of music, this book is about how to look more correctly at the world as it is. Groove is the only source we need to find our place. We access Groove at three levels or layers that are intertwined and interconnected:

Individual Groove comes from resonance in the basics, such as nutrition, sleep, and exercise. It speaks through and speaks to the peaks and troughs (upbeats/downbeats) of chronobiology and flow.
Group Groove equals resonance among and with others. It is the level of communication, multiple perspectives, and innovation/creativity. Finally,
Universal Groove taps into the totality of the surrounding environment as every human experiences it. Groove is the universal pattern, **and** it is your alignment with it.

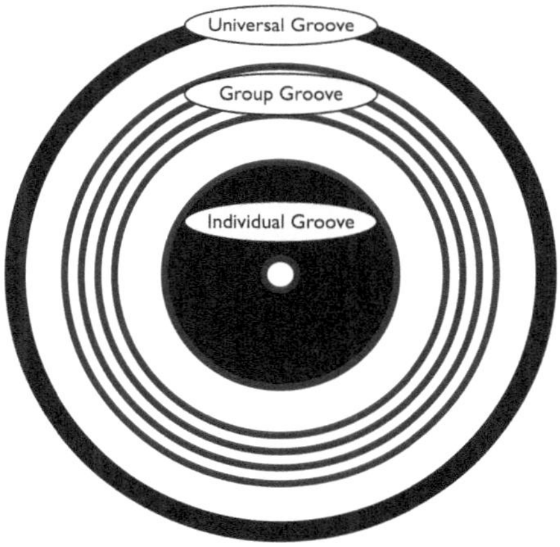

This book explores the experience of life, work, and being – as you perceive them. We do not suggest what your answers should be; we aim to guide you toward the kind of questions you might ask.

The Rhythms of Life: Flow

Efrain Toro, the great Puerto Rican musician, teacher, and surfer, uses the word groove to describe things working well together. This could be a bass player and a drummer creating magic, a football team winning effortlessly, or a researcher reaching a breakthrough in a moment of inspiration. Using the lens of physics, when a field is disturbed, movement is created in waves. With an observer, the movement patterns are experienced as rhythm. We use numbers to describe these frequencies – whether in musical rhythm, pitch or colour spectrums, or the periodic table of elements.

Think of a pebble thrown into a still pond. The ripples follow a perfect rhythmic order from the primary impact, just as in music the overtones spread outward in waves from the fundamental note. These patterns form a Groove, where everything is as it must be, and everything is contained in everything else.

All the tones in an octave are contained in the sound of middle C on a piano, although the primary note is the loudest. This is the same for every note played. Opening and raising awareness of the patterns or rhythms in and around us is a way to make sense of what would otherwise be perceived as random or chaotic. For this book, Groove conveys a state of coordination, of things working well together, applied to a far broader scope than musical rhythm.

This is aligned to the state sometimes called Flow, a term coined by the Hungarian-American psychologist Mihaly Csikszentmihalyi (2002), who used this to describe a mental state of total absorption that a person may experience when their skill or competence level is in harmony with the challenge of a task, activity, or process. In Flow, time melts away, and neither internal thoughts nor external distractions seem to interrupt or interfere. There is a sense of being fully present and connected, perhaps if only fleeting.

Groove describes the interconnectivity of all things. David Bohm called this the Implicate Order (2002). Philosopher Alan Watts, speaking on the Tao (Watts and Huang 2019), describes *Li* as all things in nature following the principles of Flow. Physics describes the state of resonance (or Groove) simply as different elements working well together. Whether we scale from tiny to massive, we see a systemic pattern that to the naive mind would seem to be a mess, "a glorious mess," as physicist Dr Richard Feynman called it. Examples of Groove in the world around us are waves at the beach, cars on bustling freeways, the heartbeat of a newborn baby, cycles in equity markets, breathe in and breathe out …

To study the phenomenon of Groove is to explore how we can improve our personal coordination with our networks, organisations, the global economy, and with nature. Musical rhythm serves as a valuable tool and metaphor to illuminate these aspects, helping to make sense of what we are calling the Glorious Mess. Rhythm can exist without melody, but melody cannot exist without rhythm. Rhythm is a universal fundamental that underpins all of nature.

How the Book Is Organised, and How You Can Use It

Chapter 1 sets the stage, beginning with this section on what we think is the overwhelming call to action sitting around us in our present context. We start by shaping our organising principle, Groove. We will introduce ourselves and set the scene for how our writing rhythm illustrates the book's point. The last section of this chapter is a more in-depth look at three concepts guiding us as we travel through the remainder of the book, which is organised into three longer chapters.

Notes

Chapters 2, 3, and 4 contain nine "Notes" each. These are collected from Barry's incredible experiences as a professional musician and world traveller. Each is juxtaposed with Chris's responses as a business school academic specialising in Management Learning and Personal Development. We chose the term Note because a note represents something fundamental in music. A single note can set the tone for an entire piece, just as one idea can transform how we think or act. In writing, a note is a fleeting thought made tangible, capturing what might otherwise be lost. As a verb, to note something is to take it on. So, our Notes, 27 in total, are meant to do all these things: resonate within you, leave a record you can return to, and ask you to pay further attention.

Barry's early musical education was self-directed. He learned by ear, replicating rhythms and sounds he encountered. It wasn't until much later, when auditioning for a prestigious music school in California, that he recognised the limitations of his purely organic approach. The rigorous demands of sight-reading and high-stakes performances required preparation far beyond his intuitive understanding. To bridge this gap, he invested countless hours in mastering the theory and application of musical notation, transforming what was once an abstract and intimidating system into a tool for increased expression and collaboration. The effort paid off, allowing him to engage with complexity, participate in ensembles, and translate intricate ideas into performance.

Years later, when starting an MBA, he was struck by the parallels between musical notation and note-taking in an academic setting. On his first day at Henley Business School, he recalls that they were encouraged to write reflectively, capturing thoughts and observations as they emerged. This practice resonated deeply with him. Much like musical notation, writing can transform flickering ideas into enduring insights.

The act of writing, of notating, has transformative power. It bridges the ephemeral and the concrete, turning abstract notions into actionable knowledge. This realisation has guided both of us in our observations, writing, reflection, and, ultimately, acceptance.

In line with the three levels of our concentric application of the principle of Groove, we group these Notes into three categories:

Chapter 2 Notes on Individual Groove: The ever-evolving conception of 'self'
Chapter 3 Notes on Group Groove: Finding and being yourself with and through others
Chapter 4 Notes on Universal Groove: Reconciling self with the widest contexts

Like all categories, these contain a certain amount of arbitrariness. It might be possible to swap them around, and the point would still be valid. Judgement, ours and yours, is always present. The underlying logic says that relationships are interconnected, and we each try to map this out in our own way. We deliberately avoided predicting or pre-construing the destination in our writing, which would contradict our thesis that life is emergent. We were open to being surprised by each other and by ourselves. We hope this element of openness to surprise comes across, and we hope even more that it rubs off on you. Barry closes the book with an Epilogue.

As you read, consider:

What rhythms currently shape how you lead or work?
Are they intentional or reactive?
Identify one area where you feel "out of sync," What one small adjustment could you make to restore alignment this week?

If you are open to *Finding Your Groove*, this book will help you.

1.2 One Question, Two Approaches

And We May Ask Ourselves, Well, How Did We Get Here?

Because this book is a dialogue between people as well as between ideas, we wanted to share how and why we decided to write it together. To help us do this, we used a tool, the Universal Values Questionnaire, taken from the Personal Development module on the Henley Executive MBA.

At their second workshop, every MBA participant at Henley is invited to explore what lies below their actions and behaviours. That top level of "What I do" is seldom a random event. It is informed by individually held beliefs that are often buried or mechanical. Once identified, these personal beliefs may feel like the final explanation. They are, however, selections from a finite set of acceptable choices within the accepted boundary of whatever collective belief systems and social principles have conditioned us. This includes our cultural background and family upbringing. Because there are differences between collective belief systems (for example, from one place to another or from one time to another), more serious conflicts can arise when there is a difference of belief between people or groups. If our different individual beliefs don't have a shared ground of a common set of principles, we will carry on arguing or miscommunicating indefinitely.

In this case, the next step is to assume that there must be common ground below our collective differences. If we cannot find this, and going there may require you to park some deeply engrained rules which have been very important in your definition of self, then there really will be no way of working on global issues. This deepest layer, the one we all share and that underpins all our differences and similarities, is a *universal* common ground. The universal must at least be assumed to exist between all human beings for open communication and the resolution of conflicts. If you don't see it and see only the differences, then you are restricted in your principles, beliefs, and, ultimately, your actions.

This is captured for us in the concept of **Universal Values**, or the basic categories of "why" that we all share, without exception. Universal means the level of zero exceptions. Having evolved, naturally, our universals are very old and impervious to change. In groups and as individuals, we work up from this common ground to discover, create, and appreciate unique communities, variations in organisational cultures, and differences between individuals. The social world is a rich web of differences and in the end, we are all seeking answers to the same questions of life.

To help our students get there, the questionnaire opens with four open-ended questions:

1. *What are the three most important words or phrases in your life, and why?*
2. *Where did you grow up? How did that place and society shape the kind of person you have become?*
3. *What have been the most important lessons passed on to you by significant people in your life?*
4. *What would you say are the three most important words or phrases in the organisation where you work? Why?*

We ask our students to make notes and refer to them as they continue their learning and studies. To begin writing this book, Barry and I each developed our narratives for this section using the questionnaire tasks as prompts. We have included the questionnaire as an appendix at the end of the book so you can do the same.

Barry

Three Important Words/Phrases: Personal Life

Energy I've always been fascinated by the creative process and the ignition of energy. I feel this as a state of flow, when an hour feels like a minute, and one is only where one is, nowhere else.

Listen My focus on listening stems from years as an improvising musician. I've realised that this critical skill is important in human-to-human awareness, and especially listening beyond words.

Authenticity Cultural authenticity enabled decades of success as a solo creative. I am passionate about this and use it as a quality filter every day. Rich stories sung in a raspy voice are so much more interesting than virtuosic karaoke!

I have further divided this personal journey piece into two life chapters, A and B.

Life Chapter A: the Business of Rhythm

I grew up on the southeast coast of South Africa in a city called Port Elizabeth, a blue-collar working town propped up by the motor industry and sprinkled with descendants of the 1820 colonial settlers. My earliest memories were of being mesmerised by the shiny drum sets played at shows and events. By age eight, I had built a drum set out of cake tins and was driving the neighbours up the wall!

My learning style was to observe, mentally record, and then re-create later, and to this day, I can absorb new knowledge best by watching rather than reading. As a 12-year veteran drummer, I realised that I could make more pocket money than my peers by playing gigs (with much older bandmates) *and* get the attention of girls. I was hooked!

Much later in life, through critical reflection and journaling, I realised that my core drivers at this early age were to move people positively through performance and the business of rhythm. The drums were a great tool, and I mastered the craft. Now I'm fascinated by the rhythm of business, and although the drums are no longer a key component, the core driver remains.

Through raised awareness of self, I realised that my broad strategy, used unconsciously throughout a career in music, was to "follow my fear." I would continuously place myself in uncomfortable situations where I would have to stretch to perform as required by the context. As soon as any feeling of comfort and complacency set in, I would disrupt my status quo, for example by moving to a bigger city and industry.

My parents supported my career choice, which in the 1980s in Port Elizabeth was a tough call. Eventually, my mother re-mortgaged her small property to enable me to attend a prestigious music college in California. This kick-started a learning journey which continued to a scholarship from the leading global contemporary music college, in Massachusetts on the East Coast. The transition from self-taught prodigy to formal learning as a student of music was a pivotal time, and I was captivated by the excitement of absorbing powerful curriculum and content, while also daunted by the complexity and time required to absorb this new understanding fully.

Many mentor figures emerged over my *business of rhythm* timeline, from teenage upstart to seasoned professional. All of these provided the same key elements in that they spoke to me as an equal, saw talent in me that I perhaps did not, and were energetic, creative thinkers. The most significant of these was Efrain Toro – performer, educator, and surfer – who resonated with my need for more than a single-minded approach to music. Intuitively, I felt that music was a tiny slice of a much bigger connected reality. Efrain had a rare combination of incredible musical talent (in my opinion, far ahead of an already stellar faculty list at this LA institution), academic depth, and formidable intellect beyond just music theory and performance, which started widening my thinking as a young music-obsessed student.

Life Chapter B: the Rhythm of Business

After decades of international-level concert tours, and as a true global citizen, I collided with Henley Business School. This was not random. For the last ten years of my touring career, I had started to feel itchy and scratchy, as if the (very necessary) singular purpose lens of the elite performer was not enough. I felt increasingly one-dimensional and bored. I still wanted to know more. As testimony to *"when the student is ready, the teacher will appear,"* I met the Dean of Henley Business School Africa, and to make a far longer story short, I graduated with an MBA, continued to learn, and began working for the business school in the UK and South Africa, tutoring on the MBA, developing business, and designing programs.

Mentors who have emerged in my more recent *business* timeline have all demonstrated the same three essential elements mentioned in my Chapter A.

The most significant one has been Chris Dalton, my co-author of this work, and the Henley MBA module convener for Personal Development. Like Efrain, Chris is a rare mix of academic rigour and formidable thinking, equally at ease in the creative world of ideas and magic making. The power of the Personal Development workshops during my MBA at Henley fed into my curiosity for "more," manifested in me being a tutor on Chris's international PD team, and has led to this book.

By the end of my MBA study in 2017, I was ready to take ownership of my identity and purpose and move on from my *"Barry the drummer"* persona. I see this as an exciting new chapter, still following the fear, and when people ask me if I miss playing music, the carefully considered answer is no. I now find the same excitement in delivering workshops to executives and tutoring on the MBA programme that I did as a teenager "jamming" for hours in rehearsal rooms. And I'm just getting started …

Three Important Words/Phrases: Career and Professional

No Free Lunch While I believe in working smart and creating the best conditions for success as efficiently as possible, showing up and doing the work is a necessity, not a choice. If the elements align, then inspiration follows simply starting …

Drone View I am determinedly building the polyrhythmic habit of seeing from above while also being immersed in the details of things.

Just Getting Started! After a lifetime in the business of rhythm, I feel the energy of my teenage self when making sense of the rhythm of business!

Chris

Three Important Words/Phrases: Personal

Ecology I've always been interested in patterns of relationship, form, and natural balance, even before I knew what these things were from a more scientific viewpoint.

Humour The shortest distance between two people.

Words I've known since school that language is where I make my home, find out what I think, and have a chance of reaching others.

Everyone grows up in changing places, and everyone grows up in changing times.

First, **place**. My geographical "where" expands or contracts depending on whom I am talking to, where we are, and perhaps why. Our stories are nested. I grew up a European, and sometimes that is my defining sensibility. This is so within the United Kingdom, my country of birth, or whenever I'm in London, my city of birth. Beyond that, am I British? English? Irish? I can claim to be any, depending on context and purpose. Is that the answer to who I am?

My formative years of education and establishing and embarking on being me were played out in a quiet, seaside town called Deal, on the Kent coast just about in sight of France. Growing up by the sea makes one wonder what's over the horizon. Doing so in a small town makes a person hungry for the city. All roads lead away.

Next, **time**. I was born in the 1960s and was too young to learn much about growing up there. I matured as an autonomous being during the crossover period in British society between 1977 and 1987, a turbulent interval politically, socially, and culturally. I left school at 17 and took myself to the capital. My London years were embroidered during this time. This growing up was me staking a (naïve) claim of having no self-doubt at the same time as having no self-confidence. That innocence led me to a sort of creative freedom and an economic dead end. I travelled, and my growing up ended one day in 1985 on a kibbutz in Israel where, without warning, I had the distinctly odd epiphany during a work shift in the gardens of discovering the profound, inner value of a day's hard work. Crucially, I was working on my own that day. I sensed the pleasure of a useful task well done for the sake of doing it well. Before that, I had a relationship with work that was haphazard, superficial, occasionally interesting and often unproductive. I was still young, and things did not change everywhere in my life, yet I had that information – intimately experienced and understood – to go to when I needed it later. Much later, I learned in Japan about "yotoku" (doing good things openly), and "intoku" (doing good things behind the scenes). This was an *intoku* realisation about good work done, without the social reward of recognition.

Back to place, and now in the family system. As the youngest of three, the budget of family expectations had been largely spent by the time schooling came to me. Brought up by a devoted and patient single mother, I was not burdened by someone else's purpose. I had a lot of freedom to explore and think for myself, which helped me develop a strong sense of independence, and I still maintain a child-like freedom to wonder. I spent much of my formative space inside my head (another version of "place"). Wonderers tend to be wanderers; this was my pattern for my first 25 years. Along the way, I met some great teachers. What they had in common was a love of thinking.

In 1992, I experienced a pivotal moment in Budapest. The timing was ideal, as I was living in a country undergoing a significant transition. I discovered a business school in need of native English speakers. Additionally, I was motivated by the responsibility of raising two young children, and I wanted to prove to myself that I had the tenacity to succeed. I have been working in management education and academia ever since. In 2005, I was determined to secure a position at Henley, and I persisted until they finally hired me.

In 2013, I experienced a third significant turning point when I obtained my Ph.D. This achievement greatly impacted my approach to working with MBAs at Henley and transformed my thinking. As Barry mentioned, this is where our paths came together and merged rather than just crossing. One of the most rewarding aspects of my work is the opportunity to connect with highly skilled and enthusiastic professionals worldwide. When I encounter someone who shares my perspective and enthusiasm, it becomes a mutually beneficial experience.

Three Important Words/Phrases: Career and Work

The Middle Distance The "between" that divides the extreme close-up of focus and concentration and the widescreen, far-off vision of the horizon. It is in the middle distance where "now" looks to find patterns. It is where leadership communication is aimed and where understanding crosses the threshold.

"Yes, and ..." The antidote to "yes, but ..." "Yes, and ..." is a form of ownership. An open and positive mindset that anchors us in the present moment, with what is actually going on rather than what we wish were the case.

Emancipation There are three kinds of freedom: freedom *from*, freedom *to*, and freedom *in*. The one that resonates most for me is the idea of education giving you "freedom in" any and every situation in life. To set yourself free from barriers and restraints to experience life as it is. I believe this is the true purpose of education.

That's the start for us. Before you read further, please visit the questionnaire at the end of the book and write a version about you.

1.3 The Essentials for Finding Your Groove

Sense-Making for Management and Leadership

In this section, we will discuss and examine three important concepts related to Groove. This will help you better understand and implement the rest of the book.

As a leader, it's essential to understand the factors that influence growth. Much management thinking and theory over the last 50 years has focused on growth as both the means and the end of doing business. Historically, we've measured organisational success simply by "more", which we have tracked in tangibles such as turnover and profit, as well as intangibles such as culture and reputation. Our society is consumer-driven, where the desired output is always more consumption. It should be noted that the word consume has a Latin root meaning to destroy, wear away, or use up, and even to squander.

We accept that this is where we must begin. We think that, if not dealt with, we will leave a toxic legacy for everyone's children and grandchildren. Our assumptions have consequences. We see the issue as a crisis of sense-making. We need to think more critically about our ignorance of sense-making.

- Until recently, our appetite for *organisational* growth was satisfied by an inexhaustible set of recipes that exploit the planet's resources.
- Our appetite for *personal* growth has increasingly been satiated by material outputs from a consumer economy. Money, of course, is a proxy for success, as are possessions, social status, and the acceleration of the speed of gratification. We prioritise shortcuts to knowledge and crave quick solutions.

These create norms. A norm describes a pattern, an unspoken set of rules designed to produce a precise result. Norms govern how we think, communicate, and make decisions, how we work together in teams, and the objectives we set ourselves. They also establish relationships among people and between organisations or industries. Because norms are taken for granted, they are rarely seen and almost never questioned.

We believe we must challenge whether the norms in organisational and personal sense-making are healthy, or, in fact, whether they align with reality.

We begin with seeing how (paradoxically perhaps) **pattern and order** are essential for creativity in leadership and management. Next, we cover the important field of **chronobiology**. We close with some thoughts on an exciting area in science, **emergence.**

Pattern and Order

Patterns are forms that can be observed in many different types of systems and phenomena, including natural systems, social systems, and abstract concepts such as language or mathematics. What is the difference between pattern and order?

1. A pattern is an *inherent regularity* between the components or variables of a system. Patterns exist whenever the conditions are right for an underlying potential to be played out in events. A pattern indicates some sort of system of organisation, and we still have to decipher what kind of arrangement or state that is. Another word for this deciphering process is "order."
2. Order is a *description* of the state of organisation or arrangement of a pattern. More precisely, order is a perception. A system may be described as in a state of order or disorder of the organisation and the predictability of its components *as we perceive them*. Order is a *social* description of how various elements within a system are connected and interact with each other.

In living systems, the essential feature of a pattern is that it carries enough information for self-organisation to be recognised as such. Complex living systems, such as natural ecosystems, are full of patterns, many of which are sophisticated systems of communication and control.

Sometimes, pattern and order are closely connected. In the **social world**, our descriptions of patterns (or order) arise from human thought and communication, and they can also develop into established patterns themselves. Social constructs describe social theory and can transform into theories in their own right. Leadership and management theories fall within the realm of social science, and the way we describe these ideas can then be adopted as a pattern. This description can then be interpreted by others, creating a continuous cycle. Being a critical thinker means you have to spot when this is happening.

A society that appears to have stable governing functions and institutions is considered to be in a state of order, while a society experiencing chaos and civil unrest is seen as being in a state of disorder. In both cases, the patterns (what is happening) are the same as the order (how we perceive it). In social contexts, understanding patterns and order can help identify trends, make predictions, and comprehend the underlying causes of social phenomena. The behaviour of a particular group can be observed and studied in terms of the regularities in its internal and external relationships, an approach that is central to the field of marketing.

However, the situation is different when it comes to underlying patterns (regularities and relationships) in the **natural world**. Nature consists of patterns that operate whether we know about them or not. Our descriptions of nature attempt to give order to a pattern. Because our descriptions are not the same as reality, they tend to be incomplete or flawed.

In living systems (natural ecosystems) and social systems, patterns are how information is transmitted and processed. Communication is more than a transfer of information. It is a transfer of *relationships* between elements. In leadership, communication is the process of creating and maintaining social patterns.

Understanding patterns leads to the next problem for you as a manager – how do you know if the order you impose on a pattern is accurate and meaningful? As an observing and curious species, we're hard-wired to look for the order in a pattern (even when there is no pattern there). That's the first problem: is there a pattern at all? The second problem is that we are looking for this through our conditioning.

As social animals, we rely on embedded social rules (biases) to define order. A good example of this is confirmation bias, which is the tendency to seek out and interpret information in a way that supports our existing beliefs or hypotheses. Many thinking biases have been identified, and these can lead to errors if we interpret patterns uncritically, favouring convenience or desirability over objectivity.

Does all that sound overly intellectual and abstract? Well, to paraphrase Albert Einstein, you can't solve a problem using the same type of thinking that caused it. If you don't know what kind of thinking you're doing, your attempts to improve things are likely to fail. It's not enough to know *what* to think; you must know *how* to think.

Leadership Application Identify a recurring pattern in your work. Is it serving you, or does it need disruption?

Chronobiology

Chronobiology is the study of how living organisms, including humans, respond to changes in light, temperature, and other environmental cues over the course of a day, month, or year. Research has shown that biological rhythms can significantly impact productivity, mood, and overall well-being. This field of biology is becoming increasingly relevant in the business world.

One of chronobiology's key findings is that our bodies have an internal circadian rhythm, a 24-hour cycle that regulates many of our physiological processes, including our sleep-wake cycle, hormone levels, and metabolism. This rhythm is controlled by a small group of cells in the hypothalamus called the suprachiasmatic nucleus (SCN). The SCN is sensitive to light and temperature changes. It receives information from the eyes about the presence of light and sends signals to other parts of the body to adjust our physiology accordingly.

In the business world, understanding the circadian rhythm can be a powerful tool for leaders to optimise their performance and that of their employees. For example, research has shown that people often tend to be more alert and productive in the morning and that their cognitive abilities decline as the day goes on. Additionally, the afternoon is when our body temperature is at its lowest, which can lead to drowsiness and decreased productivity. Therefore, leaders need to encourage their employees to take short breaks throughout the day to help them stay focused and productive.

Another important aspect of chronobiology is the circaseptan rhythm, a (roughly) seven-day cycle that regulates many physiological processes. Circaseptan rhythms regulate patterns of activity and rest, hormone levels, and metabolism. This rhythm is important to consider when planning events, projects, and deadlines in a company. For example, if a project is due on a Monday, it may be beneficial to start working on it on the previous Thursday, when our energy and motivation are at their highest.

Chronobiology also studies other rhythms, such as seasonal rhythms. These rhythms can be observed in many animals and are related to the change of seasons and the variation of temperature, light, and other environmental factors.

It is important to note that the pattern of these rhythms can vary from person to person, and it is recommended to consider individual characteristics and preferences. The same is true for organisational ecosystems.

Chronobiology is useful to illustrate some of the ideas in this book because it gives us naturally occurring patterns that influence socially agreed ones. It is a great example of how management and leadership might tackle some of the bigger problems facing us all, such as climate change and ecological degradation, more sustainably.

Leadership Application Track your energy levels for a week. When do you naturally perform best? How can you realign your schedule to reflect this?

Emergence

Leadership appears to deal with arranging for novelty and possibility. Future patterns. How do new patterns come into existence? Famously, humans are awful at predicting the future; we don't know what will happen. We agree. Our book suggests that we don't know what **can** happen.

Many of us have grown up with the rule that new things appear deliberately as constructions of ideas assembled in a new way. This **cumulative** view of patterns pervades much of the discourse in management and business theory. However, it is problematic because it is not how new patterns (or old ones!) appear in nature.

Emergence is a theory gaining ground in many contemporary fields and disciplines that deal with complexity and systems. It is an effective model for novel self-organisation in social systems. Emergence emphasises spontaneity and nonlinear, qualitative shifts, producing transformations not reducible to their parts. It is a category of change that has crossed a threshold of difference from its parts and is not the direct result of an agent.

Its importance in shaping our thinking for leadership in the next generation is certain to grow as we face momentous decisions about society and the planet. The basic idea here is that, for some things, we learn less and less the closer we look. Although we try to explain by breaking things into smaller and smaller bits and then by adding together all our smaller understandings into a whole, sometimes it doesn't work, such as with our attempts to work out the human mind, for example. Perhaps, says Emergence, we learn more and more the wider we go.

Emergence refers to how complex phenomena and patterns can arise spontaneously from the interaction parts such that explanations of the parts do not explain the whole. In social examples, these complex phenomena include social norms, cultural values, economic systems, and political structures.

It is said that leaders can study emergence to understand how organisational systems and structures develop and change over time and identify the underlying mechanisms that drive these processes. Complex social patterns can emerge spontaneously from the interactions of individual people without the need for central direction or control. This concept contrasts with more traditional views of social organisation, which often assume that social patterns and structures are imposed by central authorities or by pre-existing social rules.

A lot of work has been done to develop this idea, including in management theory. In brief, our conventional wisdom on emergence is that the whole is *more* than (or different from) the sum of its parts. This is a change from the reductionist view of the early 20th century that said the whole is made up of its parts (understand the parts, and you understand the whole). We've dropped that idea, and we now say that although we don't know what will happen when all the parts get together, in theory – if we had enough data and applied logic and reasoning – we can work it out, and then use this knowledge to make better leadership and management decisions.

Our hunch is that we are not being radical enough in defining emergence. That patterns and order can appear in reality, spontaneously and without central direction, causation or control, is a real challenge to many of our conceptions of leadership and management. The problem may be that we can *never* predict what will emerge because emergence means that not only do you not know what will happen, you **cannot** know. Reason alone is not enough to guide you. You need intuition, artistry, and open-mindedness because the future will co-create itself.

That is a heavy thought. The future world we and our descendants will live in is not unwritten; rather, in key ways, it is *unwritable*.

Leadership Application Reflect on when an unexpected outcome emerged from a project or team. What conditions led to it? How might you deliberately cultivate emergence?

Finding Your Groove: a Summary of Our Proposition

Do we need a jump in our understanding? We think so, and this is a challenge and a call to action. Making sense of emergence in life is at the heart of this book.

- Patterns can be observed, and the order within them in various systems and phenomena, including social systems, can be described. A pattern refers to a regularity among a system's components or variables, while order attempts to explain the arrangement of that pattern in a useful way.
- Understanding patterns is crucial to the functioning of a system for leaders and managers because their role involves creating and maintaining social patterns. As a leader, it is essential to be aware of your tendency to impose order on patterns that may not be real or meaningful and to recognise your thinking biases. Do not mistake the order for the pattern.
- Understanding the internal rhythms of the body, such as circadian rhythms, can be a powerful tool for enhancing performance and productivity. Chronobiology can also demonstrate, figuratively, how effective management and leadership can more sustainably address broader societal challenges, such as climate change and ecological degradation.
- Complex patterns and systems can spontaneously emerge from the interactions of individual components without the need for central direction or control. Understanding emergence can enhance your comprehension of how organisational systems and structures develop and change over time.
- The concept of emergence challenges traditional views of leadership and management and calls for a holistic approach, which includes intuition, artistry, and open-mindedness, to navigate an unpredictable future. Resonant leadership connects relational dots.

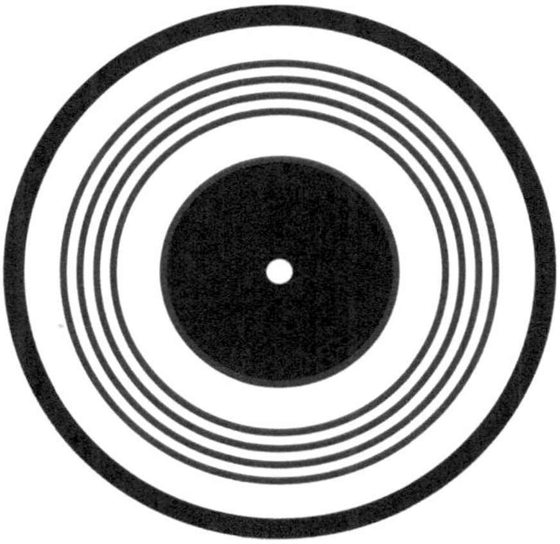

References

Bohm, David. 2002. *Wholeness and the Implicate Order*. N.p.: Routledge.
Csikszentmihalyi, Mihaly. 2002. *Flow: The Classic Work on How to Achieve Happiness*. N.p.: Rider.
Oxford English Dictionary, Oxford University Press (accessed September 2024), https://doi.org/10.1093/OED/1148132279.
Watts, Alan, and Al C. Huang. 2019. *Tao: The Watercourse Way*. N.p.: Souvenir Press.
World Bank. 2025. "Life Expectancy at Birth." World Bank Data. https://data.worldbank.org/indicator/SP.DYN.LE00.IN?end=2022&start=1960&view=chart.

Chapter 2

Notes on Individual Groove

DOI: 10.4324/9781003480655-2

Each of the nine Notes in this chapter has its own message, and each is part of a unity of focus on *Finding Your Groove* internally and in your individual uniqueness. Overall, this chapter explores the rhythms and patterns you use to define yourself. They encourage reflection, self-awareness, and conscious action.

At some point, each of us needs to tune into our own frequency. Awareness of habits, emotions, and aspirations may open the door to a deeper reshaping that aligns beliefs with principles that come into play when we encounter the wider world.

The themes cover different aspects of personal growth, from breaking routines and reframing perspectives to cultivating resilience and embracing discomfort as a catalyst for transformation. The central issue is progress, not perfection: finding small, consistent ways to move forward harmoniously with your sense of an inner self. Uncover the rhythms that resonate most deeply within you and nurture them as the foundation for everything else.

As you read, allow space after each section to reflect. Structurally, we have included two threads to help organise your reflections:

1. At the end of each Note, Barry draws out a different *Finding Your Groove Principle*, many of which also contain a call to action.
2. At the end of his response to Barry's Notes, Chris invites critical and further thinking and practice by providing three further questions for reflection.

Individual Groove is what sets the stage for creativity, balance, and meaningful action.

2.1 Just Turn Up. And Start.

Barry

It's a late Sunday night, the clock moving toward 9:30 p.m. and the supper club hums with energy. Two hundred patrons are savouring the last spoonfuls of dessert, their faces flushed from laughter and generous rounds of drinks. The air hums with anticipation for the evening's cabaret act to begin. Tucked behind the drum kit is an unexpected figure – a 14-year-old boy, the only white-skinned person in the room, who sits confidently in the cabaret backing band. At a time when the presence of someone like him in this space was legally precarious, the boy's nerves barely register. He knows he doesn't belong here officially, while intuitively he feels the deepest sense of belonging. Just hours earlier, he had slipped into the venue under circumstances that were, to put it lightly, against the rules. Welcomed with open arms by band members twice or even three times his age – he feels a part of something larger than himself. Their warmth and effortless groove dissolve any unease. Yet, one flicker of worry crosses his mind: how would he sneak back home after midnight on a school night without getting caught? This was my musical rite of passage as a fast-rising young drummer learning life's rhythms one groove at a time.

As a boy growing up in a small town in South Africa, my first great mentor, the late Taliep Peterson, instilled and inspired in me the importance of consistent practice in achieving personal freedom and success. The sense of personal freedom that comes from honing a craft, was the foundation for me to realise very personal dreams. However, I quickly realised that after the initial excitement of visible improvement has receded, the trickier part is embedding and sustaining the habit of *practice*, which at times feels mundane and relentless.

Taliep was a South African cabaret singer and composer who would later rise to international acclaim as a musical theatre producer, in partnership with local superstar and household name in South Africa, David Kramer. The duo first gained fame in 1986 with *District 6: The Musical*, based on the legendary Cape Town suburb and community uprooted and destroyed by the Apartheid government. The music from this vibrant community, a mix of Cape Malay slave descendants, Dutch settlers and other diverse cultures, became known as *Goema*. It was based on the hand drums the enslaved people would craft from brandy barrels discarded from the Dutch East India Company ships. There are still Goema drum craftspeople in the Cape Malay community in Cape Town today, and this music is unique to Cape Town. Taliep and David composed music in this style, full of humour and edgy social commentary, packaged in infectious Goema rhythms or grooves.

Their follow-up production was *Kat and the Kings*, the first musical from Cape Town to be staged in the West End in London and Broadway in New York, thereby taking the Goema tradition international. That production won the Laurence Olivier Award for Best New Musical in the West End and was nominated for awards on Broadway.

I met Taliep years before this when he was a touring cabaret artist. I was struck by his energy, presence, talent, and, more importantly, his professionalism and prodigious work ethic.

He would regularly perform at a nightclub called The Golden Fountain in Port Elizabeth that, during Apartheid times, was off-limits to a white kid like me. I was hooked when Taliep played the infectious Goema grooves, which closely resemble Samba from Brazil. Music has no boundaries, and I unthinkingly followed my intuition by smuggling myself into the so-called "coloured township" of Gelvandale by hiding under the back seats of cars, or even in their trunks. These were exciting times spent jamming with young Cape Malay and Indian musicians, including the members of South Africa's first Goema rock act, The Genuines, who were, in my opinion, the most powerful and prolific act of the day. And, of course, they were also way ahead of their time. Throughout this period, I was warmly welcomed with musical passion as our common ground, and I never experienced any racial prejudice.

Taliep would invite me into his pick-up backing band as a 14-year-old drummer, and we'd perform jazz and American soul covers on Sunday evenings at The Fountain. I loved it. After the shows, he would teach me theory, suggest study materials, and regale me with his version of what Malcolm Gladwell would, decades later, call the "10,000 hours rule." I aspired to be like him, saw that practice was my path to getting there, and realised that personal discipline was a critical element. Much later, when I heard the legendary South African golfer Gary Player say that the harder he worked, the luckier he got,[1] I knew what he was saying!

Since then, I have been on a mission to master my craft, from playing the drum set to completing an MBA and then teaching on the MBA. This route to mastery is the sometimes painful, often boring, and sometimes euphoric road to unconscious competency: the ability to lose the constraints of analytical thought and experience the joy of pure creativity. To get there, the hardest part is sustaining the relentlessness of daily application and learning. Very often, practising does *not* feel like fun. The personal code that I cracked with guidance from Taliep was to set a daily start time, without questioning emotions and energy levels, and to build a deep habit of practice.

When we watch an elite athlete, an accomplished stand-up comedian, or a great guitar player, we don't see the hours, weeks, and years of practice that are foundational to what we are experiencing. Personally, most of my practice sessions started with low enthusiasm. On an "enthusiasm" scale of 1 to 10, most of my new starts in life are never above a 3. The scale can never move up if I don't start, of course, and I have found that with determination and practice, I invariably work myself to between a 7 and 10.

So, if I had waited for my energy and appetite for practice or rehearsal to be upwards of 5 out of 10 before starting, I would never have become a professional musician or made a living by creating daily. Whether inspired or not, showing up daily enables inspiration, not the other way around. On the other hand, waiting for inspiration to start the practice will never deliver the time and effort needed for mastery, and continuing with the musical example, one could never be more than an enthusiastic hobbyist: a weekend warrior! My professional life has been built on this model of focused resilience, which transfers into all aspects of life: for example, does one ever feel inspired when waking up for an early morning run in winter, or does one get inspired once on the road with all senses alive?

> *My* ***Finding Your Groove Principle:*** *Starting a new practice with low energy or enthusiasm is normal. What matters is starting anyway. Start without letting emotions or thoughts get in your way. Set a fixed time each day to work on your skills, regardless of how you feel. On good days, inspiration and flow will follow. Track how often you start with low enthusiasm but end up feeling more engaged.*

Chris

Deliberate practice and hard work are essential for achieving mastery and personal freedom. The road to mastery is often tedious and difficult and ultimately it leads to the ability to perform without conscious thought and experience true creativity. Deliberate practice refers to the idea that mastery comes from focused, consistent practice over time.

Buried deep in my childhood memory bank is a BBC television show called *Record Breakers*, presented by Roy Castle (an English dancer, singer, comedian, actor, television presenter and musician). The show brought to the screen people who had succeeded or were working to succeed in holding a world record, as adjudicated by the Guinness Book of Records. Castle would end each show with a song titled *Dedication*, the sub-text for all achievements and ambitions to excel. Dedication is not the same as perseverance because dedication is the state of mind needed to get going, while perseverance is the state of mind of not stopping once you have begun. Perseverance is grit over time, usually. For some, it's a label for perfectionism.

What is the theoretical basis in this area? Barry mentions the 10,000-hour rule, popularised by Malcolm Gladwell in his best-selling book *Outliers* (2013). The work ethic of Taliep Peterson made a strong impression on Barry, and the research quoted by Gladwell in his book came originally from Swedish psychologist K. Anders Ericsson (Ericsson, Krampe, and Tesch-Romer 1993). Briefly, the idea was that exceptional levels of success could not be attained or explained by innate talent, intelligence, ambition, or ruthlessness alone. Success is a web that includes support from others and, crucially, sufficient time dedicated to the right kind of practice. Gladwell interpreted this as the 10,000-hour rule, and many agree that some activities need many hours of guided practice to master. Ericsson stressed that the continual setting along the way of goals that are just out of reach constitutes deliberate practice; the figure 10,000 was, well, figurative. Nevertheless, mastery means repeatedly becoming a beginner again, which Barry experienced in his journey to mastery. This is the lesson: be ready to sit back down and work up your expertise to the next level (relative to you) – it will always be hard work, even if you are a genius.

The 10,000-hour number has proved controversial in part because it did not quite capture the complexity of the original research into the connection between expertise and deliberate practice, and in part, we all want to believe it. It's a great soundbite and has been simplified to mean if I practice *anything* for 10,000 hours, I will become an expert in it. Ericsson later distanced himself from this interpretation, but Gladwell's book had started the myth. Inner effort alone cannot do that, although many studies have demonstrated that dedication to deliberate practice does make a difference.

The concept of deliberate practice still appears as a walk-on part in continuous improvement models such as the Toyota Way (Liker 2020), a system developed in Japan after the Second World War, and Carole Dweck's concept of the Growth Mindset (more on this later), which is frequently associated with dedication and effort to overcome inertia and internal challenges to improvement.

Creativity requires that you show up on time for your own meeting, stay there long enough for your presence to matter, and become obsessed with showing up. You need the will *an*d the discipline of dedication to be present. In fact, to be a starter.

Questions for Reflection and Groove

Try disrupting one routine tomorrow. What changes? What stays the same? What did you notice?

Think of a habit you have struggled to maintain. What is one way to "show up" for it, even on low-energy days?

How might you apply Barry's principle to team dynamics at work in starting new initiatives?

2.2 Say Yes and Figure It Out

Barry

As a new music student in California, I had a profound experience during my orientation week. Tommy Tedesco, the most recorded guitarist in history, spoke to our cohort of 900+ aspiring musicians. It was an inspiring commencement address filled with warmth and humour that centred on the themes of self-belief and working hard and smart. Tommy had worked in Hollywood recording studios for decades, playing as a studio musician on everything from TV advertising jingles to movies and albums for singers and songwriters. He arrived at our school in his convertible Rolls-Royce, which made a great impression on all of us!

Some context is needed here before I continue my Tommy story.

The need to say yes to secure an opportunity can be very powerful in the professional music business. In this context, the term "busking" (unlike the musician in a tube station playing for donations) refers to making it up on the spot while projecting an air of self-confidence, even if one is massively unsure of the job at hand. This behaviour is often driven by a competitive environment with more musicians than available work, through hubris, as a learned strategy, or a mix of all three. Music is an art form that is so vast and dynamic that it's impossible to be prepared for every situation. However, in the top tier of performance professionals, where the mandatory "entry fee" is thousands of hours of preparation and practice, "saying yes and then figuring it out," otherwise known as "busking," is a tactic and brand-building strategy.

Back to Tommy.

Tommy presented a commencement speech which was a masterclass in this strategy, beginning with a story about arriving decades earlier at an L.A. studio for one of his first engagements. This was after accepting the gig as a Hawaiian guitar specialist, despite not being one. With less than 10 minutes of preparation time available, he realised that he could easily adapt his mandolin expertise to meet the brief. So he put on a floral surf shirt and headed over to play the session. Tommy delivered the ten-second guitar flourish for a TV commercial with panache. He made such a good impression, both musically and socially, that he was on his way to ongoing calls from this production facility.

The message he conveyed to us was to prepare broadly by mastering theory and technique while absorbing many styles of music. Then, say yes – the session musician's equivalent to a minimum viable product!

I first applied what I shall call the "Tedesco method" at music school and have continued it into my career, first as a session musician and then as an international performer. To achieve success, I always maintained a high level of situational awareness and engaged in ongoing broad preparation through consistent listening, practice, and learning. This approach has been successful 80% of the time, with the remaining 20%, the disappointments, used as a mechanism and chance to learn missing skills and absorb missing theory. I found this to be a good ratio for sustaining my career.

An example of leveraging a broad platform of preparation was "following the fear" by raising my hand to have a crack at sight reading and playing complicated arrangements in the Big Band performance class at music school. I did this without a moment's hesitation. Paradoxically, this was a mental state that took me many months to achieve. At another time, it was me confidently agreeing to perform a style of music in a professional setting that was far outside of my comfort zone. Neither example is simple foolhardiness. On the contrary, these are instances of me being willing to stretch beyond my comfort zone, based on hours of preparation.

Later in my life, I used the same approach when deciding to pursue an MBA. The context here was a mix of serendipity and intuitively arriving in the right place to make a significant change. After 30 years as a high-performance musician, I started to lose my energy and excitement for the business of playing and producing music. A strong signal, in hindsight, was checking my social media feeds on stage between songs in front of an audience of 20,000 people and impatiently waiting for the show to end to get back to the hotel and unwind. In other words, the spark was no longer there!

Over my career, I have always been interested in the business aspects of creativity, especially the notion of entrepreneurship and start-ups (terms I learned later on), and this interest was growing. At this time, I met the leadership of Henley Business School, introduced through music and my membership of an iconic touring/recording act. We resonated immediately, and conversations started informally. I expressed my interest in the commercial aspects of music and creativity. Before long, the MBA was mentioned – rightly so, as the generalist structure of the programme was perfectly aligned with the intuitive change I was making. The serendipity part was that the school had started to look for unusual candidates for the flagship MBA from the creative industries as a new strategy.

I had heard people talk about doing their MBAs, the amount of work involved, and the benefits, so I knew this could be a powerful process of change and development. After agreeing to submit my proposal for a place in the programme, I asked a simple but very important question: "What do the letters MBA stand for?" I transferred my music business strategy to the world of business education by saying yes and knowing that I would figure it out later.

> *My **Finding Your Groove Principle:** Groove develops through habit. Small, consistent actions lead to mastery. Rather than going narrow and deep into a single area, adopt a wide and shallow approach. Explore broadly, experiment, and gain insights from a variety of experiences. Embrace uncertainty by taking risks and saying yes to opportunities, even without full confidence. Confidence grows through action. Repeatedly and consistently facing new challenges helps identify skill gaps, refine abilities, and build lasting habits. (An MBA is a great way to get prepared.)*

Chris

Barry's Note, "Say Yes and Figure It Out," revolves around accepting new challenges by taking calculated risks and utilising hard-won knowledge to seize opportunities beyond one's comfort zone.

In business and management, theoretical inputs that align with this are those dealing with Strategic Risk-Taking and Adaptability.

Sir Richard Branson's Philosophy of Entrepreneurship

The British serial entrepreneur Richard Branson often advocates a "screw it, let's do it" attitude, which resonates partly with Barry's approach of saying yes first and figuring things out later. This philosophy emphasises seizing opportunities even when full knowledge or preparation isn't possible, trusting in one's ability to learn and adapt on the fly. Branson's career has been marked by what he described at Henley in 1985 as risk-taking "at a gut level" (Branson 1985, p. 5). He operates with a series of decisions where risk would be very difficult to rationalise. Rationalising risk is, for him, a hindsight activity because reasons for failure are generally impossible to identify at the time of the decision. More importantly for Barry's point, Branson's number 1 tip for risk-taking is "Know the Business," and this is where we see a close correlation to the notion that saying yes to something is much less of a risk when you are fully informed about the basics of what you do.

Herminia Ibarra's Work on Identity Transition and Adaptability

Ibarra's theory of Working Identity explores how professionals evolve their careers through self-reflection, iterative trials, and experiential learning. Her concept supports the idea that saying yes to opportunities, even unfamiliar ones, plays a critical role in personal and professional growth by forcing individuals into new roles and identities where they can acquire and refine skills. Experimenting with new professional identities is a very open-ended way of avoiding the career trap of not making a move unless we are sure that we can succeed.

Herminia Ibarra's influential work, particularly her book *Working Identity: Unconventional Strategies for Reinventing Your Career* (2004), provides a powerful framework for understanding how professionals can transition into new roles and redefine their career trajectories. Ibarra challenges the conventional wisdom of deep introspection as the sole route to career change, instead proposing that real change happens through a process of "crafting experiments" with new professional activities and identities.

Such experiments are small steps that you take outside your current roles to test new professional possibilities. This involves trying new activities that can lead to profound insights and career shifts. Barry's willingness to say yes to new challenges, like taking on gigs that stretched his abilities or transitioning into an MBA programme, aligns with this idea. Each choice acted as an experiment, allowing Barry to explore and eventually embrace new facets of his professional identity. Each new musical challenge or genre he embraced helped him build confidence and skills transferable to other areas, including academia and business.

Another of Ibarra's key concepts is shifting one's social and professional networks to open up to new fields, ideas, and practices. Barry's narrative hints at this when he talks about meeting leaders from Henley Business School and how this connection led him to consider and eventually pursue an MBA. By integrating into a new network, Barry could access different thinking and opportunities, which is crucial for facilitating a career shift. As Barry shifted from music to business education, he also shifted his professional network, a pivotal element in Ibarra's model. This new network supported and facilitated his transformation, providing new perspectives and opportunities.

Ibarra also discusses the need to make sense of one's story as changes occur. This narrative reconstruction is vital as it helps individuals understand and articulate who they are becoming during their career transitions. Barry's reflection on his career – recognising the loss of passion in his music career and seeing the MBA as a new chapter – illustrates how he reinterpreted his professional life's story to align with his evolving identity. Barry's transition from a session musician to an MBA student and business thinker significantly reshaped his professional identity. Reflecting and making sense of this shift was crucial for Barry to integrate his past experiences with his new ambitions, a process central to Ibarra's theory.

Questions for Reflection and Groove

Think of a recent opportunity you hesitated to take. What would have changed if you had said yes?

What is one skill you could develop *now* that would make future 'yes' moments easier?

What is an unconventional opportunity in front of you right now? What is stopping you from saying yes?

2.3 The Art of Practice

Barry

Attending music school in Hollywood, California, came with an incredible value add: the chance to attend masterclasses almost every night, led by the music industry's top professionals. Glimpses into the careers and minds of the best in the business. One evening in early 1990, the legendary Ricky Lawson took the stage for a much-anticipated masterclass. Over 200 students, mostly drummers like me, packed the room. I was already a fan of his work with the progressive jazz act, The Yellowjackets. However, Ricky had shifted by leaving the jazz scene to join pop music's biggest acts, prioritising financial stability – a move he addressed openly that evening.

At the time, Ricky was Michael Jackson's drummer, working for the biggest pop star in history. Fresh off Jackson's record-shattering "Bad" tour, which set Guinness World Records for the highest-grossing tour and largest audience attendance, Ricky was the world's highest-paid session drummer. Most of us expected a technical showcase – a demonstration of "chops" on the massive acoustic & electric drum rig his team had set up.

Ricky surprised us.

For most of the session, he didn't touch the drums. Instead, he sat casually at the edge of the stage, talking to us. What he shared was more valuable than any technique showcase. He emphasised the importance of practising strategically: investing focused, distraction-free energy into every session, guided by a clear methodology. He said talent was merely the "entry fee," accounting for only about 20% of success. The other 80%? Professionalism, which he defined as being reliable, respectful, and consistent in both behaviour and mindset. It was a revelation. Here was someone at the top of his game, reminding us that humility, intention, and work ethic mattered just as much as technical skill. It wasn't just advice – it felt like a roadmap to a sustainable career in music. Then, as if to remind us why he was the master in the first place, Ricky got behind the drums and played along to some of Jackson's biggest hits. His sense of groove was mesmerising.

From the age of ten, I dedicated myself to becoming a professional musician, without exploring any other career options. Pursuing a music career is similar to pursuing a career in sport, as it requires countless hours of practice to attain mastery. In the initial stages, progress can be made quickly and easily as you learn the basic skills and techniques. However, as you develop a deeper understanding and mastery of the craft, progress becomes more incremental and harder to achieve. For instance, you may be able to run 100 metres in a certain average time, and it requires a lot of hard work and dedication to shave off seconds and minutes from your time. Similarly, you may be able to learn a broad range of drumming techniques quickly, but it takes months of practice and refinement to incorporate the nuances and subtleties into your performance.

The time spent practising can shift from the excitement of acquiring new skills to a focus on effectiveness and results. This is measured by what I term ROIH, which stands for return on invested hours. It refers to the measurable improvement in performance achieved over the total amount of time invested, and is more qualitative than quantitative.

At this point, the principle of "simply starting" is critical. It is crucial to follow the practice of starting every day and dedicating a committed amount of time to it, regardless of whether or not you feel motivated. Once you establish this routine, the focus should shift towards increasing efficiency and output. After all, it's essential to maximise the results of the time and effort you put in.

In a study by Daniel Chambliss titled *The Mundanity of Excellence* (1989), it was discovered that the primary differences between elite and local club swimmers were their technique and mindset. Despite using the same facilities and investing similar amounts of time, elite swimmers developed a more effective technique and a powerful internal narrative reinforced by their chosen peer groups. Similarly, elite musicians use their practice time to its full potential by following a carefully considered process, along with a powerful narrative achieved through "words to self" and surrounding themselves with strong and capable teammates, who are often better than themselves. Now, while the measurement of excellence can vary, the results from small mundane daily actions are clear and profound for the athlete or musician who is so "tuned-in" to their physical and mental performance. And as mentioned by Ricky Lawson, talent matters far less than we think!

While studying music in California, I developed my process of practising, which I call the "art/science of practice." I used the insights provided by the faculty and masterclasses to create a practice system consisting of 60-minute cycles.

It is important to understand that practice involves working on areas that you have not yet mastered, which is known as conscious incompetence. On the other hand, playing refers to performing the areas that you have already mastered, known as unconscious competence.

The following is a methodology for practising. In my case, it is a musical instrument, and it could easily be adapted to any skill, including the numerous skills needed for management and leadership, such as making a presentation:

1. Allocate 60 minutes for practice.
2. Divide the time into four equal segments of 15 minutes each.
3. Study theory, such as reading music or ear training, in the first segment.
4. Work on motor skills, such as rudiments or coordination exercises, in the second segment.
5. Take on a new challenge in the third segment, such as a foreign rhythm or improvisation.
6. In the fourth segment, have fun and play without judgment.
7. Use a timer to keep track of time.
8. Move on to the next segment as soon as the timer goes off.

Practising daily for shorter periods is more effective than practising for a long time once a week. To practice for more than 60 minutes, repeat the 60-minute routine or split 120 minutes into 30-minute segments. Take a 15-minute break between each hour of practice. During the break, meditate, move around, or stretch using yoga techniques.

Improve It: the SGC Model

When learning new knowledge and skills, it's important to follow what I call the SGC model; Slow, Gradient, and Context.

Slow Begin by practising at a very slow pace, even slower than you might think necessary. Then, halve that pace and continue practising.

Gradient This slow and gradual approach allows your brain and body to absorb the new techniques and patterns fully. Once you have mastered the technique at a slow pace, gradually increase the speed in small increments to allow yourself to calibrate to the new speed.

Context Finally, when you're comfortable with varying speeds from slow to fast, try using your newly acquired knowledge and skills in different settings to understand better how they work in different contexts. In my case, this could involve using a new drum riff in various music genres, ranging from jazz ballads to speed metal.

*My **Finding Your Groove Principle:** Deliberate practice is most effective when structured – set a dedicated time, follow a clear process, and let consistency drive progress. A timed neuroscientific approach is a powerful method for learning and mastery in any field. I applied it while completing my MBA and continue using it to develop new skills. By integrating this structured approach, you can amplify focus, retention, and long-term success in any area of growth.*

Chris

Barry's Note is about the best method of improvement when one already has a high skill level from practice. Barry's story emphasises the significance of dedicated and disciplined practice from the start and highlights that significant accomplishments result from everyday incremental improvements.

Does this apply to improving as a business manager or leader? Does it apply to the more general idea of an organisation improving what it does?

Let's look at the four main ideas highlighted, starting with Dedicated Practice and Incremental Improvement. It is not too hard to see how this principle can be applied to your professional development. Few would reject the idea that consistent effort and a focus on continuous improvement, even in small steps, may be linked to excellence in our respective fields.

Is there a catch?

Not if we already know and agree on what counts as improvement. Usually, becoming a better top athlete is defined by compliance with the laws of a given sport and performance compared to others and (perhaps more meaningfully) past self. In the creative arts, such as music, dance, or the performing arts, what counts as performance is (generally) well documented, and improvement is, therefore, easy to connect with for the individual, group, or even community. Improvement is more difficult to pin down if we are less sure of the rules or boundaries of what to measure.

Management is contextual, and while there are some universally agreed standards for performance, such as those reflecting financial and material inputs or outputs, we often struggle to say with certainty what things management and leadership consist of. This means you get to decide what good practice is, what it is part of, and what counts as improvement. The downside? Your time and resources for this are not infinite. You need to prioritise.

The ROIH Principle and Efficiency

Return on hours invested (ROIH) stresses the importance of deliberately measuring the efficiency and productivity of time spent on any activity. In a business setting, this can help optimise performance and ensure that time is dedicated to maximising the returns on your efforts. This can be achieved through various means, such as skill development, team management, and strategic planning.

Although no single theory defines ROIH, it has roots in several principles that have influenced management thinking over the years. Time and effectiveness management models help align with this, as does Human Capital Theory (Becker 1993), an economic model which proposes that formal investment in skills and education creates value for individuals in their careers. As a side note, it's interesting to think whether there is a tension between Human Capital theory's framing of education, training, and acquired skills as an investment in one's productivity and future earnings (and perhaps the logic for doing an MBA), and the organisational question of sunk cost. A sunk cost refers to unrecoverable resources (time, money, effort) already spent. Ideally, these should not affect future decisions. However, if you become overly attached to the investment you have already made in yourself, you may continue on a path even if it is no longer optimal or makes you miserable. It's never easy.

The SGC Model for Learning New Skills

The Slow, Gradient, and Context approach is a structured methodology for learning and mastering new skills. You can use this approach to develop both personal and professional skills, especially in mastering complex tasks. This approach can be particularly helpful in developing leadership capabilities, problem-solving skills, and adapting to new organisational roles or challenges.

As mentioned in Note 2.1, one of the voices behind the idea of a deliberate slowing down for better performance is Swedish psychologist K Anders Ericsson, the person Malcolm Gladwell featured in his book *Outliers*, which introduced us to the controversial idea that it takes 10,000 hours to master a skill. That was rejected by Ericsson, who said that what makes the difference is your prolonged application of mental representations of the boundary of current excellence until there is a breakthrough. For Ericsson, the components of this kind of practice were:

1. Have in mind a specific goal (managers might choose a behaviour).
2. Maintain an intense focus on this (consistency).
3. Make sure that there is immediate feedback from every attempt.
4. Operate always just at the edge of where you feel comfortable (tolerating mistakes).

The deliberate and determined effort in the task is framed by a wider, overall goal, which is to reach a solid, creative insight, now internally absorbed. The idea of a Gradient step is partly the revving back up of the deliberately slowed "learning motor." However, it also speaks to theories of Incremental Learning, such as Russian psychologist Lev Vygotsky's Zone of Proximal Development (ZPD), which brings in the importance of context. ZPD was first introduced in the 1930s to explain how some performance improvements can only be made with the guidance of someone with a higher skill level. In education and training, this is often called scaffolding, and this helps us understand how coaching and mentoring are often used today. For Barry, this technique uses speed as a way to achieve competence in the skill of what he can play. For you as a leader or manager, this will require first a period of raising awareness of your current situation and context to identify, perhaps in dialogue with others, what aspect of your craft needs to be mastered in this way.

Practice vs Play – Conscious Incompetence vs Unconscious Competence

The distinction between practice and play highlights the difference between working on skills or areas that still need to be mastered and performing skills that are so well learned that they become automatic. In Barry's case, as a musician, play is a synonym for performing what has been learned through practice. That is certainly enjoyable and recreational (in line with how we usually define the word), but performing may also be purposeful (which playing for fun wouldn't necessarily have to be) because it is his profession. This concept can be applied to professional growth, where leaders must balance developing new skills by stepping outside their comfort zone and leveraging their strengths where they are most effective. Does the idea of "work" carry more than one sense? Is being good at what you do analogue to having the freedom also to "play"?

Take note of some of these concepts, which will be the basis for your development work. Reflect on how these principles, extracted from music practice, can be implemented in developing management and leadership skills. The objective is to adapt the discipline, methodologies, and mindset that come with drumming into valuable lessons that can help you find and maintain your Groove in the professional world.

Questions for Reflection and Groove

What deliberate practices can you implement to improve a skill critical to your role?

How can incremental improvements lead to larger transformations in your personal or professional life?

How be might the SGC (Slow, Gradient, Context) approach applied to foster organisational learning?

2.4 Multi-Level Groove

Barry

"The Hotfoot Symphony Orchestra live at the Bassline tonight at 10 p.m."

This sign was a familiar sight outside the iconic Bassline Jazz Club in Johannesburg during the early 2000s. The 'Hotfoot' was no ordinary band – it was a 12-piece mini-big band, daring in its complexity and packed with improvisational energy. I had the privilege of being its drummer, an exhilarating role that pushed my musical limits.

The founder of this provocative ensemble was Bruce Cassidy, a mercurial Canadian trumpet player, composer, arranger, and bandleader who had made South Africa one of his creative homes. Decades before, as a young boy, I'd sat in awe as my mother took me to see a Blood, Sweat & Tears performance, where Bruce served as both musical director and trumpet player. That concert was a transformative moment for me, where I saw and felt the highest level of performance, intellect, and emotion first-hand for the first time. Years later, when I found myself mentored by Bruce and playing drums in his band, it felt like life had come full circle – the groove of connectivity bridging past and present.

Playing with the Hotfoot was unlike anything I'd experienced. The music defied conventional genres, demanding a level of thought and creativity far beyond simply following a score. Bruce selected musicians not just for their technical prowess but for their intellectual and emotional depth. Sight-reading was a base level requirement, followed by playing technique, and third was a good understanding of different music styles. However, the real challenge was another level up; interpreting the music by blending notation with abstract cues. A score might include not only melody and rhythm but also cues for styles, emotions, and vivid imagery – for example, a sentence scribbled above the stave to evoke the chill of winter, the vastness of a solar system, or the serenity of a watering hole, and perhaps asking for the style of Frank Zappa meets Willie Nelson!

This layered approach to music-making was a revelation. It wasn't just about playing; it was about embodying the music, painting with sound, and channelling imagination into every note. For me, it was a masterclass in multi-dimensional thinking, a journey into the emergence of what it means to become more than a group of musicians.

Richard Feynman, an American physicist, conducted experiments on time, rhythm and simplifying complex systems. He discovered that counting silently was a more accurate way to approximate 60 seconds than simply imagining it. He also found that he could practice this internal counting while reading or during physical activities without losing track. He found that visualising patterns or groups helped establish the number of sentences on a page or pairs of socks in his washing. This is exactly the way that a session musician quickly manages a complex score – by learning how to recognise groups of bars and patterns of notes.

What he could not do was talk while counting, as his unique neural network was fired by counting imagined words. However, he later observed that some people were able to count a full minute while speaking by using non-counting visualisations, such as mentally picturing a measuring tape or imagining their fingers tapping. This highlights the effectiveness of visualisation techniques and the energy of Bruce Cassidy's ensemble.

Music rhythm, or beat, can be divided into two elements, namely, metric and cyclical. Metric rhythms are a combination of upbeats and downbeats arranged into groupings of 2 or 3 and can be counted metronomically. Cyclical rhythms, on the other hand, are free to start and finish without constraints. An example of metric rhythm is Queen's *We Will Rock You*, while Phil Wood's saxophone solo in Billy Joel's *Just The Way You Are* is a complex cyclic improvisation over a metric grid (Liberty DeVito's beautiful drum groove, underpinning Joel's song form). This demonstrates the highest level of abstraction, connection and mastery, that is, the equivalent of *high levels of imaginary counting while grouping socks!*

Daniel Kahneman, in his book *Thinking, Fast and Slow* (2012), also suggests that creative processes (cyclic) should be layered on algorithmic processing (metric), thereby improving decision-making. There is so much to learn here about simplifying complexity by layering patterns, one level at a time. This skill is useful beyond musical improvisation and is transferrable to any work or social environment. It involves reading news, recognising opportunities or problems, and improvising with options while understanding the big picture, or letting the imagery of a solar system guide the performance by a provocative mini-big band!

> *My* ***Finding Your Groove Principle:*** *Mastery is achieved by layering structure with improvisation – learning the rules, then bending them. Use visualisation to mentally map out ideas, allowing you to see the bigger picture while navigating details. Build structured systems, but leave room for improvisation – adapting to new challenges and responding creatively. This approach merges the predictable with the spontaneous, enhancing decision-making, problem-solving, and creativity in any field.*

Chris

Barry's account of rhythmic and visualisation techniques got me thinking about whether it's possible to simplify complexity to enhance cognitive function in business. It certainly sent me off to revisit Queen's iconic 1-2-3 beat in *We Will Rock You*, and pay attention to the saxophone in the Billy Joel track and how it floats effortlessly within the beat of the song.

How does this principle manifest in organisational life? Does it have an equivalent in how an individual functions within such a system?

For organisations, there is some evidence that it does, beginning with Barry's reference to Kahneman's work.

Dual-Process Theory in Decision-Making

Thinking, Fast and Slow by Daniel Kahneman explores dual-process theory and suggests that we have evolved to use two systems of thought: System 1, which is fast, instinctive, and emotional, and System 2, which is slower, more deliberative, and more logical. In the book, he discusses the importance of combining creative and algorithmic processes to make better decisions. This mirrors the integration of intuitive and analytical thinking in decision-making.

Kahneman said that in our chase for quick results and solutions, we focus more on System 1. Sometimes, this is to the exclusion of the longer-term benefits that System 2 would bring. As an organisational leader, you can promote a better balance between the two by creating an environment that values and refines intuitive insights through analytical processes, leading to better-quality decision-making.

The concepts of "metric" and "cyclic" rhythms, borrowed from music theory, can be intriguingly applied to business and management to describe the structured and unstructured patterns of work, decision-making, and strategic planning. Metric rhythms in business and management accumulate through repetition over time. Here are some examples:

Quarterly Earnings Reports: Like the steady beat of a metronome, quarterly reports provide a regular, predictable rhythm to a company's financial reporting. They allow stakeholders to measure performance against benchmarks and make more informed decisions.

Annual Budget Cycles: The yearly planning and allocation of resources follow a structured, predictable pattern similar to a metric rhythm. This ensures that strategic and operational planning is aligned with financial constraints and goals.

Scheduled Check-ins: In agile management practices, for example, daily stand-up meetings serve as a regular pulse, helping teams synchronise their activities, report progress, and identify blockers, much like the downbeats and upbeats in a metric rhythm.

Project Milestones: Set milestones at regular intervals (the clue is in the name!) and create a structured timeline for teams to follow, ensuring progress is measurable and aligned with the project's overall timeline and objectives.

Cyclic rhythms represent more fluid, flexible, and often creative or adaptive processes within business and management, which may start and finish without constraints. Here are some examples:

Innovation and Product Development: Unlike the predictable cadence of metric rhythms, the innovation process is more cyclic, with ebbs and flows in creativity, brainstorming, prototyping, and testing. This cycle is iterative and can vary in length and intensity based on the project's nature and the insights gained during the process.

Market Trends and Consumer Behaviour: Fluctuations in market demand, consumer preferences, and trends operate on a cyclic rhythm, often influenced by external factors such as social, economic, and technological changes. Businesses must adapt to these cycles by pivoting strategies or innovating products.

Organisational Change and Transformation: Change initiatives often follow a cyclic rhythm, marked by periods of intense change efforts followed by times of consolidation and integration. These cycles are influenced by internal and external factors and require adaptive leadership and flexible planning.

Creative Brainstorming and Problem-solving Sessions: Unlike the structured approach of regular meetings, creative brainstorming sessions are more free-form and cyclic, allowing ideas to flow without rigid constraints.

Understanding both metric and cyclic rhythms in management practices can enhance your ability to navigate the structured and unstructured elements of business more effectively. The trick is to see how they interact with each other. Here are some organisations that have approaches that align with a layered approach:

3M's Innovation Culture

3M is well-known for its Post-it Notes, a product innovation that originated from the work of 3M employee Spencer Silver. In the late 1960s, Silver was experimenting with adhesive formulas to create strong new adhesives. By chance, he developed an adhesive with a very weak bond, which initially seemed like an idea without a problem to solve. In the mid-1970s, another 3M employee, Art Fry, took advantage of the company's policy allowing employees to spend office hours on new projects. He envisioned an application for the weak adhesive on paper, where the ability to peel items off and reapply them would be beneficial. After five more years of design, testing, and especially branding efforts, Post-it Notes were officially launched in the USA. The rest, as they say, is history.

3M's '15% Culture' fosters a unique environment that blends structured research and development processes with employee-driven innovation projects. This approach integrates performance metrics and scheduled evaluations from its R&D processes with opportunities for employees to freely explore new ideas and solutions. Combining these structured innovation processes and unstructured creative freedom has established 3M as a continuous innovation model.

Google's 20% Time Policy

Inspired by 3M, Google has become equally well-known for its policy that allows certain employees to spend 20% of their work time on side projects of their choice, away from their regular duties. This policy combines two different approaches to work; metric rhythm (the structured work tasks that are part of one's job role) and cyclic rhythm (the unstructured and innovative work). The successful combination of these two approaches has reportedly led to the creation of some of Google's most popular products, such as Gmail and AdSense, although there is some debate regarding the authenticity of this narrative.

Agile Project Management

Agile methodologies are widely used in project management as they demonstrate the perfect balance between metric and cyclic rhythms. Scrum, an agile framework, is a prime example of how structured sprints, typically lasting two to four weeks, can be combined with the flexibility to adapt and iterate on work based on feedback. This combination allows teams to remain disciplined in their execution while being flexible in their approach to product development, resulting in faster delivery of value to customers.

Toyota Production System (TPS)

The Toyota Production System (TPS) was initially developed as a method of continuous improvement in manufacturing for the Japanese company's plants. TPS aims to eliminate waste by removing manufacturing activities that do not contribute to value, such as bottlenecks, defects, and workflows. The mindset of pursuing perfection is the driving force behind TPS, which promotes immersion in the present moment. TPS allows decisions to be made where the problem is identified. Individuals are empowered to take action when they identify an issue. At the same time, TPS promotes team decision-making based on evidence that must be shared openly throughout the system.

The Toyota Production System gave us the Just-In-Time (JIT) manufacturing principle, which combines metric and cyclic rhythms. JIT uses precise metrics to manage inventory levels and production schedules (metric rhythm), while also encouraging continuous improvement practices (Kaizen) that enable employees to identify inefficiencies and develop innovative solutions (cyclic rhythm). The team and social bonding fostered by a spirit of restless search for incremental improvement (*kaizen*) can also promote health and well-being benefits for the organisation. This dual approach has earned Toyota a strong reputation for producing high-quality products and achieving operational excellence.

These examples illustrate that when leaders and organisations skilfully integrate the structured, predictable aspects of management (metric rhythms) with the adaptive, innovative processes (cyclic rhythms), they can create environments that excel in operational efficiency and thrive in innovation and adaptability. This synergy can be a key differentiator in today's fast-paced and constantly evolving business landscape.

Cognitive Flexibility and Innovation Using Visualisation

As Kahneman illustrates, dual approaches are part of our individual cognitive make-up. Feynman's internal counting method and the musicians' technique of managing complex scores are also examples of cognitive flexibility – the ability to adjust one's thinking or attention to changing goals or environmental stimuli. Leaders with high cognitive flexibility can navigate complex situations more efficiently and inspire innovation within their teams. By encouraging the development of such skills, leaders can enhance their team's ability to think creatively, adapt to changes, and improvise solutions in uncertain or complex situations.

Feynman's experiments have proven that visualisation techniques are effective. You can use visualisation to set personal goals and inspire and guide your teams toward a shared vision. This involves visualising success, picturing the steps required to achieve it, and mentally rehearsing the actions needed to overcome any obstacles. It's no accident that many leaders employ metaphors when conveying their ideas to others.

Combining metric and cyclic rhythms in business and management can create powerful synergies, fostering environments that balance predictability with adaptability and structure with innovation. The distinction between metric and cyclical rhythms and their application to work processes can optimise workflows and enhance productivity. By understanding the natural rhythms of their teams and tasks (metric vs cyclical), leaders and their teams can better structure work, allowing for periods of focused, algorithmic work interspersed with creative and strategic thinking phases. This can lead to a more dynamic, flexible, and productive work environment.

Questions for Reflection and Groove

How can you re-balance structured processes with creative freedom in your decision-making?

In what ways can identifying patterns improve problem-solving within your organisation?

How might layering thoughts enhance collaborative innovation in your team or work environment?

2.5 If You Can Sing It, You Can Play It

Barry

Taka. Takita. Takadimi. Takadina Ga. Takadina Geynaga.

At first glance, these phrases might sound like an alien language from a distant Star Wars galaxy. But they're not. These rhythmic syllables were part of the language that the late Joe Porcaro, a much-celebrated percussionist, recording artist, and educator, brought to life for his students at the Percussion Institute of Technology in Los Angeles.

Joe, who mentored me during my studies, was not just an extraordinary musician but also loved teaching, which he did with respect and humility. He was the father of three brothers who co-founded the chart-topping rock band Toto alongside guitarist Steve Lukather. Joe's name appears in the credits of Toto's albums as a percussionist, and his son, the late Jeff Porcaro, was a legendary LA studio drummer often described as the heartbeat of Toto's sound.

Joe introduced us to the foundations of a South Indian rhythmic system, a vocalised method of learning and performing complex patterns known as tala. The syllables shared above – groupings of two, three, four, five, and seven – were initially foreign to our ears but became fluid with practice. This system became an invaluable tool, helping us navigate odd metres and intricate groupings in the world of Jazz, Big Band and other improvisational styles.

While studying with Joe and others at college in California, I encountered the world of American Big Band culture. This art form has an unbelievably exciting drumming tradition. Listen to renowned drummers such as Art Blakey, Buddy Rich, or Steve Gadd, and you will get the idea. With finesse and mastery, these drummers powered large ensembles of fabulous instrumentalists in impressive displays of virtuosity, volume, and showmanship.

The way this rhythmic art form is taught is interesting and points to a much larger system of resonance and rhythm. It uses a first-principles approach of isolated steps to build mastery and understanding. The drum student learns to interpret musical notation by first slowly counting out loud the mechanical beats of each measure while playing the written phrases on the drum set, which are mostly syncopated, or in the opposite direction to the beats. This requires much repetition and practice because much of what is written "dances" around the grid created by counting measures of 4 (or 3) beats, and is a challenge of brain versus body independence. Once this part is mastered, the student starts *singing* the rhythmic phrases while keeping time on the drum set, which is step one in reverse. Once the mechanical grid of beats has been internalised, the final step is singing and performing the syncopated phrases simultaneously and then gradually increasing speed to reach the desired written tempo.

This approach to Big Band drumming draws inspiration from *Tala,* the Indian rhythmic system which is cyclical rather than constrained to the shorter measures of notation used in Western music. In this tradition, students learn their parts first by singing the phrases (which become longer as mastery is built), then by playing while singing, and only at the end by playing without singing.

I remember spending many hours while at college singing the "shout chorus" of a piece, accompanied by a metronome, using a system of phonetic sounds that translate the stress and duration of the notes that make up phrases of rhythm. The shout chorus is the climactic section in a big band piece where certain instruments phrase big rhythms in unison, usually the drums and the horn section. Play any up-tempo work by Count Basie's band, and you'll hear this beautifully demonstrated. After being comfortable singing these rhythm sentences with a sense of feel or *voice*, the next step (playing and singing) was less of a stretch and a bridge to the ultimate state – playing without singing or thinking.

My core message is that after achieving mastery, counting and singing cease to be explicit and remain implicit in the player's subconscious. They form a grid or roadmap that provides the freedom necessary for real improvisation. This overlaps and segues into other domains, such as physics, problem-solving, and complexity management.

I am passionate about the natural intersection of physics and music. I am drawn towards the first principles approach of taking a basic set of assumptions as a roadmap to solve problems and the purest route to innovation. Made famous by Elon Musk, it has been around for some time. This involves a three-step process. First, it requires questioning what we already know. Second, we identify and define our assumptions. Third, we break down our goals into their fundamental parts to create new solutions from a pure space. This approach mirrors the three-part big band drumming process I have just shared.

In his tour-de-force work *Principles: Life and Work*, Ray Dalio suggests a stepped approach, similar to the big band and tabla students practising improvisation techniques, and he includes the metaphor of a jazz quartet to illustrate how to navigate complexity and solve problems.

Developing creative ability as a musician means starting at the beginning, without letting our egos and preconceived ideas interfere. It's about adding one element at a time, just as I described in my big band and tabla analogies, and then being free to soar in a sky of innovation.

The whole process of leadership and creative problem-solving is very similar. It begins with seeing things as they are, identifying the primary elements, and accurately describing them using words and pictures. Then, additional elements are added, options are dashboarded, and complexity is carefully increased without building the gradient too soon, as that can lead to confusion. It is not easy, and it *is* worth the time and energy required to develop this practice as a learned ability!

> *My* ***Finding Your Groove Principle:*** *Break challenges, opportunities, or ideas into simple, tangible elements. Sing them, sketch them, embody them – immerse yourself in the process. When ideas become part of you, execution flows effortlessly.*

Chris

Barry's Note on the intersection of music, learning, and problem-solving offers a rich tapestry for exploring learning methods. I was fascinated by the role of verbalisation in the mastery of drumming skills, and it got me thinking about the application of these principles to leadership and management creativity.

Theoretical Background on Verbalisation In Learning

The method of learning that includes verbalising or vocalising while engaging in a task has roots in cognitive and educational psychology. This approach is often associated with the Cognitive Theory of Multimedia Learning proposed by Richard E. Mayer (2014), which suggests that people learn more effectively when engaged in active learning processes that include verbal and visual information processing. Verbalisation is a cognitive tool that helps learners articulate their understanding or confusion, facilitating deeper engagement with the material.

One of my favourite examples of an effective technique is called Commentary Driving. This method is used for advanced driver training in emergency (blue-light) services, such as the police. Commentary Driving involves verbally expressing what you are doing and why you are doing it – *while* driving. This can include explaining how you are avoiding potential risks. The most powerful aspect of this technique is that it benefits experienced and learner drivers alike. It works by engaging multiple areas of your mind. Most of us drive without giving much thought to our actions since road conditions are usually stable and predictable, which is often sufficient. However, by intentionally minimising distractions and verbally articulating every relevant detail about your situation, you create a strong framework for effectively handling unexpected challenges and achieving your goals more successfully. Over time, you learn to commentary drive non-verbally, freeing your potential to add more value. For those of you wondering how a police car travelling in the opposite direction can tell in a flash that you're using your mobile phone or don't have your seatbelt on – it's because of this training.

Situational awareness is well-known in management theory, particularly regarding decision-making. Verbalisation, whether used to master music or navigate complex driving conditions, enhances situational awareness by encouraging continuous verbal analysis of the environment. It may not be a literal translation for better decision-making, and there are many subtle ways of introducing a verbal commentary or description at work, such as in meetings.

Some of the reasons for this are explained by the Cognitive Load Theory, developed by John Sweller (1994) and colleagues in the 1980s, from the work of American psychologist David Geary, who differentiates between two types of biological knowledge: primary and secondary. Primary knowledge consists of anything you learn without explicitly having to learn it. Recognising faces, first language acquisition, and social interaction are no small feats, and none of us had to learn *how* to do them. Your brain is processing in the background, leaving you free to focus on a conscious use of what you are learning. Much human ingenuity and creativity fall into this evolved category of knowledge and use our enormous mental capacity for processing from long-term memory (including, usually, autobiographic, semantic, and procedural memory). Secondary knowledge deals with anything we *haven't* evolved to learn without needing to be conscious of how we do so. This includes most cultural skills and norms and involves heavy and expensive use of short-term memory (sensory or working memory).

For much of our biological evolution, cultural advancement has been slow. This has changed. For example, since writing was invented about 5,000 years ago, we have all had to be taught how to read and write to capture and process how we speak and think. This was quite a leap in our social development. Since the Industrial Revolution, the demands on us for cultural learning have grown exponentially. To meet this, we have formed elaborate systems of education to create or replicate the contents of our culture.

Barry shows us how learning can happen more effectively when short-term memory is not overloaded with information. We distribute the cognitive load by employing our primary learning abilities alongside our secondary. Situational awareness aids decision-making in business, where dynamic and potentially hazardous situations require a multi-level understanding of what is happening in the environment.

Dual Coding Theory, proposed by Canadian psychologist Allan Paivio (Paivio and Csapo 1973), suggests that cognitive processing operates through two distinct channels: verbal and non-verbal. This may be how the examples given engage both channels by requiring drummers, or police drivers, to observe and process visual information (non-verbal) and then articulate their observations and intentions (verbal), leading to a more comprehensive processing of information.

Leadership and Creative Problem-Solving

Next, still drawing on the traditions of Big Band drumming and Indian tabla as well as anecdotal evidence of its use by icons such as Elon Musk and Ray Dalio, Barry makes a compelling argument for a first principles approach to learning and innovation.

As mentioned, first principles thinking is not new. You can go back to the Greek philosopher and polymath Aristotle for the roots of the tradition. When applied to learning, it may embrace a whole category of theories and approaches to problem-solving and logical reasoning. What they all have in common is the aim of establishing the most fundamental elements of every task or situation. If you have ever come across Bloom's Taxonomy (1965), for example, when it states that analysis is required before you get to synthesis, you are dealing with first principles thinking. More precisely, Elon Musk's work developing Space X is a good example of problem-based Learning (PBL), in which complex, real-world issues are first understood through critical thinking, which embeds reasoning as it searches for a practical solution. Whether spending billions on space exploration is a good idea falls outside the scope of Space X as a problem-solving process because *that* question is a problem in a higher category with its own first principles.

This is a big subject that we will no doubt expand on in other Notes in *Finding Your Groove*. However, Barry's *Finding Your Groove* Principle translates these learning principles to leadership and creative problem-solving and underscores the importance of breaking down complex challenges into their fundamental elements. This mirrors the cognitive process of chunking, whereby information is broken down into smaller, manageable units, making it easier to process and understand. By verbalising these elements, leaders can create a clearer roadmap for navigating complexity, fostering a culture of innovation and flexibility within their teams.

Barry beautifully articulates the synergies between music, learning, and leadership, providing a holistic view of how verbalisation and a first-principles approach can flower into mastery and innovation. Applying these principles fosters a culture of deep learning, adaptability, and creative problem-solving. This approach enriches personal development and also equips organisations with the tools to navigate the complexities of the modern world, echoing the timeless rhythms of music that Barry so vividly describes.

Questions for Reflection and Groove

How can putting complex challenges into words help you manage uncertainty?

In what ways can visualisation enhance your problem-solving and leadership effectiveness?

How might integrating analytical and intuitive thinking foster innovation in your organisation?

2.6 The Power of Words

Barry

Two things have resonated with me while touring the world as a drummer in a band. One is carefully choosing the words that make up the stories we tell ourselves, and the other is developing the reflective practice of writing these words down at the same time each day.

It has taken me several decades to understand the importance of the stories we tell ourselves. This stuff has always felt too simplistic, perhaps revealing a personal bias about the effectiveness of what I would have called esoteric or "soft and fluffy" practices.

Until that is, I tried it.

I was a musical prodigy. By the time I was ten, I was celebrated in my small part of the world. I had no doubts about my ability or mission and wasted no time with self-destructive stories to myself. Over the years, this changed, and I developed the freelance creative's habit of self-deprecation, copied from my peers and role models. This was a way of belonging to a tribe and fitting in through behaviours, humour and jargon.

In Johannesburg or Cape Town, professional musicians engage in a typical banter that uses humour, self-deprecation, and even sarcasm about one's abilities as a performer. This is a coping mechanism to deal with the precarious nature of their profession, where they live from one engagement to the next with minimal formal contracting and no private or public support structures. When you are literally "as good as your last gig," self-deprecation creates an illusion of carefreeness and is a preparation to lessen the pain of possible failure.

The network effect creates the phenomenon of the majority of a city's professional session musicians becoming part of a neurotic and insecure community that never shares its fears, with members who don't realise how far they have shifted from their teenage selves. This shift is often brought about by words received externally in banter and stories told internally in narratives.

It's interesting to note that during my three decades of studying and performing in the United States, I experienced very little of the negative behaviour that I encountered in my home country. I believe this is due to the massive scale of the industry there, the support structures in place, and a culture of professional respect. While I appreciated these pockets of relief while in North America, I still felt the negative norms when I returned to the "reality" of home.

In essence, this process of over-humility and self-ridicule is a slow-release toxin that can eventually stunt one's creative growth, success, and enjoyment. This was my lived experience, even though I was part of an elite pool of freelance professionals working at the highest level and a member of one of the most commercially successful South African acts of all time.

My journey into a second chapter beyond music started in 2015 with an MBA. This new path taught me the power of raised self-awareness and one's internal narrative. It helped me identify blind spots and uncover old, buried experiences triggering reactive behaviours and feelings.

I came to realise the damage that can be caused by the words we use to describe ourselves, both internally and to others. Our brains form new neural pathways from these instructions, and if we use dark humour and messages of stupidity, forgetfulness, slowness or mediocrity to describe ourselves enough times, it can and will influence our behaviour.

During my MBA, I was introduced to coaching as a practice, which turned out to be a revelation. The aspects of fully engaged listening and lack of advice or fixing intrigued me, so I decided to work with a coach as an experiment. The results were so remarkable that I have continued this practice, and even after eight years, I am still astounded by the positive impact of coaching.

Through coaching, I reshaped my internal story and began the habit of writing daily reflections on what I was noticing. I jot down my thoughts, emotions, behaviours, and physical sensations. This simple practice of pen to paper, transferring from brain to body, produces deep and powerful results. To add to this, I record certain key statements from this writing on my iPhone, for a daily playback session of self-coaching.

I make a conscious effort every day to change my words and thoughts from scarcity to abundance, from fear of failing to trusting the process, from uncertainty to intentionality, and from self-doubt to belief in my abilities. Even choosing the words to construct that last sentence gives me a boost – causing me to put my shoulders back and focus on the relaxed energy emanating from my core.

The neuroscience and psychology of our stories have been brought to life for me, and I have experienced firsthand the series of small wins (which must be celebrated!) that then snowball once in motion. At the same time, I have become aware of the potential harm caused by toxic narratives and limiting behaviours that prevent us from reaching our full potential and pursuing our dreams.

> *My* ***Finding Your Groove Principle:*** *Choose empowering language, reflect daily, and celebrate progress. Eliminate limiting and damaging words. Reframe your story to yourself with uplifting language, and daily written reflections. Record energy-filled audio statements to reinforce your mindset. Finding groove is in the journey, not in waiting for future goals to bring fulfilment.*

Chris

Barry presents a deeply reflective exploration of the transformative power of language, particularly through personal narrative and the process of self-reflection. I see three main themes at play here, each with interesting theoretical backgrounds:

The Impact of Self-Narrative on Personal and Professional Development

All good stories are about how relationships change over time. By making a habit of daily reflection, Barry illustrates how this practice serves as a foundation for identifying and changing limiting beliefs and behaviours, and one of the best ways of making sense of these is as a narrative. Barry's observations underscore how the stories we construct about ourselves loop back around to shape our self-perception, our professional trajectories, and our interactions with others. From unconsciously adopting a self-deprecating narrative, influenced by peer behaviours and cultural norms within the professional music industry, there is a conscious shift towards empowering self-talk. And note how this makes sense only in hindsight.

Narrative Inquiry (Clandinin and Connelly 2000) is a research method that suggests individuals interpret the world and construct their identities through the stories they tell. These narratives are fundamental to our experience and understanding of the world, influencing how we see ourselves and our potential. Barry's transformation through changing his self-narrative aligns with this view of narrative's power in mapping reality.

When we make sense of our identities through stories, we are doing two interesting things at the same time. First, we can introduce new elements without destroying our existing identity, and second, we can maintain a sort of sameness or "permanence over time," as French philosopher Paul Ricoeur once put it. Our lives contain many examples where different things can happen, yet they are somehow all part of the same thing.

The Role of Reflective Practice in Personal Growth

Donald Schön's book *The Reflective Practitioner* (1983) started a conversation about reflective practice in management and learning that remains part of the professional development landscape. He distinguished between reflection-in-action and reflection-on-action, advocating the first as a continuous dialogue with one's own experiences to improve understanding and practice. Barry's daily reflective writing supports Schön's observations, fostering self-awareness and professional growth. Since Schön, many have tried to model the type of reflection that can be done after the event (many will be familiar with project wash-ups or lessons learned events at work). There is a danger of making all this too procedural and model-laden.

For example, inspired by (among others) the work of American philosopher and educational reformer John Dewey, experiential learning began as a human-centric critique of 1930s Scientific Management. David Kolb's work on experiential learning theory was extensive, and it has only been the Experiential Learning Cycle, framed in the 1980s, which has made the crossover to the mainstream, a diagram shown at almost every team-building to model learning. This I know firsthand from my years as an outdoor organisational development trainer in the 1990s. Although Barry's account of reflective practice and its impact on his personal development echoes an emphasis on the reflective component of experiential learning, I think it is much more subtle and complex than that. Many theories about reflection tend toward rigid outcomes.

The good news in your *Finding Your Groove* is that Schön's book was subtitled '*How Professionals Think in Action*'. Most of his text was about thinking on your feet in response to a world constantly in motion and always (just) out of rational grasp. Reflective practice improves most when you bring awareness of language, hidden assumptions, and a critical thinking mindset much closer to the present moment.

The Neuroscience and Psychology behind Change

Barry touches on the scientific underpinnings of how words can, so to speak, rewire our brains. As an aside, the wiring/programming metaphor in neuroscience is showing its age. An oversimplification, it carries a static connotation of linear and fixed circuits that are being reconnected. This does not capture the dynamic, constantly changing nature of the brain's plasticity. It overlooks the incredibly complex and relational biological processes contributing to brain function and adaptability. We would, for example, be better advised to think about change in the brain as gardening. Cultivating a garden certainly involves interventions (pruning the unnecessary connections and nurturing useful ones). Sculpting might be another.

By changing the language we use to describe ourselves, in his case, shifting from a language of scarcity and fear to that of abundance and confidence, we can alter neural pathways and, subsequently, behaviours and outcomes. Neuroplasticity refers to the brain's ability to reorganise itself by forming new neural connections throughout life. Even though it is not a single theorist's model, this scientific principle supports Barry's experience of changing thought patterns and behaviour. It's exciting to see how neuroscience and psychology can be practically applied to achieve personal transformation, emphasising the power of language in this process. The processes in the brain have become much better understood in the last 20 years, and the capacity to change networks via narrative input is already integrated into therapy to deal with brain patterns for a range of negative states and promote new ones for positive outcomes. In management, leadership, and everyday life, we are only at the start of this journey.

It highlights the possibility of transformation through altering one's narratives and practices as the brain adapts to new ways of thinking and being. For example, in her theory of mindset, Carol Dweck (2012) distinguishes between fixed and growth mindsets. She proposes that humans have a continuum of mindset that determines how they react to challenges in life. At one end of the spectrum is the **fixed** mindset, which assumes that people are born with a certain amount of talent and outlook that cannot be changed. This leads to behaviours such as avoiding challenges, giving up easily after failure, and being unresponsive to criticism or feedback. Individuals with this mindset tend to stick to their natural abilities (which may be considerable). While they may experience early success, they often plateau and become guarded about their achievements.

At the other end of the continuum is the **growth** mindset, which believes that a person's attitude, persistence, resilience, and ability to handle failure can be developed and improved. Much of Dweck's book is dedicated to exploring how this mindset can be encouraged and what benefits it can bring. Barry's shift from a self-limiting narrative to one of growth and possibility exemplifies the adoption of a growth mindset, which Dweck argues is crucial for achieving one's full potential.

American psychologist George Kelly's *Personal Construct Theory* (1965) is also worth mentioning. This suggests you develop unique, personal constructs about how the world works, and you use these to make sense of your experiences, much like a scientist who formulates hypotheses and theories, tests them against reality, and revises them when necessary. When first published, Personal Construct Theory provided a new lens to look at personality and psychological disorders. Individuals form unique mental frameworks, or constructs, to interpret and predict events. These constructs shape how people perceive, understand, and respond to the world, guiding their thoughts, feelings, and behaviours. Uncovering and possibly changing these constructs can lead to different interpretations and experiences of the world like Barry changing his narrative from self-deprecation to empowerment.

Putting It Together

These ideas converge to offer a holistic view of the power of words as a means of communication and a vehicle for profound personal change. Through Barry's journey, we see the potential for narratives to confine and liberate, underscoring the importance of consciously crafting our stories.

The lessons from this Note may apply to a deeper personal understanding of, for example:

Diversity in Workplace: where and how each employee constructs their reality differently. This awareness can improve communication and conflict resolution and better navigate interpersonal differences.

Leadership Development: by fostering a mindset that values adaptive thinking and flexibility.

Innovation and Creativity: by encouraging managers to question and revise their existing constructs and self-assumptions, they can become more open to novel ideas and alternative perspectives, crucial for creative problem-solving and innovation.

Personal adaptability: lifelong learning is continuously adapting and acquiring new knowledge and skills through life. Awareness of narratives supports this by emphasising the fluidity of personal constructs.

Personal accountability: this places you as an author at the centre of your learning experience, actively seeking out and engaging with new knowledge that challenges or expands your existing worldview.

Career Transitions: as you discover them through stories, the shifts in identity and role accompanying new professional landscapes can help you integrate new professional roles and environments.

Questions for Reflection and Groove

How does your internal narrative shape your professional and personal identity?
What practices can help you reframe limiting beliefs into empowering thoughts?
How can storytelling be used to align team goals and foster shared purpose?

2.7 The Groove of Physicality

Barry

Boxing has always fascinated me for its mix of power and brain-to-body coordination. Coming from a family with boxing roots, it felt inevitable that I would eventually step into some training myself. One day at a local gym, I noticed a boxing trainer working with a client, calling hand combinations on the pads. It was Groove personified.

I took his number and soon began a training routine. Progress was painfully slow as I worked to unlock what felt like wooden feet and hands, and no coordination ability for skipping! Yet this experience was a revelation. It heightened my awareness of how our bodies are designed to move, the incredible potential for resonance within us, and how much of that resonance we've lost as a sedentary species mostly focused on thought work.

In conversation on this topic, my trainer shared his experience of coaching children and observed that kids in low-income, inner-city schools ran without shoes, climbed walls, and played various games, while kids from higher-income schools participated in organised events wearing expensive sports shoes from a very young age. As a result, the lower-income kids were noticeably stronger, faster, and more enthusiastic about sports activities. In contrast, the higher-income kids displayed stunted natural strength and agility and were less enthusiastic due to being overly restricted from early childhood.

While delivering a team training programme on body language, a colleague mentioned an American study on mugging (being robbed in the street). The study looked at why muggers chose certain victims over others. Video footage and interviews with perpetrators revealed an interesting commonality: people who walked awkwardly were attractive victims. For the mugger, this awkward way of walking is a primal and subliminal indicator of weakness, much like how a hunting lion chooses the herd animal that is limping.

After reflecting on this, I concluded that urban humans have educated away certain natural behaviours and even basics such as walking have become confused.

This brings up resonance again and the way different elements work together. My example of the kids from different backgrounds highlights natural development (resonant) versus forced behaviour (dissonant). Similarly, a person walking in a natural flow (resonant) is perceived as stronger than a person walking in an uncoordinated way (dissonant).

The miracle of biological design is found in something as simple as walking, which is something we all know how to do and have forgotten how we learnt. The limbs work in a sophisticated rhythm of cycles and recovery or peaks and troughs. The left leg strides ahead, the right arm moves forward, while the left arm moves back to prepare for the next advancement by the right leg. It requires perfect synchronicity and is a wonderful demonstration of groove when done effortlessly. However, a largely sedentary urban life, the absence of uncertain terrain to navigate, and induced self-consciousness from media and group insecurities have resulted in people somehow unlearning the process of walking without thinking about it.

Similarly, natural creative things like singing, dancing, laughing and dreaming are being unlearned.

The good news is that this stuff is embedded and can be recovered with a bit of practice.

Here is an exercise (adapted from Efrain Toro's research and writing in his manuscript and course, *The Essence of Rhythm*) to practice as you walk daily. It uses the mix of rhythm, physics, and nature that we have called Groove.

Notice in your walk that the body will tend to balance itself so that if you count your actions, you could say **One** (1) to your left foot and then count **Two** (2) to your right foot (*no problem if you prefer to lead with your right foot, simply reverse this).

1. In this sequence, you will notice that your arms swing opposite your feet.
2. When the left foot is forward, the right arm is forward to match and then the reverse.
3. Observe that your arms touch the sides of your body exactly in between the count of your feet producing a **1 + 2 +** sequence, so use the word **"and"** for the "+" signs.
4. Count **1 + 2 +** evenly while you walk, coordinating your limbs with the counting system.
5. Feel how this heightens your awareness.
6. Practice this slowly and carefully, counting out loud (so that you can hear your own voice).

After 30 days, you will have relearned what you knew anyway!

When we walk, our body performs many complicated movements without us even realising how complex these are. Our subconscious mind takes care of these movements, allowing us to react quickly to our environment. And it works. For instance, if a skateboarder is heading towards us while we're walking, our body quickly (we might say unthinkingly) responds to avoid a potential disaster. These coordinated actions happen instinctively, without us having to think about them or make a decision consciously.

Right now, though, let's focus on practising these coordinated movements. This is the most fundamental idea in rhythmic flow, and the way the body does it is a natural wonder. A feeling of groove that manifests in all elements of life.

> *My **Finding Your Groove Principle:** Try this vocalised counting system to guide your walking pace. Your body's rhythm shapes your presence and confidence, feel how you move with awareness and intention. Practice this coordination in two stages: first, bring focused awareness to refine it; then move to effortless, natural movement. By mastering this rhythm, you develop greater control, balance, and confidence in both movement and mindset.*

Chris

This Note strikes me as being about two things. First, it speaks to an awareness and coordination of how we as *individuals* show up with others, physically and mentally. It therefore begs the question, "Who is doing the showing up?" Our modern, conventional answer involves three ideas: a conscious self, a subconscious self, and an unconscious self, and it is difficult to think of a bigger, more complex, and mysterious chain of concepts than that. Then, attention to walking is useful as a metaphor that helps us understand more about *organisational dynamics*. That draws us toward a different sort of awareness and coordination, one that is collective in nature.

The Components of Consciousness

We cannot survey all views of selfhood over the last 2,000 years, and we may never know how the ancients answered the question, "Who am I?" (though they surely asked it). Nor can we fully map the myriad ideas in the world's many cultures.

In the 19th century, after science eliminated many religion-based explanations for the natural world, a similar attempt was made to explore the mind without recourse to a medieval belief in a dualism of an immaterial and immortal self (the soul) and a material body (the person), a vessel to express, and a person's thoughts.

Western culture, the dominant voice in commerce, management, and leadership, has largely adapted to a view of the self that takes for granted the language used by Sigmund Freud to map out consciousness. Today, *ego* is unquestioned as shorthand for self, which can be very useful, and also as an explanation for what we do, think, or say, which can be much less useful.

Physical and Mental Coordination of the Self in Leadership

Self-awareness and self-regulation are key to effective leadership. However, they are easier said than done.

Barry's exercise on relearning the natural rhythm of walking underscores the connection between physical and mental coordination. This theme is particularly relevant for managers and leaders, who must maintain balance and coordination in their professional lives. Just as walking with a natural rhythm enhances physical presence and confidence, maintaining mental coordination through structured thinking and preparation enhances leadership effectiveness.

This translates to maintaining balance and coordination in leadership roles in a business context. Effective leaders, much like skilled walkers, must synchronise their actions and decisions to navigate the complexities of the business environment. Leaders who can maintain mental coordination through structured thinking and planning are better equipped to handle challenges and inspire team confidence. This coordinated approach enhances leadership presence and effectiveness, akin to the confident and resonant walking style Barry describes.

The Natural Flow of Leadership and Organisational Dynamics

In the same way that Barry discusses the intricate and often unconscious coordination required for walking, effective leadership involves understanding and harnessing the natural rhythms and flows within an organisation. "Walking" can serve as a metaphor for the seamless operation of a team or organisation. This natural flow is essential for fostering a productive and satisfying work environment. When employees immerse themselves in tasks that feel natural and unforced, they are more likely to experience job satisfaction and increased productivity (see *Flow*).

As leaders, it is crucial to create conditions where this flow can flourish. This involves recognising the inherent dynamics of teams and workflows and facilitating an environment where tasks and roles feel natural and unforced. Just as walking involves a sophisticated rhythm of cycles and recovery, organisational success relies on the smooth coordination of various elements working together harmoniously. Effective leadership requires the coordination of team members and resources to achieve common goals.

Resonance and Dissonance in Leadership

Dissonance is the state of being in disagreement with. This is stronger than just having a different view. There is an obstructive, perhaps destructive, element present, and this will often result in the source of the conflict being ignored, buried, or denied.

Resonance is a state of a harmonious echoing, of being in tune with. This strongly indicates agreement and reinforcement. Resonance (like dissonance) is a feedback loop, often to amplify a positive intention.

Barry's insights into natural versus forced behaviours offer a valuable lesson for leaders. *Resonant leadership*, as explored by Richard Boyatzis and Annie McKee (2005), involves Leaders attuning to their own and others' emotions. This creates a motivating and harmonious work environment (think back to the earlier references to EQ, SI, and EI, and you are in the right ballpark). This resonance fosters engagement, motivation, and a positive organisational culture.

Conversely, dissonance, characterised by misalignment and forced behaviours, may lead to stress, reduced performance, and high turnover (although there's also an argument for dissonance acting as a powerful force for creativity, a point I will make later). Those working in organisational structures should work to cultivate a resonant culture where employees' natural talents and energies are harnessed effectively. Leaders can enhance organisational cohesion and performance by fostering an environment of emotional intelligence and alignment.

Practical Exercise: Enhancing Leadership Presence Through Resonance

Barry's exercise on relearning the natural rhythm of walking can be adapted for leaders to enhance their presence and effectiveness. Here's a modified version for you to practise:

1. *Observation*: Begin by observing your natural leadership style and interactions. Notice how you communicate and coordinate with your team.
2. *Awareness*: Develop an awareness of your emotional state and how it affects your leadership. Pay attention to how your actions and words resonate with your team.
3. *Practice* mindful leadership by consciously aligning your actions with your intentions. Use a vocalised counting system, like Barry's walking exercise, to maintain a steady rhythm in your interactions.
4. *Reflection*: Reflect on the outcomes of your mindful leadership practice. Notice any improvements in team cohesion, motivation, and overall organisational resonance.

By incorporating these practices, can you enhance your leadership ability with presence, resonance, and effectiveness? You cannot know this without trying it and examining the results. This is where dissonance, failure, awkwardness, doubt (and so on, the emotional list is long) should be embraced. Resonance and dissonance arrive as twin potentials, and neither makes sense without the other. Ultimately, finding your own groove in this complex dance of organisational dynamics.

Questions for Reflection and Groove

How might you intentionally "relearn" other innate skills or behaviours (beyond walking) that have become stifled by modern habits or self-consciousness?

How could simpler physical practices (e.g., posture, breathing) deepen your presence and leadership impact in the workplace?

How can you encourage your team or colleagues to re-engage their natural strengths or instincts for greater well-being and productivity?

2.8 The Theory of Reassembly

Barry

It's 10:30 a.m. in a conference room in Barcelona. Seventy sales managers clap and count through a complex rhythm, fully engaged and unafraid of mistakes. On the stage, the facilitator sits on an upside-down metal trash can, playing it like a cajon with his hands. The energy in the room builds, and a shared groove begins to take shape.

This was me, leading a series of global workshops for sales teams from a multinational company. The 2-against-3 rhythm game, when gamified and without any theory, always succeeds in connecting and energising participants. From Lagos to London, Boston to Copenhagen, this exercise demonstrates the transformative power of creative reframing and repackaging familiar concepts, turning rhythm into a universal tool.

I have been using rhythm as my compass for decades in my career and life. Understanding frequency, patterns, or cycles (all words for rhythm) has been a powerful tool for me as a musician. I have learned that musical application, although obvious and explicit, is only a tiny part of a much greater system – the intricate and implicit universe that theoretical physicist David Bohm described.

By assigning whole numbers to rhythmic events, we can understand frequency in music and other fields, such as the colour spectrum or the periodic table. When combined in a particular way, the frequencies 1, 2, and 3 create a powerful groove template, in musical terms a polyrhythm. When these frequencies start together and resolve together, they form a harmonic rhythm, as opposed to starting and/or ending separately, which would form three linear rhythms. This underpins all modern music, from early Blues and Rock and Roll to Hip-Hop and Afrobeats. In the same harmonic order, these frequencies are found in nature, in physics, and in chemistry.

When performing this polyrhythm in a musical setting as a type of rhythmic scaffolding, we can create distinctive "beats" that define popular music styles by adding accents, ghost notes, and dynamics, all influenced by cultural environments. As if by magic, Afrobeats from Lagos, Rai from Tunis, Indie-Rock from Seattle, Rhumba from Havana, or Blues from Austin all seem to emerge from the same basic rhythm skeleton!

This demonstrates that what we usually think of as different styles are all nuanced versions of what is already there. This may not be surprising. After all, in contemporary Western music, we have 12 notes to play with (12 semitones in a chromatic scale) and three rhythms (1, 2, or 3, then multiples of these frequencies). That's it!

Innovation is often perceived as being something entirely original. In reality, it often involves reorganising existing elements in a novel way. Creativity is largely about repackaging existing components in a highly innovative manner, which can obscure their basic, shared nature. For example, in jazz, a soloist can blur the fundamental structure of a song. This illustrates an emergent phenomenon where the whole is greater than the sum of its parts.

In 2012, I performed all the percussion and beat elements in a recording session for the South African rap group *Die Antwoord*'s new song, "Fatty Boom Boom." Die Antwoord is arguably the most prolific and commercially successful South African act of the past twenty years, and the official video for this song has had 75 million views on YouTube.

The producer wanted a high-energy rhythmic bed that sounded like a large group of tribal drummers. I layered multiple percussion instruments to achieve this, resulting in a huge tribal beat. However, we felt it sounded too natural and traditional, which didn't match the band's persona. I suggested a more nuanced approach: keeping the same rhythm while performing on unusual "scrapyard" instruments, inspired by the visuals of the Mad Max movies and a barren dystopian setting.

To find new sound sources, I gathered a variety of metallic and interesting objects from the studio kitchen and workshop. The result is a rhythmic mix of traditional and unusual sounds: a driving traditional drum pulse peppered with what sounds like scrap metal scavenged from the set of the last Mad Max shoot! It was the same rhythm and elements of improvisation from my first attempt but then reassembled using unexpected sounds. The crazy bursts of metallic improvising that build through the piece were performed with inverted wire brushes on a large pasta pot lid from the kitchen!

> *My **Finding Your Groove Principle:** Creativity isn't about reinventing the wheel, it's about reframing and reassembling ideas in fresh, exciting ways. Innovation comes from shifting perspective, not starting from scratch. Make this a habit: spend 5 minutes daily crafting a brief-to-self in an area of interest, then generate five ideas without overthinking. This simple practice sharpens creativity, fuels inspiration, and builds momentum, turning imagination into action.*

Chris

Watching seventy sales managers transform their individual claps into a shared groove is more than just a metaphor for leadership and teamwork. It demonstrates how we rarely create new ideas completely from scratch; we remix, adapt, and repurpose. The moment of collective understanding when fragmented beats suddenly fall into sync is a vivid example of what happens when individuals align with a system larger than themselves.

After all, if rhythm is a guiding compass for a musician's creativity, then business leaders and managers should be able to find their equivalent principle in their equivalent structures. All sorts of innovations are possible using only the most basic and existing ingredients. These can become part of a manager or leader's identity and effectiveness when practised and balanced over time.

Understanding and Leveraging Patterns

Barry's discussion on rhythm and its foundational role in music and nature reflects the importance of recognising and leveraging patterns. In management, this concept is related to the theory of Systems Thinking. Popularised by thinkers such as Peter Senge in *The Fifth Discipline* (2006), Systems Thinking involves understanding the interrelationships between individual elements of an organisation (including you) and recognising how these can lead to sustainable success. Another word for such relationships is pattern.

Seeing and describing patterns is central to systems thinking. When relationships are mapped out in the processes and workflows within their teams, it becomes possible to identify recurring issues and then understand how different elements interact. This holistic view lets leaders pinpoint leverage points where small changes can lead to significant improvements. For example, as Barry uses polyrhythms to create complex musical pieces, managers can use system dynamics to innovate and optimise organisational processes. Companies can apply systems thinking to address imbalances within the complex interplay between external social determinants and internal cultural factors.

Elsewhere in the book, we focus on organisational examples and initiatives, as well as the wider environment, and our interest in this chapter of *Finding Your Groove* is you as an individual. That is an appropriate lens because the self is a system, too.

Innovation Through the Reassembly of Existing Elements

Barry illustrates how innovation often results from reassembling existing elements in novel ways rather than creating something entirely new from scratch. This aligns with the concept of **Combinatorial Creativity**, a term popularised by Steven Johnson in his book *Where Good Ideas Come From* (2011). Johnson argues that new ideas often emerge from the combination and reconfiguration of existing knowledge and the resources you have available at the time. He suggests that an inward culture of combinatorial creativity is possible by encouraging the same kind of cross-functional collaboration and knowledge-sharing principles you may already be using at work. In organisations, for instance, workshops and brainstorming sessions that mix employees from different departments can spark innovative ideas as diverse perspectives converge. How Barry created a unique sound for Die Antwoord by using kitchen utensils and scrap metal illustrates how unconventional thinking and resourcefulness can lead to groundbreaking results. The same basic principles will also operate for you in your relationship to creativity.

Reassembly suggests that progress, whether in learning, career development, corporate strategy, or self-awareness, is not about discarding the past and starting fresh from a blank slate but cutting up any of the elements that are already there and reordering them in a way that produces something that was *not* there before. I sometimes do this with MBA alumni and students at Personal Development retreats, with an exercise on reorganising narrative identity and the stories we tell ourselves. I get everyone to write down and read out "life chapter" summaries in the presence of others, one by one. For the author, this can become a surprising opportunity to find release from source scripts and plots. For the group (the audience), listening to each person's story is now material for reviewing their narratives from a different angle. New pathways can emerge by shifting perspective and reassembling past lessons, skills, and influence.

Many of us reach moments where we feel stuck or unable to move forward. Often, this is not because we genuinely lack new opportunities but because we view our abilities and experiences through a static or outdated framework.

Another insight from Barry's Note is that innovation does not require originality in the way we typically assume. The idea that breakthroughs result from unique, ground-breaking origination is a myth perpetuated by cultural narratives about genius and creativity. Many of the most significant advancements in science, art, or business result from recombination rather than out-of-the-blue invention.

The four-part documentary *Everything Is a Remix* by Canadian filmmaker and writer Kirby Ferguson (2023) argues that all creative processes are based on copying, transforming, and combining existing elements. The notion of a singular, inspired genius is misleading; instead, innovation is about recognising the potential in what already exists and rearranging it to create new meaning. There are many examples of this:

- The Beatles drew on skiffle, rhythm, and blues, gained experience covering older songs, and eventually drew directly from Indian classical music. They used current technology to fuse everything into something that felt new. Significantly, others drew directly from them to do the same. The writer William Burroughs and recording artist David Bowie gained much from the cut-up technique for text (novels and song lyrics, respectively).
- Steve Jobs and Apple revolutionised consumer technology not by inventing the personal computer but by integrating and refining existing ideas into an elegant, user-friendly design. When the iPhone launched in 2007, nothing in it was completely original.

Are great leaders those who impose radical change from scratch or those who can take existing structures and assemble them into something that better aligns with the needs of the moment? Does this mean that progress is less about discarding what has come before and more about learning how to recombine past influences in innovative ways? Barry's framing of rhythm as a tool for engagement reminds us that learning itself is a process of iterative reassembly. We take in information, break it apart, reconstruct it, and apply it in new contexts.

Integrating Content With Theory With Practice

To effectively integrate these themes into managerial practice, consider the following steps:

1. *Systems Mapping*: Conduct systems mapping exercises regularly to identify patterns and interrelationships within your organisation. Use these observations and insights to identify what might happen if existing resources could be rearranged (make it visual and tactile if possible).
2. *Cross-pollination and a Safe Environment for Experiment:* Create opportunities for employees to collaborate across departments. This can be facilitated through joint projects, rotational programmes, and informal idea-sharing platforms. Don't set outcomes or objectives for these; just communicate permission to see what emerges and a forum to capture ideas. Provide the necessary support and resources for a culture that encourages experimentation and views failures as opportunities.
3. *Daily reflection:* Implement Barry's *Finding Your Groove Principle* by encouraging colleagues, co-workers, etc., to spend a few minutes each day reflecting on a specific brief and brainstorming ideas. Keep or start a **commonplace book.** Not a diary, this is a curated way of capturing the bits and pieces of life and arranging (then revisiting and rearranging) elements later. Indexing by subject, for example, allows you to collect snippets you read or hear (often quotes from others) over time and connect various elements to spark new ideas. This practice can help keep the creative juices flowing and lead to unexpected innovations. You will be in good company. The poet John Milton, philosopher John Locke, scientist Charles Darwin (who learnt the technique from his grandfather, Erasmus), and author Virginia Woolf all kept commonplace books.

We see ourselves as complex systems composed of various rhythms, conscious and unconscious. From daily routines to career decisions, our choices are guided by an underlying structure that, when mapped, can reveal patterns of action and thought that may be holding us back or propelling us forward. Progress may also come from cutting up our maps and rearranging the pieces in new assemblies just to see what we find. To gain control over your personal groove, you must first recognise what elements are already in play. What rhythms are shaping your life? What resources – skills, networks, past experiences – can be repurposed?

Look for Patterns Before Looking for Change

Before assuming that you must completely overhaul a system, a career path, or a personal habit, first map the existing rhythm. Where is the groove flowing? Where is it disrupted? What small shifts could create a major impact?

Experiment with New Combinations

Creativity and problem-solving are rarely about starting from scratch. They come from reconfiguring in novel ways what already exists. If you are stuck in a leadership role, a project, or a learning plateau, try remixing existing elements rather than searching for a brand-new approach.

Reassemble, Don't Replace

True reinvention is rarely about throwing everything away and beginning again (although it can occasionally be). It is usually about disassembling, understanding, and reconstructing the pieces to better serve you.

This applies to organisations, self-identity, learning, and resilience. Rather than fearing change, what if we saw ourselves as living compositions, constantly evolving, remixing, and fine-tuning the elements that make up who we are?

Your groove isn't something you have to find from scratch, it is something you shape by reassembling the rhythms already within you.

Questions for Reflection and Groove

How can you identify and repurpose your core strengths to adapt to evolving challenges?

In what ways can repackaging existing resources lead to innovative solutions?

How can organisations foster a culture of reassembly to stay competitive in dynamic industries?

2.9 The Balance

Barry

The year is 2010, and I am in a recording session for Annie Lennox's new album, "A Christmas Cornucopia." I was hired for my understanding of African rhythmic styles, combined with the ability to read music, follow direction, and work comfortably with a click track, the metronomic pulse essential in most recordings. My task is to improvise creatively, with little preparation, while staying fully aware of the song's sections and overall structure. Finding a state of groove between the polarities of emotion-driven "feel" and analytical theory is a delicate balance.

My lived experience of playing a set of drums at the highest level in so many different settings has taught me that analytical thinking with an excessive focus on theoretical underpinnings can impede the creative flow needed to generate new ideas. Over-analysis can stop the creative sparks from flying. At the same time, however, *some* level of analysis and structure is needed. If it is missing, that will also negatively affect creative quality.

It is a delicate balance. Using musical improvisation as a metaphor, the two extremes are (1) free improvisation with no boundaries and not underpinned by theory or technique, and (2) the tightly bound technique and theory-dependent "solo" pieces used in classical orchestras.

From my perspective, the most fertile ground for creativity lies just to the left of the centre, leaning into freedom but still scaffolded by theory and technique. First, one must master the necessary theory and techniques to be able to improvise with any meaning. Once one has attained a state of unconscious competence, the true creative narrative can be unleashed – a story unencumbered by concerns over technical ability or analytical thought. By taking risks and exploring uncharted territory, we can enter the highest levels of creative flow and acute present time, where anything is possible.

In music performance, the ability to read notation saves the performer time and allows them to avoid the opportunity cost of committing a complicated arrangement to memory. However, relying too much on reading can drain the energy needed for creativity, leading to a dull and uninspired performance. So, when playing a piece of new music in a large ensemble guided by a chart (a *road map* or sheet music score), the creative and analytical brains must work together in a more defocused way. Getting that balance right requires a lot of effort and practice!

The process requires a decoupling of analytical and creative abilities so that while the "reader" is rooted and aware of progress and milestones on the map, the "player" is unencumbered by any gravitational pull and free to create and innovate. While this may seem challenging at first, with practice and perseverance, it becomes a natural part of the musical journey, allowing you to express your creativity to its fullest potential.

Psychologist Daniel Kahneman has defined two types of thinking: System 1, which is quick and instinctive and defocused, and System 2, which is slower and more deliberate, focused and logical. In my experience, the defocused state allows a person to examine multiple things at once, slipping in and out of conscious and subconscious awareness. On the other hand, the focused state can only handle one or two things at a time. To be creative while also analysing a musical chart, one must be able to dance between the two systems of thinking. I suggest that the primary approach should be a broad and defocused one, where one has blurry attention to the notation, similar to watching the countryside pass by slowly from a high-speed train while allowing for unforced creative output to take centre stage.

Performance anxiety can negatively impact a musician's creativity by triggering overwhelming analytical thinking due to perceived pressure. This, in turn, can ruin the state of flow necessary for creativity. To combat this, the musician must develop a mindset of self-trust through preparation and learn to reframe stress energy into a defocused state of flow.

However, this confluence can only be achieved once the musician has mastered the craft at the highest level. For a musician, this involves spending years learning to sight-read scores and thousands of hours practising musical theory, technique, and real-time application. Once the musician has achieved mastery, a dance between analytical and creative thinking begins, and from within the patterns of technique, a unique "voice" emerges with stories to tell.

I remember experiencing all of this as a music student in California, especially in our performance classes. Initially, the written music (which I would have accessed from the library before the class and pre-absorbed) would constrain my performance. I would be so consumed with the act of reading that my performance would be robotic, and my "time" would be unstable (i.e. no groove). This only started to shift once I'd managed to integrate the brain/body connection of reading (sense-making) and performing (meaning-making) as one process, which required many hours of practice and a change of mindset (from fear of failure to the gift of an exciting opportunity). Once this happened, I was confident enough to volunteer for the ultimate risk-taking experience each week: sight reading, which was to perform a new piece, in the moment, without any preparation. Decades later, this same process enabled my studio performance for Annie Lennox's Christmas album!

> *My* ***Finding Your Groove Principle:*** *Innovation thrives on the balance between focused and defocused thinking. Allow ideas to flow freely, without judgment or time pressure, while staying anchored to clear opportunities rather than random ideation. By aligning creativity with a "jobs to be done" framework, you ensure that innovation serves a purpose – solving real problems and unlocking meaningful possibilities. This structured yet flexible approach transforms inspiration into impactful action.*

Chris

Barry's insights on creativity and structure in music offer a compelling metaphor for leadership, decision-making, and innovation. His experience illustrates a paradox that applies equally to business and personal mastery: true creative freedom is not the absence of structure but the ability to move effortlessly with and within it.

This resonates with a fundamental tension in learning, leadership, and creativity, one that has been explored in diverse disciplines, from Zen philosophy to complexity theory. The challenge is toggling analytical and intuitive thinking and integrating them into a dynamic, fluid state where both coexist and amplify each other. Knowing your stuff so well that it just melts into action without thought is the essence of mastery.

The Art of Holding the Tension

Barry describes the interplay between structured analysis and creative flow as a dance, a process of switching between Kahneman's System 1 and System 2 thinking. But what if we go further? Instead of viewing them as opposing forces, we can explore the notion that they are two aspects of the same phenomenon. You can't, in other words, have one without implying the other. They are complementary, coexisting, and mutually reinforcing.

In complexity science, this is akin to the concept of the *edge of chaos* – the zone between order and disorder where systems are most adaptive and innovative. If you stay too structured, you stagnate; if you lean too far into pure improvisation, you collapse into randomness. The sweet spot – the groove Barry speaks of – is a state of poised instability, where control and surrender coexist.

A useful analogy comes from *The Inner Game of Tennis* by Timothy Gallwey (2024). Gallwey argues that peak performance emerges when the conscious mind (which analyses and corrects) gets out of the way, allowing the unconscious mind (which acts and adapts) to take over. For me, this division between the conscious and unconscious mind is a simplification and not a literal separation. Rather than two distinct systems, we might see them as different labels for one overall mode of attention. We sense they are always in dynamic relationships with each other, shaping, constraining, and enabling one another in an ongoing process rather than acting as isolated forces.

This is roughly what Barry describes: deliberate practice builds structure, but the musician must relinquish control and trust the body's learned intelligence at the moment of performance. For you, this means seeing systems as structured enough to provide guidance *and* loose enough to allow emergence and novelty. Frameworks like Agile and Design Thinking may work on this principle. They create conditions for creativity by introducing just enough constraints to direct energy without suffocating it.

Mastery and the Illusion of Knowledge

Barry's reflection on *unconscious competence* raises a crucial question: what does it mean to "know" something in an era of almost infinite information?

Traditionally, mastery involved accumulating vast reserves of knowledge and experience, stored in memory and refined through practice. Today, the very notion of expertise is shifting. With AI models capable of generating solutions, insights, and even artistic expressions in seconds, is knowledge still something to be stored in us, or is it increasingly about *navigating* and *synthesising* knowledge available whenever we need it from an external source?

Remember that Donald Schön argued that the most effective professionals don't just apply pre-existing knowledge, they engage in *reflection-in-action*, constantly adjusting, experimenting, and reshaping their understanding as they go. In a world where AI accelerates access to knowledge, our value may not lie in what we know but in how well we dance with knowledge, in the here and now. This is going to be part of what we call intuition. AI may also allow us to automate certain repetitive tasks to free us to think at higher levels of abstraction. Perhaps, paradoxically, this forces us to deepen our *human* capabilities of imagination, ethical reasoning, and the ability to find patterns in ambiguity.

Creativity in the AI Era

Barry hints at a question that is perhaps the most urgent of our time: How does technology affect creativity? If improvisation in music only requires deep internalisation of structure, what happens when AI can instantly generate "improvised" pieces that sound indistinguishable from human creativity?

The work of French philosopher Bernard Stiegler (2016) warned that automation risks replacing not just manual labour but also *human individuation*, which is the process by which we create originality through struggle, failure, and mastery. If AI can create without that practice, will we lose something fundamental about the process of becoming? Or, are we going to harness this incredible, generative processing power and let it carry out some of part of our focusing and defocusing to free ourselves up for higher level thinking, and performance? For Steigler, knowledge and memory are melded with human technology (and have been for millennia), so this is a really interesting time to be living and learning in. The question is, what is going to happen to our capacity to think and create?

Questions for Reflection and Groove

How can you balance developing technical expertise and fostering creative freedom in your personal or professional life?

How might your team's approach to problem-solving improve if they focused on creating a balance between structured processes and the freedom to innovate?

How can your organisation support both the development of technical skills and a culture of creative exploration? What role does AI have?

Making the Transition to Group Groove

Having honed your individual Groove, discovering personal rhythms, building consistent habits, and embracing the power of self-reflection, you now possess the foundational insights necessary for deeper collaboration. The lessons of personal resilience and self-awareness pave the way for collective creativity. As you close this chapter, consider how your unique rhythm might enrich team dynamics. Reflect on how your personal practices can influence and elevate the energy of those around you. This bridge from personal mastery to collaborative harmony invites you to envision a space where every voice contributes to a shared cadence, setting the stage for building resilient, high-performing teams.

Note

1. Gary may have been repeating a much older quote, possibly originating with Thomas Jefferson, much streamlined, and re-used by entrepreneur and venture capitalist Peter Thiel.

References

Becker, Gary S. 1993. *Human Capital: A Theoretical and Empirical Analysis, with Special Reference to Education, 3rd Edition.* N.p.: University of Chicago Press.

Bloom, Benjamin. 1965. *The Taxonomy of Educational Objectives: Handbook.* N.p.: Longman Higher Education.

Boyatzis, R. E., and McKee, A. 2005. *Resonant Leadership: Renewing Yourself and Connecting with Others Through Mindfulness, Hope, and Compassion.* N.p.: Harvard Business School Press.

Branson, Richard. 1985. "Risk Taking." *Journal of General Management* 11 (2) (Winter): 5–11.

Chambliss, Daniel. 1989. "The Mundanity of Excellence: An Ethnographic Report on Stratification and Olympic Swimmers." *Sociological Theory* 7 (1): 70–86.

Clandinin, D. J., and F. M. Connelly. 2000. *Narrative Inquiry: Experience and Story in Qualitative Research.* N.p.: Wiley.

"Cognitive Theory of Multimedia Learning." 2014. In *The Cambridge Handbook of Multimedia Learning,* 2nd edn. Edited by Richard E. Mayer, 43–71. N.p.: Cambridge University Press.

Dalio, Ray. 2017. *Principles: Life and Work.* N.p.: Avid Reader Press/Simon & Schuster.

Dweck, Carol S. 2012. *Mindset.* N.p.: Robinson.

Ericsson, Anders, Ralf Krampe, and Clemens Tesch-Romer. 1993. "The Role of Deliberate Practice in the Acquisition of Performance." *Psychological Review* 100 (3): 363–406.

Ferguson, K. (2023). *Everything Is a Remix* [Video series]. Retrieved from https://www.youtube.com/watch?v=X9RYuvPCQUA

Gladwell, Malcolm. 2013. *Outliers: The Story of Success.* N.p.: Penguin.

Ibarra, Herminia. 2004. *Working Identity: Unconventional Strategies for Reinventing Your Career.* N.p.: Harvard Business School Press.

Johnson, Steven. 2011. *Where Good Ideas Come from: The Seven Patterns of Innovation*. N.p.: Penguin.
Kahneman, Daniel. 2012. *Thinking, Fast and Slow*. N.p.: Farrar, Straus and Giroux.
Kelly, George A. 1965. *A Theory of Personality: The Psychology of Personal Constructs*. N.p.: W.W. Norton.
Liker, Jeffrey K. 2020. *The Toyota Way, Second Edition: 14 Management Principles from the World's Greatest Manufacturer*. N.p.: McGraw-Hill Education.
Paivio, Allan, and Kalman Csapo. 1973. "Picture Superiority in Free Recall: Imagery or Dual Coding?" *Cognitive Psychology* 5 (2) (September): 176–206.
Schön, Donald A. 1983. *The Reflective Practitioner: How Professionals Think in Action*. N.p.: Ashgate.
Senge, Peter M. 2006. *The Fifth Discipline: The Art and Practice of the Learning Organization. N.p.*: Random House Business Books.
Stiegler, Bernard. 2016. *Automatic Society, Volume 1: The Future of Work*. Translated by Daniel Ross. N.p.: Polity Press.
Sweller, John. 1994. "Cognitive Load Theory, Learning Difficulty and instructional Design." *Learning and Instruction* 4: 293–312.
Timothy Gallwey, W. 2024. *The Inner Game of Tennis*. N.p.: Pan Macmillan.
World Bank. 2024. "Self-employed (Total % of Employment)." https://data.worldbank.org/indicator/SL.EMP.SELF.ZS?end=2019&start=1991&view=chart.

Chapter 3

Notes on Group Groove

DOI: 10.4324/9781003480655-3

The Notes in this chapter focus on *Finding Your Groove* within and between groups. Being among other people is where the energy of collaboration, diversity, and a shared purpose drives individual and collective growth. Musicians know this space well.

We explore how working in tune with others, in teams, as communities, or just in spontaneous collaborations, can amplify creativity, sharpen skills, and inspire new perspectives.

Each Note delves into different aspects of group Groove, from the dynamics of high-performing teams to the magic of collective problem-solving. It examines how shared goals, mutual trust, and a culture of inclusion can turn a group into a thriving ecosystem where everyone contributes their unique strengths. The Notes also highlight how diversity, when embraced fully, becomes a catalyst for innovation and resilience.

The spotlight shifts from individual rhythm to the symphony of group dynamics, where we are finding out about harmony within the complexities of working with others, balancing our own voice with the collective sound. By engaging fully with the Group Groove, you tap into a powerful source of inspiration, learning, and achievement that transcends what any one person can accomplish alone.

3.1 From Big Band to Genuine Brand

Barry

It's 9 a.m. on a Thursday in 1990 at a renowned music school in Los Angeles. Seventeen musicians are set up in a large performance room. The student rhythm section – drums, bass, guitar, and piano – waits quietly while the rest of the band, all seasoned Hollywood session players, trade banter and drink coffee. These are pros, the kind of people who make Oscar-winning movie soundtracks and hit albums happen.

The bandleader, Dave Pozzi, calls for a sound check. They tear into an uptempo piece. Steve Houghton, a faculty member and one of the best big band drummers in the world, is on drums. His playing is so powerful, and joyous, and the groove so undeniable that the band ignites and the room shifts. And me? I'm a student taking it all in. What I experience isn't just music, it's an unforgettable masterclass in authenticity, confidence, and emergent groove.

The Big Band drumming tradition in America significantly influenced my early drumming education when I first arrived in Los Angeles as a young drum student in the early 1990s. Before my arrival, I had been listening to Big Band recordings in South Africa, largely due to my mentors' encouragement to expand my listening and deepen my understanding of the jazz tradition. Jazz was particularly important in the so-called "townships" during Apartheid South Africa. I was captivated by the power of these Big Band recordings and sought out whatever I could find in my culturally limited hometown.

I vividly remember immersing myself in the arrangements, horn lines, and drum performances on vinyl records from Frank Foster's legendary band, which I would later experience live at the Village Vanguard in Manhattan. However, it wasn't until I attended school in California that I truly grasped the intricacies of this art form. My education provided a structured approach to breaking down its immense complexity into manageable parts, incorporating theory, ear training, technical skills, and understanding the various styles. Once I began to make sense of the music this way, I was hooked. I became truly passionate about it and dedicated long hours to progressing from basic competence to mastery of the craft.

A typical Big Band consists of seventeen seated players, divided into two sections: a rhythm section (drum set, bass guitar, piano, and electric guitar) and a horn section (two alto saxes, two tenor saxes, one baritone sax, four trumpets, and four trombones). The band leader is sometimes a conductor, but most often, they are an instrumentalist and frequently a drummer. Great examples of band leaders in this tradition include Buddy Rich, Art Blakey, and Louis Bellson.

This setup is also known as a Swing Band, due to its triplet (a grouping of three notes) based rhythmic approach, which directly links to the African roots of Jazz, Rock & Roll, and Blues. All African rhythm has a rolling or swinging feel of three and four at once!

However, some context is first necessary to avoid turning this into too much of an ethnomusicology piece! The musical styles from the early days of the barbaric slave trade between Africa and the New World were influenced by the exchange of people between West Africa and the cotton plantations in the southern region of North America. This cultural exchange led to a blend of African and European musical styles, forming what can be described as a musical melting pot, or *gumbo*.

Due to restrictions placed on these displaced West Africans, they were not allowed to play indigenous instruments, sing traditional songs, or practice their own religious beliefs. Instead, they were forced to learn English and practice Christianity. In response to this oppression, slaves demonstrated ingenuity by adapting Western marching band instruments to play traditional music and rhythm, laying the foundation for early forms of blues and jazz. Additionally, African melodies were incorporated into music with English lyrics, contributing to the earliest forms of the Gospel tradition. To continue their worship of culturally relevant deities, they coded their beliefs into Catholicism, which eventually evolved into practices described as Santeria or Voodoo worship. This adaptation allowed them to carry on their traditions under the radar of plantation owners.

The modern drum set is a direct result of an innovation that allowed a single seated percussionist to play instruments that four marching band members previously played.

This gradual shifting and reframing in the use of marching band instruments was reflected in the journey of emancipation from New Orleans to the industrial cities in the north. It introduced new, popular music styles to North America, including R&B, blues, rock & roll, and jazz (including Big Band). Big Band jazz is now considered an American art form and is taught in high schools across the USA. As a young South African in the twentieth century, the art of Big Band was completely unfamiliar to me, especially when I was faced with its purest and most sophisticated form. Not to mention that my instructor was ranked as the #2 practitioner in the drum media's international polls.

Nevertheless, something about the sound and the rhythms resonated with me on a fundamental level, and I was determined to master what initially felt overwhelming in its complexity. Looking back, it's now easier for me to understand the roots of this resonance – the rhythms were African!

Eventually, I realised that success in my role in this environment was dependent on confidence and posture, qualities that had not been instilled in 1990s South Africa. The country had only just emerged from decades as a pariah state, culturally sanctioned due to Apartheid. This created an inferiority mindset across a generation of musicians whose talent was denied the creative oxygen of global exposure. For a full academic year, I sat in the back of Steve Houghton's Big Band class, too fearful to raise my hand when he asked for volunteers to demonstrate their abilities. Finally, after much careful preparation, I gathered the courage to try. His reaction is burned into my memory – "*Very cool, great job! Where do you come from, you sound different?*"

At that moment, I felt seen and appreciated, and this changed my game in a few seconds.

I soon made the connection. For me, standing out from the crowd was about being "*that different-sounding player from Africa*" who could master American-based theory and pedagogy and then use it in a slightly new way. The approach was not that far removed from the African musicians in the 1800s when they learned and rearranged European music on the cotton plantations of Louisiana.

I worked harder, developed resilience and tenacity, brushed aside some bumps in the road, loved the affirmation, and became fearless. By year two of my studies, I would raise my hand and volunteer without knowing the material to be performed, which was a level few students attained. This represented the first step toward establishing my unique brand, which I retained and nurtured for over 30 years. The authenticity around my brand as a Worldbeat specialist created resonance for decades when working with groups of musicians and producers.

(As a play on words in the title of this Note, my middle name is actually Brand!)

> *My **Finding Your Groove Principle:** Leverage your uniqueness within the group. Confidence, authenticity, and resilience turn your voice into a lasting brand.*
>
> *Here is a **Team Groove** checklist:*
>
> 1. *Does your team have a shared rhythm or cadence for work?*
> 2. *Is there a balance between individual autonomy and collective alignment?*
> 3. *Where is there dissonance in your team, and what might resolve it?*

Chris

Most of us have felt like a fish out of water in our personal or professional development at one time or another. Barry's reflection made me wonder about the lessons and themes of this experience for management learning.

There are many threads to choose from. I'm going to highlight three:

1. Cultural Adaptation and Innovation

Barry highlights how African slaves' adaptation of Western instruments and merging of African rhythms with European music formed the foundation of many modern American music styles.

This theme is significant in management as it shows the power of cultural adaptation and innovation in overcoming constraints and creating new value. However, it also models the role of power relations in directing, sometimes forcing, people to do or not do something that is part of their cultural heritage. You cannot achieve one without the other. The trick is to know what's going on and stay in tune with the present moment without being held too fast by the past or pulled too much by an imagined future.

Cultural Intelligence, or cultural quotient (CQ) (Earley and Ang 2003), is the capability of an outsider to relate to and work effectively across cultures other than their own. Barry's adaptation to the Big Band tradition in LA is a practical example of a developing CQ. He navigated cultural differences *as* cultural differences, understood and respected the new musical culture, and integrated it with his African roots to create a unique sound.

CQ is a member of a family of social intelligence concepts and theories, including Emotional Intelligence, which is said to be part of intelligence in general and leadership in particular.

According to Earley and Ang, CQ has four components: *cognitive* (knowledge of cultural norms), metacognitive (knowledge of the *process* of knowing cultural norms), *motivational* (the universal drive to adapt), and *behavioural* (abilities or capacities to act appropriately in different cultural settings). Barry exhibited all four, learning the technical aspects of Big Band music, being motivated to excel despite initial fear, and eventually performing confidently and authentically.

2. Overcoming Fear and Building Confidence

At a very personal level, Barry's journey of overcoming fear and building confidence in a foreign musical tradition underscores the importance of resilience and self-belief. This theme is crucial for managers who need to foster a culture of courage and continuous improvement within their teams.

When seen in a group context, Barry's story connects with important aspects of *Transformational Leadership* (Burns 2004) (Bass and Riggio 2006), where leaders offer themselves as visionaries to inspire and motivate followers to exceed self-interests for the good of the group. In this case, his instructor, Steve Houghton, played a transformational role by recognising and affirming Barry's unique talent, inspiring him to reach his potential.

As popularised by Bernard Bass, the concept of Transformational Leadership integrates humanistic considerations for employee welfare and empowerment with objectives related to driving change. The leader aims to inspire others to bring about collective and individual transformation. They achieve this by leveraging their personality, values, and skills across four key areas:

Idealised Influence: being a role model.
Inspirational Motivation: leading to trust and admiration and the wish to work harder.
Individualised Consideration: *having a* genuine concern for others.
Intellectual Stimulation: challenging others.

Houghton's approach in recognising Barry's talent and giving him positive feedback embodied these elements, fostering an environment where Barry felt valued and motivated to excel.

3. Differentiation through Authenticity

Barry's realisation that his unique African sound could be his differentiator teaches an important lesson in branding and personal development. Managers can learn the value of encouraging authenticity and leveraging unique strengths to stand out in a competitive environment.

Here, we are again in the realm of *Personal Branding.* This term borrows heavily from theories associated with marketing and sales. It includes two main elements: a process of defining, which involves a lot of reflection and self-analysis, and a process of promotion, which involves strategic positioning to stand out in a given context.

At work, my definition of personal branding is that it is (i) a belief that it would be best for you to align your knowledge and experience with what others think/do, (ii) by managing expectations and presenting a credible image as being useful or suitable in a role, (iii) a strategy of being perceived as a trusted ally for decision-makers or key stakeholders.

Almost all of us need to consider our personal brand in organisational life. The counterpoint, or perhaps evolution of this, would be Thought Leadership, which I take to be (i) a belief that it would be better for *others* to align their knowledge and experience with what *you* think/do, (ii) by taking your knowledge, expertise, and insights out into the world, (iii) in a strategy of becoming a trusted authority for decision-makers.

Barry's journey from reluctance to confidence and the importance of his unique sound highlight the process of personal branding. His self-discovery and strategic use of his African musical heritage to create a unique identity in the Big Band world are textbook examples of how effective and healthy personal branding can start.

"Big Band to Brand" offers rich insights into management learning, particularly in cultural adaptation, overcoming fear, and leveraging authenticity for differentiation. By examining theoretical frameworks like cultural intelligence, transformational leadership, and personal branding, you can understand the principles underlying Barry's experiences and apply these lessons to your management practices.

Questions for Reflection and Groove

How can you cultivate the habit of "agreeing to" without the pressure of "agreeing with" in your professional or personal relationships?

What systems or practices could you implement to encourage multi-perspective thinking and collective problem-solving in your organisation?

Reflect on a recent situation where you misjudged someone else's viewpoint; how might pausing judgment have changed the outcome?

3.2 Forming the Band

Barry

After four decades as a professional drummer and producer, I have been amazed and pleased by the many valuable music industry principles that can be applied to any business relying on teamwork.

By age twelve, I was already a veteran drummer with eight years of informal practice. At that young age, I instinctively understood the concept of personality types and the balance between talent, skill, and social EQ (Emotional Intelligence).

When forming a band to perform at the school year-end concert, it was important to address several issues while looking for talent in a limited pool. The main criteria included figuring out who owned any equipment and whether they could play it. This was followed by an assessment of how they showed up socially. Last came whether they had any musical talent. This approach was very practical and driven by the available resources. As a result, many kids would end up as the bass player or singer in the band simply because their parents had invested in equipment or had allowed the group to use a garage or basement as a rehearsal space.

Then, it was up to three or four personalities to figure it all out. They did this by showing up, spending hours developing personal mastery and group synergy, and fearlessly attempting to conquer their neighbourhood. Some succeeded, most did not, and a handful of outliers conquered the world. Many hugely successful acts, such as U2, were formed exactly this way. They embedded these principles of trust, loyalty, and a relentless work ethic throughout their careers, serving as a model for high-performance team building.

The shift from enthusiastic amateur to practising professional means a change in the order of events, and elements such as talent, skill mastery, and social adeptness become more important than owning equipment or rehearsal space. However, the basic formula stays intact.

During my formative years, I discovered the power of chemistry and the resonance that occurs when the right mix of individuals comes together in a creative space. Time seems to fly by during these moments, and creating incredible music feels effortless. This instinct has been refined over many years, and I've learned to trust this feeling of potential creative flow completely.

Years later, I still vividly remember walking onto a stadium stage for a guest spot with Carlos Santana's band, alongside Johnny Clegg, guitar player Andy Innes, and bass player Trevor Donjeany. Earlier that afternoon, we had only a 10-minute rehearsal session, a talk-through, under Carlos's warm and wonderful guidance. When showtime arrived, it felt to me like a beautiful jam session in a garage, a conversation with inspiring creatives. Percussionist Karl Perazzo beamed positive energy on the riser next to me while Carlos, at centre stage, controlled the flow with his amazing spirit. The huge audience faded from consciousness, and we were left with just the band, communicating effortlessly at the highest level.

In the realm of business and leadership development, I've come to appreciate the significance of mastering the dynamics of team resonance. I've overlooked that this knowledge I've acquired over many years of working in rehearsal spaces and experimenting with various forms and configurations of creative talent is not commonly understood.

Upon reflection, I have come to understand three things:

1. Talent and mastery are not different words for the same thing. Many talented individuals have not persistently worked on developing mastery and, as a result, have never progressed beyond the stage of being enthusiastic amateurs.
2. How one is with others, especially in a high-performing team like a band, is more important than talent or mastery. For instance, the Beatles disbanded after a few years, while the Rolling Stones have remained in business for six decades.
3. The chemistry that creates resonance may appear simple and repeatable when it occurs, but it is quite elusive. This makes it the most valuable commodity we humans possess.

When you feel a surge of inspiration and creative energy that makes anything feel possible, it's important to take it seriously while also allowing yourself to enjoy the moment and surpass your limits.

> *My **Finding Your Groove Principle:** Trust your gut. Team chemistry is felt before it is analysed. When it's right, complexity feels effortless.*

Chris

"Forming the Band" provides valuable insights into team formation, the evolution from amateur to professional, and the importance of chemistry and resonance in creating high-performing teams. There are several themes relevant to management learning that this chapter could illustrate, perhaps the most important three of which are:

1. *Team Formation and Dynamics:* Barry emphasises the importance of appreciating and valuing personality types, and balancing talent, skill, and social-emotional intelligence (EQ) when forming a band. This highlights the critical role of team composition and the dynamics involved in creating a high-performing team.
2. *The Evolution from Amateur to Professional:* The transition from being an enthusiastic amateur to a practising professional necessitates a shift in priorities, with greater emphasis on talent, skill mastery, and social adeptness. This theme is one we have met before, and here, what is underscored is the continuous development required in a professional setting involving others.
3. *The Importance of Chemistry and Resonance:* Barry's reflection on the power of chemistry and the resonance that emerges from the right mix of individuals

working together is a crucial insight for team building. This theme points to the intangible yet vital elements contributing to a team's success.

Here are some ideas to help you follow these as themes in your organisation and work with teams.

Team Composition: Tuckman's Stages of Group Development

A team is its connections and interrelations. Like most things we think of as work, effective performance **in** a team to achieve consistent or effective performance **as** a team requires self-awareness and effort. Various theorists have studied how this happens when it happens (and very frequently it does not, or not all the way). One of the best-known is Bruce Tuckman's model (1965), which outlines the stages of forming, storming, norming, performing, and adjourning that teams typically go through. To an extent, Barry's experiences align with this, particularly in the forming and storming stages, where initial team dynamics and social interactions play a significant role. Briefly, Tuckman's stages of group development look like this:

- *Forming*: happens when a team first comes together or reforms itself for a fresh start after major changes in task or personnel. Typically, all members are polite and positive at this stage. Completing the task is not a high priority.
- *Storming*: after a while, the wish not to conflict begins to compete either with unresolved tensions (personal or contextual) leading to frustration that "nothing seems to be happening" or clashes between members. This stage is where team members may begin to assert ideas.
- *Norming*: assuming the team doesn't implode during Storming, a new order establishes itself in accepted norms or newly cohesive and authentic relationships. All team members accept these "ground rules" internally. This doesn't equate to the task being performed, however.
- *Performing*: it's not always obvious, even to those involved, at what point a team starts to click personally and productively in the task, and there is no guarantee that it will reach this stage, which is a high level of functioning. When it happens, everyone feels the synergy, making the group a powerful source of identity and positive results. For a time.
- *Adjourning*: Eventually, all teams and all groups disband (except perhaps the Rolling Stones), whether by completing the task, running out of time, or moving personnel away. Those who do so after achieving their goals take this success with them. A group's break-up or dissolution is a good moment for learning and reflection, either from successes or failures.

In practice, much teamwork, including being part of a band, doesn't follow this linear path. There are stops, starts, setbacks, and failures. Being forewarned may allow you to be forearmed when it comes to minimising any setbacks and doubt as a newcomer to a group or more decisiveness in decision-making as a leader. To build on this, American management consultant Patrick Lencioni (2007) put forward a list of five dysfunctions and their remedies:

- *Absence of Trust:* Team members remedy this by being open to each other. Trust is your willingness to accept the risk of failure, which is not often discussed in new or evolving teams.
- *Fear of Conflict:* Teams can minimise this by using trust to allow for disagreement and critical questions.
- *Lack of Commitment:* It is difficult to keep people involved, as team energy will sap over time. Early conflict resolution and opinion sharing do allow for genuine buy-in later on.
- *Avoidance of Accountability:* Commitment allows teams to hold each other accountable for decisions and actions.
- *Inattention to Results:* Overcoming all of the above lets the team focus on the charter (collective goal).

Social Intelligence (SI) in Team Performance

It has been fashionable to talk of *Emotional Intelligence* (EI), a concept now most often associated with the work of Daniel Goleman (1996). This focuses on self-awareness and motivation and has limitations as it takes the spotlight away from the nature of group interaction. *Social Intelligence*, an idea that has been around for at least 100 years, is an essential competency for managers. It draws a distinction away from emotional intelligence and is equally crucial for effective leadership and team dynamics. Because SI is about understanding and navigating the social dynamics and interconnected emotions of others to foster effective interactions and relationships, it is largely interpersonal, as we saw in Note 3.1 (EQ) and how you apply your awareness of social and cultural cues to interact successfully with others. SI underscores adapting behaviour and communication style to fit the social environment or context, which is essential for building networks.

As Goleman notes, though, Emotional Intelligence and Social Intelligence are intertwined. Being attuned to your emotions (EI) can help you better understand and respond to others' emotional states, supporting effective social functioning (SI). Similarly, observing social cues can inform how you manage and express your emotions in varying contexts.

Social intelligence involves active listening, empathy, and proficiently adopting different social roles. These skills enable individuals to navigate diverse social scenarios confidently and with finesse, often known as *social self-efficacy* (Bandura 1977).

Developing SI requires the same sort of deliberate practice Barry has already referred to and a keen understanding of various social norms and behaviours. It demands intelligent listening, where one pays full and credulous attention to others, as well as the ability to manage and resolve conflicts smoothly. To an extent, SI can be measured and developed over time, helping individuals enhance their interactions and achieve their objectives in social and professional contexts. If you can develop and incorporate your social intelligence into your management practice, it can significantly improve team cohesion and overall organisational performance. By fostering an environment where social dynamics are understood and valued, you can better motivate your teams and navigate the complexities of workplace relationships.

Flow and Optimal Experience

Barry's description of the effortless and resonant experience of playing with Carlos Santana's band can be related to Mihaly Csikszentmihalyi's concept of Flow (2002). Flow is the state of being completely absorbed in an activity, where one's skills are fully utilised, and the experience is intrinsically rewarding. I like to think of this as a sort of trance state, and usually a very pleasant one.

Characteristics of Flow

Classically, *complete concentration* on the task at hand is essential, allowing you to focus your mental resources fully and efficiently. It's an interesting debate as to whether this is a pre-requisite and something you can set up, or is itself just another way of describing the feeling when Flow comes in. I believe it can be either, and either will involve some kind of induction or ritual.

Then, *clarity of goals* and *immediate feedback* further enhance this focus, ensuring that every action is purposeful and aligned with the desired outcomes (which may be very broad and open-ended). Very often, there is a sense that *time transforms*, either speeding up or slowing down, and you can find yourself deeply immersed in your work without reference to the clock. This immersion makes the *experience intrinsically rewarding*, as the joy and fulfilment derived from the task itself become evident. Moreover, when tasks are approached with *effortlessness and ease*, stress is minimised (perhaps because there is no strain on you), leading to a more pleasant working experience. Crucially, achieving *a balance between the challenge and your available skills* ensures that tasks are just at the edge where learning and production meet. It is neither too easy nor too difficult to maintain engagement and prevent or postpone boredom or anxiety. This harmonious blend of elements fosters an environment where managers can thrive, consistently performing at their best.

Questions for Reflection and Groove

In your experience, how does a leader's ability to embrace mistakes influence team morale and innovation?

How can you integrate humility and confidence into your leadership style without undermining either?

What steps can your organisation take to nurture a culture where people can experience Flow?

3.3 The Pain of Failure (When the Student Is Ready, the Teacher Appears)

Barry

How my sources of inspiration have changed over the decades!

I started with early musical giants like Led Zeppelin and the Rolling Stones, then moved on to Miles Davis and Frank Zappa's experimentations and, later, the African source code of musicians such as Salif Keita and Paco Sery. And then I came back full circle to Zeppelin and the Stones. Everyone was pushing creative, individual boundaries using the same tools of melody, beat, and storytelling, while also building staying-power and learning from mistakes.

Over the past five years, I have been inspired by the work of intellectual icons such as Richard Feynman, Seth Godin, David Bohm, Alan Watts, and Ray Dalio. This has not been a complete departure from music. It is a fresh way of looking at the same subject matter from new perspectives. It has given me new insights into learning, creativity, and connecting with ourselves, others, and the world around us. And the power of being guided by principles.

In his masterful book *Principles for Life and Work* (2017), billionaire hedge fund manager Ray Dalio talks about using the pain of failure as a valuable learning tool. He drew on significant personal failures from the early years of his business, Bridgewater Associates, to build theories and principles that have created and sustained the world's largest hedge fund. Bridgwater's emphasis on human and analytical innovation in areas such as transparency, open-mindedness, and speaking truth to power has embedded resonance in the company culture.

The key learning from this piece can be summarised as follows: embrace mistakes and failures as opportunities for self-reflection and positive change (that is: to prevent the same thing from happening again). This approach becomes a method for developing personal algorithms or principles, which are preferred ways to respond to specific situations. Similar situations will always reoccur, albeit with different individuals involved. In other words, as Dalio puts it, it is important to tolerate a mistake the first time as a chance to learn and improve, and not to tolerate the same mistake to happen repeatedly two or three times.

As a professional musician for hire, I've had many moments of anguish. I have feared that I would be fired and ridiculed or even that my career would be over. If your world is one where you truly feel as good as your last gig, this perceived reality influences everything. One strives for peak performance, with a total focus on infusing a particular performance with soul and passion. This can often get adverse reactions due to elements that are out of sight or out of my control: a band leader with a hangover, a recording engineer's marriage problems, or a singer's bruised ego from a recent TV interview. It could simply be that I had an off day or was unable to prepare. Whatever the reason, I may have to deal with rejection or insulting behaviour. Without a clear set of guiding principles, it could damage my creative psyche for life!

Interestingly, our brain cannot differentiate between physical and mental pain, and it uses past physical experiences as a proxy when needing to feel abstract or imagined pain. So the pain of failure is very real when it happens (Eisenberger, Lieberman, and Williams 2003). Understanding this simple truth has helped me enormously.

I came to understand the potency of pain many years ago when I was a young music student in California. After dedicating much time to building my confidence, I eagerly participated in a variety of ensemble opportunities on campus, including big band, rock, blues, Latin, funk, and more. Each day brought a new experience.

One notoriously tough nut to crack was the Six Horn Band ensemble class facilitated by the late Jeff Berlin, an iconic bass player that I had followed for years on vinyl albums that I bought as a kid in South Africa.

The Six Horn Band classes were organised as follows: a horn section of six seasoned Hollywood session musicians was paired with a rhythm section consisting of three students playing drums, bass, and either guitar or piano. As the director, Berlin would randomly select a piece of music from a stack of manuscripts and distribute the individual parts – charts – to everyone in the room. With minimal time to review their parts, he would count the band in, and the piece would either come to life – or not.

When my turn arrived, fate intervened: the student bass player didn't show up. As a result, Berlin himself stepped in to play bass, which dialled up my anxiety levels! Midway through the performance, Berlin stopped the band and told me I was dragging the tempo, causing him and the ensemble to fall asleep. He even slid off his chair in a mock display of fatigue. I had to pack up and leave, embarrassed, crestfallen, and disheartened.

At that moment, I had to make a tough decision. My first instinct was to accept the humiliation and go home. However, I realised I needed to reflect on what went wrong, work on it, and face the challenge again. I chose to trust my abilities, summon some fighting spirit, and practice harder to stay just ahead of the beat, which requires energy and confidence. This is especially important when playing with a larger ensemble, as the drummer needs to drive the energy, especially with horn sections that can be sluggish and pull back the tempo. I put in plenty of effort, listened attentively, and practised a lot.

After two weeks, I returned to the Six Horn Band session and requested to replay the same piece of music. By then, Berlin had forgotten about my previous attempt. After we finished, he got up, shook my hand, and said, "Great job!"

This was a significant moment for me, and it has since become one of my anchor visualisations. I use it when I need to dig deep, move past a bruised ego, and use pain as my teacher to learn and improve.

> *My* ***Finding Your Groove Principle:*** *Failure is a cue to pause, learn, and adapt. Acknowledge mistakes without judgment, identify what went wrong, and commit to change. Fill the gaps – whether through learning, adjusting behaviour, or avoiding pitfalls – and fully own your growth.*

Chris

Barry reflects on a profound appreciation for the diverse expressions of creativity. This cultural evolution is not merely about music but encapsulates a broader spectrum of intellectual and emotional growth, especially evident in his recent alignment with thinkers outside music.

Barry's journey of evolving inspiration is both fascinating and deeply resonant. As I see it, he is getting at three themes applicable to development for managers and leaders:

1. *Growth Through Adversity:* The role of resilience in enhancing leadership performance and strategies to cultivate resilience among leaders.
2. *Pain as a Teacher:* Emotional Management at work and how pain and passion influence leadership effectiveness and culture.
3. *Strategies for Overcoming:* Good practices for overcoming various educational challenges and preventing, or at least mitigating, future failure.

Barry finds meaning in Dalio's philosophy and outlook, introduced in *Principles for Life and Work.* This outlook calls for embracing an interconnected reality (the world of "things as they are") where pain or suffering, combined with reflection, equals productivity.

This underscores a critical theme: the constructive power of pain and failure. Dalio's approach to using personal and professional failures as learning tools aligns perfectly with the concept of growth through adversity. I have found similar insights in my own exploration of management learning and personal development. Research suggests that resilience and personal growth often stem from facing and overcoming adversity. Dalio sets out a 5-step process for this, which is very goal-oriented. There is some evidence supporting this as a strategy. Dalio's advocacy for open and transparent communication, a mission to foster a working environment that feels meaningful in its culture, and an evaluation of ideas based on merit and not hierarchy all make sense.

Leaders who navigate challenges with an open mind and a reflective attitude can transform setbacks into stepping stones. While an epiphany may take just a second to occur, there is no shortcut to getting one. Deep, personal self-awareness is a prerequisite, and this is not a simple recipe.

In Barry's anecdote about the humiliating experience with Jeff Berlin, I found a vivid illustration of pain as a teacher. The emotional pain he felt when criticised publicly could have easily led to defeat. His decision to reflect, practice, and ultimately overcome this challenge highlights a crucial neurobiological and psychological insight: our brain can process physical and mental pain in similar ways. That is, the same parts of the brain are activated whether there is a physical injury or an emotional disruption(from, for example, social rejection). Much of our idiom to describe emotional strain, such as "gut-wrenching," reinforces this overlap (Eisenberger 2012).

There is a link here to the idea of universal values. Whether I belong or not is a potent driver for health and well-being, so social exclusion may have just as damaging and painful an effect as being punched in the gut. Understanding this is vital for anyone in a creative or high-performance field, where the fear of failure can be as debilitating as physical injury.

An organisational leader must also show compassion and steward the collective well-being of the group. Many thought leaders have echoed the principle of embracing mistakes and failures as opportunities for growth in the professional realm. For instance, in educational leadership, emotional management and resilience are recognised as key to navigating the complexities of guiding others. In business, leaders who foster a culture of transparency, open-mindedness, and continuous improvement often find their organisations more innovative and resilient.

This Note's *Finding Your Groove Principle* brilliantly encapsulates these ideas. It aligns with Dalio's principle of creating personal algorithms to respond to specific situations, thereby preventing repeated mistakes. This approach is concerned with avoiding errors and has an extra emphasis in systematically improving one's responses to recurring challenges. This reflection, acceptance, and proactive improvement method is central to developing effective leadership strategies.

Moreover, Barry's experience highlights a broader theme of strategies for overcoming personal and professional obstacles. A strategy is always contextual. Effective leaders employ various strategies to manage and mitigate challenges, including fostering a supportive culture, encouraging open communication, and continuously learning from setbacks.

Questions for Reflection and Groove

How can you reframe a recent professional or personal failure as a catalyst for growth rather than a source of defeat?

In your leadership approach, what structures can you put in place to ensure that mistakes become stepping stones to greater performance?

How might you encourage team members or colleagues to harness the lessons of failure without dwelling on blame or regret?

3.4 The Rehearsal Trap

Barry

I'm twelve years old, with years of drumming experience already behind me, and all I want is to spend hours playing radio hits with a guitarist, bassist, and singer – the band setup of the time. I've been introduced to a well-known local band and invited to one of their rehearsals. Their drummer is way more advanced than me and five years older. I absorb everything he does with the pure joy of learning a craft I love without feeling intimidated or inadequate.

During a break, the lead singer turns to me and asks if I can play the drums well. Without hesitation, I say, "Yes, I can." He then asks if I want to join another band looking for a drummer to prepare for a Battle of the Bands performance for a large audience. My response is immediate: "When can I start?"

That was my instinctive approach as a kid – to dive in headfirst, knowing I'd have to stretch and learn along the way. But the growth and development was where the excitement lived.

When I started learning to play the drums, my goal was to develop enough skills to play with and for others. If I had waited to achieve some far-off, high level of mastery as my entry fee, I would surely have lost the excitement and never progressed.

I experienced the joy of making music in a team very early, and it was addictive. My learning style was to watch more experienced players, and then, once back in my bedroom/practice room, I'd attempt to mimic what I'd absorbed. This was done with a carefree, do-it-yourself (DIY) attitude, and I figured out technique hacks to duplicate the sounds I "felt" while observing these more advanced musicians. I had memorised the experiences as sounds and images which then made my own.

This combination of curiosity, desire, practice and talent worked well for me, and I progressed rapidly. My guiding principle was clear, though not consciously articulated at the time: develop just enough ability to perform in a present-time situation. I neither waited for perfection nor became anxious about failure (although that did develop much later!). My focus was unwavering. Hours felt like minutes, and I was consumed with developing my offering as a drummer, musician, performer, and band member.

What I've described above is a textbook method for Silicon Valley startups. As LinkedIn co-founder Reid Hoffman said in 2009, "If you're not embarrassed by the first version of your product, you've launched too late."

In time, and as my skills improved, I noticed a phenomenon I call *the Rehearsal Trap*. This is the constant struggle between practising in the cocoon of a rehearsal room and the reality of performing in front of an audience. Both activities are important, and the timing and strategic process are even more crucial. Here's what I mean:

1. Rehearsing in a fun and structured way is a necessary step in creating a live performance, and having some experienced-based leadership can be very helpful (which is why professional acts usually have a musical director to project manage the rehearsal process).

2. At the earliest opportunity, a small, supportive audience (like family and friends) should be invited when the show, which is still a work in progress and a rough draft, can be played from start to finish.

There is nothing quite like an audience to highlight the cracks in what you and your band members might think is a fantastic and fully formed set of songs. Interestingly, understanding what works and what doesn't is mostly achieved by experiencing the energy in the room and, much less, via direct verbal feedback. It's as if having people observe your isolated and intimate creative output forces you to get out of your own way and gain a wider perspective of what you're doing.

I have spent weeks rehearsing for projects that built up to a seemingly well-prepared performance, only to be dismayed by how off-target and robotic the event felt. My first Battle of the Bands performance mentioned at the start of this note comes to mind. I worked for weeks with a group of fellow teenagers to construct a setlist of songs in the hope of a standing ovation and a prize. We loved the process, and it sounded better and better as we rehearsed. To our ears, that is. On the night of the show, we were beyond nervous and dismayed by the prowess and talent of the competing acts. The audience gave us a lukewarm response, and the reality of the entire experience humbled us. At that point, the potential for learning would have been massive … had we just got over ourselves and looked for feedback about how to do it better next time and the next.

My lived experience has proven that continuous long hours of isolated rehearsal will produce diminishing returns if not interspersed with test audiences. Perhaps this is because when creatives are at work, they explore stuff they love and collectively self-endorse their output. But is this *really* their best work, and when do they begin to drink their own Kool-Aid?

The swiftest route to world-beating performance is to stress test as early as possible by asking the world, that is, an audience. Starting with friendly faces is perfectly fine. However, this must always be done *before* you are ready. For musicians, a rule of thumb could be that when you feel that two more weeks of practice are needed to perfect the show, that's the day for audience #1.

The methodology is as follows:

Perform to Audience #1 then reflect, accept, learn, react and re-adjust. This will include the songwriting and running order edits. Then, more rehearsal.
Perform to Audience #2. Repeat the process.

After two or three more iterations, this act will have sprinted toward battle readiness, far ahead of a similar group that is not leaving the safety of the rehearsal space. At this point, the timing is good for that first outing into the world of ticket-paying audiences, where the chances of winning hearts are hugely increased! Critically, the process of learning, reacting, and adjusting must meanwhile continue.

This is one example of the entrepreneurial start-up process. The founders are a singer, guitarist, bassist, and drummer. Their offering to the world is their songs, performed with attitude and a mission to move people.

> *My **Finding Your Groove Principle:** Share your work before you're ready. Feedback fuels progress, so test, adjust, repeat.*

Chris

Two themes strike me from this Note, which is a slice of the reality it takes to become and perform well as a group:

1. *Perfectionism and Procrastination*
   With his approach of developing just enough ability to perform and not waiting for perfection, Barry highlights the importance of overcoming these tendencies to achieve progress and success. He subtly underscores the pitfalls of the twin ideas of perfectionism and procrastination, concepts for which some underlying theory exists.
2. *Agile Techniques in Management (Rehearsal and Real-World Testing)*
   Barry introduces the concept of the "Rehearsal Trap," or the error of remaining too long in isolation from the kind of feedback only to be found in the performance in front of an audience.

   This theme is crucial in management as it emphasises the need for real-world testing and feedback to refine and improve performance. Barry's iterative process of performing, learning, reacting, and adjusting mirrors agile management principles.

Perfectionism and Procrastination

Perfectionism is the tactic of never letting something go, by never accepting that it's ready to stop. Procrastination is also the tactic of never letting something go, by never accepting that it's ready to start. These are both delaying tactics and, in Barry's context, the delay refers to allowing the practice to extend to the live performance. With very few exceptions, if we see contact with the customer, market, recipient, client, user, learner – or whatever is the appropriate term for your situation – as being outside the scope of the creative process, then we have failed to understand the nature of our business and the correct design of our business model. Barry's warning not to wait or expect perfection *before* a performance aligns with the idea that striving for perfection can hinder progress and innovation.

Research by Dr Piers Steel in his book *The Procrastination Equation* (2011) suggests that perfectionism is a significant predictor of procrastination. Individuals can overcome procrastination and achieve their goals more efficiently by focusing on iterative improvement rather than perfection. Related to this is the concept of *satisficing*. This was part of a theory of decision-making introduced to cognitive psychology and economics by the American political scientist Simon Herbert (Herbert 1956). It involves aiming for a satisfactory rather than an optimal solution, thereby reducing the paralysis that perfectionism can cause. This was intended as a pragmatic approach to selecting whichever (available and viable) alternative that would cover most of the aims or goals in mind, which draws from a rich vein of American philosophical thought called Pragmatism.

Agile Techniques in Management

In general usage, agility is the capacity – whether in action or thought – to respond to feedback and then move or change rapidly, easily, and with energy. As a specific term used in business and management, *Agile* originated in the 1990s as a methodology, an extension of developments in productivity improvement in manufacturing systems. This was then formally introduced in the software development industry with the Agile Manifesto in 2001, created by a group of 17 technologists who sought to address the limitations of traditional, plan-driven approaches to software development.

The manifesto set out four preferences as guiding principles:

1. *Individuals and interactions* over processes and tools. People and their interactions are what achieve project success.
2. *Working software* over comprehensive documentation. Focus on delivering functional products rather than extensive documentation.
3. *Customer collaboration* over contract negotiation. Foregrounding iterative collaboration with customers to meet their needs.
4. *Responding to change over following a plan,* preferring adaptability and flexibility in response to changing requirements and environments.

The Agile approach, now widely used in project management, involves iterative cycles of planning, executing, testing, and refining. As a method, it allows teams to respond to feedback and make adjustments quickly, hopefully leading to continuous improvement and better outcomes. What are the main advantages of Agile as an outlook or mindset? Here are a few:

1. Reframe how you define delivery. Delivery isn't a one-shot, final "ta-dah!" It is the whole messy process with many points of contact. This is most useful in contexts or industries where contact and, crucially, feedback from the customer are a major part of the product, and a feeling for that is a major part of the process.
2. Collaboration among the team and between the organisation and its customers or clients can lead to massive improvement and benefits from the process. This ties well with continuous improvement through an iterative repeat of the process.
3. Crucially, Agile should lead to better results when results are measured. Rapid, not perfect. Lean, not wasteful.

Equally, certain caveats and barriers must be considered if you plan to introduce these principles in your workplace (or understand them properly if they are already present). Again, three examples as prompts:

1. As with all changes of direction or culture, adequate communication and plenty of time are needed, including tolerance of failure (a meta-level of Agile methodology).
2. Be prepared for parts of the organisation or team to lose sight of their previously written-in-stone goals and for less control over forecasts and budgets. Equally, new ways need to be found to prevent or avoid runaway costs.
3. Less documentation and record-keeping can feel (and sometimes be) a risk. Scheduling still matters but is no longer the point of the project. Things become *much* less predictable (counter-caveat: things are inherently rarely predictable anyway). The set list and the date of the gig are important, and they will be better for emerging from the process leading up to them, not the other way around.

Rehearsal and Real-World Testing

That last point brings us back to what Barry noticed about the relationship between performance and feedback and his notion of the Rehearsal Trap. This illustrates the importance of balancing practice with real-world testing. The book also features some other (emerging) ideas on how we learn that have been featured elsewhere in management. This can be seen as the wider need to move beyond planning and into execution and feedback loops.

Eric Ries's Lean Startup methodology (2011) also emphasises the importance of early testing and feedback. This methodology advocates the Build-Measure-Learn feedback loop, in which products (or live performances) are developed iteratively, with each cycle providing valuable insights for refinement.

Questions for Reflection and Groove

Where have you fallen into "rehearsal mode" for too long, and what "minimal viable test" could you launch sooner?

What area of your work or personal projects might you benefit from launching early and learning live rather than rehearsing in isolation?

In what areas of your work or personal projects might that be the wrong approach? What is the difference?

3.5 A Freelancer's Medley: Talent + Hard Work + Authenticity

Barry

I started my freelance career at twelve, leveraging my natural musical talent, which I had developed over six years of experiential learning. It was my way of avoiding rugby and cricket, and it was also a superpower when it came to peer recognition, not to mention early-stage attention from girls.

Financial reward was part of the equation. I quickly understood that charging an entrance fee to performances was a simple and effective way of generating revenue: supply and demand in action. After a single Saturday afternoon of "working," I earned four times more than most 12-year-olds receive in pocket money for the month.

Fast-forward a decade: I was a music student in California. I was the personification of a heat-driven purpose. Nothing had wavered in my trajectory. I had the singular objective of becoming a master of my craft, with a burning drive to explore and express an overflow of creative narrative. Everything I did, from where I went, what I did, who I engaged with, and what I read, was a means to an end. Everything.

At this point, I had achieved unconscious mastery. I was spending every waking hour in pursuit of my dream: a career as an internationally respected drummer, performing and recording all over the world. I love reflecting now on this singular pursuit, namely, the journey of action-learning by observing and then modelling the best practitioners I could find.

What changed this purity?

I needed to generate regular income! To do that, I needed to engage in equally critical practices such as being consistent, reliable, and open-minded. These are super important for reputation and network growth but were super dull to me as a young man with the world as a playground. In short, I burned some bridges and learned how quickly you can destroy something that takes years to construct. I used these errors of judgment to develop certain principles, learning from painful experiences and not repeating them. This way of being was endorsed decades later by the inimitable Ray Dalio in his book *Principles: Life and Work* (2017), as referenced in a previous Note.

The first principle I learned was that getting along with your team and partners is more important than having talent and mastery of a skill. For example, while at music school in the USA, I heard three frequently repeated themes from faculty and visiting clinicians, all successful players in the music business: (i) The talent-to-hard work ratio is roughly 20/80. (ii) Avoid arrogance. (iii) Be kind to yourself and those around you because success today is not guaranteed tomorrow, and those that you offend on your way up will remember you on the way down! It didn't make sense then, but it stuck with me.

While at the same music school, I had a profound ah-ha moment. After 18 months of trying to outdo my American classmates, I realised that being different was more powerful than being better. They had grown up with similar theories, cultures and role models, so trying to compete on that basis was unnecessarily swimming upstream. As mentioned in the opening Note of this chapter, while performing in ensemble classes, I found I would grab everyone's attention when playing what was natural – rhythms from my African heritage. People are drawn to something expertly executed and mastered, but also with a touch of the exotic.

The second principle here was that cultural authenticity, referred to as *terroir* in French, is the key to differentiation. If your roots are in South Africa, stop trying to fool the world that you grew up in Hollywood. This can significantly increase your chances of long-term career success.

Then third, as I developed my freelance brand, I found it incredibly valuable to develop instinctive principles for survival. It was an iterative process of landing in painful places (getting fired, losing contracts, getting rehired elsewhere), learning from this and ultimately adapting my behaviours. The freelance music business is not predicated on qualifications. What matters is having the necessary skills on demand for particular contexts, which could change several times in one day. As they say, "You're only as good as your last gig."

This training was beneficial for my freelance music career, which was unpredictable and sometimes challenging, with unexpected events such as the fallout from the 9/11 attacks, the global recession in 2008, and the global pandemic in 2020. All of this against the backdrop of a tech-driven disruption of the music value chain - affordable, powerful software distributed at scale, a shift in consumption from ownership to access, and the devaluation of recorded music due to subscription-based streaming on demand.

Using the metaphor of a circus performer, I have developed a high level of expertise in "plate spinning" and, most importantly, not dropping too many! In other words, the capacity for responsiveness, adaptability, and managing complexity

> *My **Finding Your Groove Principle:** Freelancers thrive on trust, relationships, and authenticity, not talent alone. Trust is sacred, relationships matter more than expertise, and authenticity is everything.*

Chris

The freelance economy is flourishing in an increasingly personalised and digitised world economic system. According to the World Bank, almost 47% of the global workforce is self-employed (World Bank 2024). An estimated 59 million Americans (36% of the US workforce) engage in some kind of freelance, gig, or contracted freelance work. In the UK, the figure is 4.3 million, and the European Union estimates that 27.66 million people are self-employed. This shift towards gig and freelance careers underscores the significance of adaptability, cultural authenticity, and foundational principles for navigating a volatile landscape.

Managers and leaders must understand these dynamics for personal development and for fostering a culture of innovation and resilience within their teams and organisations. So, this is a great subject.

Building on Barry's three parts to his Finding Your Groove Principle, the Freelance principle may apply to running and guiding an organisation as well as to an individual's career.

The Interpersonal Realities of Freelancing

The freelance economy is transforming the way people engage in work. Freelancers enjoy the flexibility of being so close to "supply and demand" by setting their schedules and working independently. They use their unique skills to create sustainable careers and must have a strong understanding of their value proposition and the ability to adapt to market changes. In organisations, this highlights the importance for managers to foster a culture that values entrepreneurial thinking, continuous learning, and the ability to pivot strategies as market dynamics evolve. Because you cannot do or know everything on your own, all of these entail maintaining strong and sustainable relationships with others, including people in other institutions or systems. It's a mindset that is useful for creating a workforce that is more proactive, engaged, and motivated by more than just financial rewards. For leaders, these factors are essential for driving innovation and maintaining a competitive advantage.

There is an *intrapersonal* side of this, too. The freelance model emphasises the importance of financial independence and the ability to generate income through one's talents. This means empowering yourself to take ownership of your projects and view yourself as an entrepreneur. If you work in an existing organisation structure, the same thing is true, although, in your role, you may define it as "our" projects.

Key Principles of Freelancing

Drawing from Ray Dalio's *Principles: Life and Work,* Barry's narrative emphasises the importance of foundational principles that guide decision-making and behaviour in personal and professional contexts. For leaders, this underscores the necessity of establishing clear values and principles that are a compass for the organisation's direction and culture. These principles should emphasise the importance of relationships, trust, integrity, and authenticity – critical for long-term success and resilience. In practice, this means fostering an organisational culture where trust is paramount and employees feel valued and supported in their authentic expressions.

There are no shortcuts here. These principles must start with you as an entrepreneur or manager and be visible to others in your actions. Trust always has to radiate out from its source. People who say "Trust me," but don't start by trusting you have not understood the nature of trust.

Additionally, when Barry talks about learning from failure, that adaptability speaks to the importance of fostering a growth mindset within organisations. Leaders should encourage experimentation, tolerate calculated risks, and view failures as learning opportunities. This approach drives innovation and equates to resilience as individuals and teams learn to navigate challenges and adapt to unforeseen circumstances.

Cultural Authenticity and Differentiation

The concept of *terroir* expresses the unique flavour that one's cultural background brings to one's work, a potent differentiator in today's homogenised world. Generally used in the wine industry, terroir is derived from the French words for soil or earth and encompasses every part of the ecology that results in something distinctive. It's a suitably systemic way of deriving principles for healthy differentiation.

In the shared narrative, the individual's embrace of their African heritage set them apart and added a unique value that was highly sought after. This illustrates a broader lesson for leaders: the power of diversity and the competitive edge it offers. Encouraging teams to bring their whole selves to work, including their cultural backgrounds and unique perspectives, can foster a more creative, innovative, and resilient organisational culture.

This approach requires leaders to create an environment where diversity is tolerated, celebrated, and leveraged as a key strategic asset. It challenges the traditional paradigms of conformity and highlights the importance of building teams with a rich tapestry of backgrounds, experiences, and ways of thinking. In doing so, organisations can enhance their adaptability and innovation, which are crucial competencies in navigating the complexities of the modern business landscape.

Questions for Reflection and Groove

How can trust and cultural authenticity become strategic advantages in your organisation?

What lessons from freelancing resilience can be applied to navigating uncertainty in your career?

How might a focus on relationships over assets transform your leadership approaches?

3.6 Tempo of Leadership

Barry

Paul Shaffer is taking a break from his role as bandleader for *Late Night with David Letterman*, the longest-running and arguably most successful night time talk show in American history. In his absence, drummer Anton Fig steps in, with his signature green Yamaha drum set moved to centre stage, a mix of acoustic instruments and electronics. Anton leads the band with a perfect mix of confidence and humility, cueing the musicians while trading banter and drum rolls with Letterman.

As a student in the USA, this was my favourite show, partly because Anton Fig is South African. I'd been a fan of his since hearing his work on Joan Armatrading's albums. On Letterman, a role he occupied for over 30 years, I was struck by his powerful presence and his ability to use humour, sometimes self-deprecating, as drummer and sometimes bandleader of "The World's Most Dangerous Band." Many years later, while touring North America frequently with the Johnny Clegg Band, I met Anton, and we became friends. Whenever we performed in New York, I'd stop by the Ed Sullivan Theater to watch a taping of the Letterman show. Those visits sometimes ended with a cold beer and a good chat at a nearby music bar.

Previous to this, as a Letterman-watching student in the mid-90s, I had developed some understanding of the dynamics when playing in these types of medium to large-sized ensembles. This included everything from overcoming stage fright to building confidence while performing with the Tuesday Big Band or smaller-style ensembles. We'd join these classes daily to rack up performance credits. The sessions paired student drummers and bassists with a rotating cast of seasoned but often disinterested and grumpy LA session musicians hired for the day. Perfect training for the real world!

I prepared for my first Tuesday Big Band experience by spending hours in the practice room, learning the chart (music score), singing the phrases, and paying attention to dynamics and style notes (whether to play loud, medium, or softly, and annotations that guide the player regarding the stylistic nuances that cannot be scored). This careful preparation abandoned me on the day, faced with a cold room of session musicians and a sea of music students, and I let nerves and fear of embarrassment take over. Dave Pozzi, a veteran Los Angeles sax player and band leader, walked over, took away my chart, and told me to forget the reading and simply keep time. I was terrified!

What had happened?

Upon reflection, I realised that I had been so consumed with all the intricate details of the score that I had forgotten my main role as a drummer: keeping the tempo, or time, steady so the band could play the music. This was an important lesson in prioritising the fundamental, core function with high situational awareness, managing nervous energy, breathing, maintaining the tempo, and *then* tackling the technical details. Groove is the desired result here, and when emergent, it is felt by everyone in the band and audience.

One year after learning from this painful experience, I was playing as many slots as possible at each Tuesday Big Band class, with no preparation, sight-reading the score, and hoping for the big, complicated pieces with long drum solos that required the drummer to cue and lead the ensemble. I had grown from a nervous follower into a confident leader, and so when I saw Anton Fig leading the Letterman band, it resonated deeply.

This outcome was underpinned by many hours of often mundane practice, listening, and raising of awareness; small, private steps daily that manifest in a winning public result. This is a process of preparation for an unknown situation, in order to respond with confidence rather than to react with fear. Looking back, this was an exercise in confidence, authenticity, and leadership that aligns with anything in the executive leadership world.

In big band culture, one of the lead instrumentalists is usually the official band leader, and drummers have often led successful bands, if you consider Buddy Rich or Art Blakey. However, whether band leader or not, the drummer informally leads the way.

The drummer's role of keeping tempo, providing stability, and providing some signalling for critical moments is true for most contemporary music groups but is critical in big band jazz, where the drummer steers the ship by constantly signalling and signposting critical information and by being totally on top of the master score. This is achieved by simultaneously reacting to multiple inputs, such as reining in any fluctuations in tempo, highlighting the "roadmap" (master score) with accents and flourishes, articulating rhythmic lines with the horn section, feeding improvisational spirit behind soloists, managing band dynamics, feeling the band's energy, and all the while interpreting the notated drum score.

This level of leadership can only be achieved with equally high levels of preparation, confidence, active listening, open-mindedness, and flow. These ensembles personify meritocracy and a distribution of leadership throughout the system. Each instrumentalist takes ownership of their part, and each section leader takes ownership of their section, all in service of the overall system and, ultimately, the music being played with a feeling of groove.

The drummer is the overall systems thinker, highlighting the way for the group.

In terms of raw power, a big band drummer's closest equivalent would be found in heavy/speed metal. Nothing has been more satisfying in my career than being in flow, in the driver's seat, behind a thundering and grooving big band!

In Big Band drumming, prioritisation is critical, and as shared in my anecdote, focusing on less important details instead of the primary function, which is "time," will result in a train wreck. This brings me to another important point: mistakes. When making a mistake in the detail or nuance of the drum performance, nothing is worse than stopping to play, thereby disrupting the core function of keeping time for the collective. We all make mistakes; however, in this context, if the drummer spends even a second on self-criticism or panics and loses their place in the music, it's over for everyone. Therefore, the learned behaviour is that mistakes need to be noticed, acknowledged, accepted, and then instantly moved past without missing a beat. Any forensic analysis and reflection can come later.

Building on the leadership theme, a good drummer or leader will focus on the big goals and ignore distracting details and ego for the good of the collective purpose. Once on track, space can be made to revisit the details.

In hindsight and with reflective practice, I have gained a lot of valuable learning and wisdom from my music performance journey. For a long time, I thought that the long hours spent developing habits, skills, and creative capacity were only applicable to music. However, I have come to realise that these principles are valuable to any ambitious practitioner in any discipline.

> *My* ***Finding Your Groove Principle:*** *Healthy leadership is earned through confidence, humility, communication, preparation, and positive intent. Learn from mistakes without dwelling on them, but avoid repeating them. Mistakes are powerful lessons when used to grow.*

Chris

Two cultural biases influence our mainstream conception of leadership. The first favours using hierarchical power to explain leadership, made worse by an obsession with the person at the top – their skills, experience, and temperament. We tend to focus on the lead instrument or the conductor and forget that what the band needs to function is also distributed among its members – all of whom are there for a reason, not just to make up a crowd to make the leader look good. This is a reasonable description of what we see when we study how modern organisations function because, when asked about it, everyone working there assumes leadership to come from the top. So, that's what theorists measure.

The second is our tendency to treat our conclusions about the study of leadership as a dyad. We frame it as a question of only two elements: a conversation between two people or between a single person and a group, which amounts to the same thing.

So, what are the key themes here?

Prioritisation and *focus* are certainly important. At a personal level, Barry highlights the importance of prioritising core functions over getting lost in details, whether keeping time in a band or maintaining focus on key objectives in leadership.

Attaining informal leadership through *preparedness* and *confidence*, Barry's journey from nervousness to confident leadership in the big band setting underscores the value of thorough preparation and the development of confidence.

Regarding handling mistakes and developing resilience, Barry's ability to move past errors without disrupting the overall performance is also a crucial theme in leadership. We cover these elsewhere in the book, so what interested me about *this* experience was the realisation of informal leadership as a synchronising tempo in a group setting.

Sensorimotor Coupling and Leadership

If you take 100 metronomes, stand them on a suspended platform in rows of ten, lines on a plank, and set each one in motion at different times, it looks (and sounds) chaotic and disordered. What happens is that within three minutes, all 100 devices are synchronised (phased) with each other in a mesmerising unity of clicks.

The concept of *sensorimotor coupling* highlights the importance of synchronisation between a leader and their team. This coupling concept has been studied in terms of the connection between music and the psychology of a sense of "feeling the groove" (as an emotional response). In leadership, this can be likened to a leader's need to set the tempo and maintain cohesion within the team, ensuring that everyone is working in harmony. This is coupled with an inherent, receptive quality present in the other people in the organisational ensemble. When a part of the whole maintains a consistent tempo, the group is more likely to coordinate successfully. However, a sudden change in the tempo somewhere in the system can disrupt this coordination, leading to potential challenges within the group.

Barry's experience as a drummer in maintaining a steady tempo was crucial for the band's cohesion. In leadership, consistency while being responsive to the group's dynamics can enhance team performance. Nearly every organisation maintains a hierarchy with the role of "Leader" at the top, but leaders are part of a system of complex relationships. They must balance setting the pace with the flexibility to adapt when necessary, ensuring the group remains coordinated.

Impact of Leadership on Group Cohesion

Group dynamics are helped when the presence of a leader increases the perception of cooperation and connectedness within a group. Even when the leader introduced a perturbation (a change in tempo), the group members reported increased feelings of being followers and of group cohesion.

This finding is relevant to Barry's observation of the drummer's role as an informal leader in a big band. Just as the drummer's tempo guides the band, a leader's consistency and ability to manage changes effectively can foster a strong sense of unity within the team. In leadership, clear guidance and consistent communication can create an environment where team members feel connected and cooperative.

The Challenge of Coordination in Medium-Sized Groups

Maintaining coordination in medium-sized groups is complex due to the integration-segregation challenge. Individuals must decide whether to follow the leader's tempo or maintain their rhythm. This decision-making process reflects the cognitive load involved in leadership, where leaders must manage multiple inputs and guide the team through complex tasks.

Finding Your Groove is an embodied process. In music, a certain rhythmic complexity invites players and audience alike to fill the space with their body movements. It just emerges spontaneously, though not without great skill. Similarly, in business or management, a certain organisational complexity (a deep awareness of the leadership team, for example) invites colleagues to move in that same rhythm. Again, it will feel like it is a spontaneous emergence when it happens, but there is serious craft and wisdom in the playing.

So this complexity mirrors the challenges leaders face in organisations, just as it did in Barry's Big Band organisation, where balancing individual autonomy with team coordination is crucial. Barry's reflection on the drummer's role in managing the tempo, dynamics, and flow within the band can be applied to how leaders must manage both the macro (overall direction) and micro (individual contributions) aspects of leadership to maintain group cohesion.

Consequences of Perturbation in Leadership

When someone changes the tempo, regardless of whether they are a formal or informal leader, it disrupts the group's coordination. This suggests that while change is necessary, how the leader introduces it can significantly impact the group's performance.

Barry's loss of place in the music due to over-focusing on technical details can be compared to leaders who might lose sight of the bigger picture when managing changes. Successful leaders must introduce changes thoughtfully and ensure their team can adapt without losing overall cohesion. Emphasising the importance of consistency, the impact of leadership on group cohesion, the complexity of coordination, and the careful management of change can provide a rich theoretical backdrop to the practical insights Barry shares in his chapter.

Questions for Reflection and Groove

In high-pressure situations, how do you balance the need to keep in mind the big picture with the temptation to micro-manage details?

When you make a mistake as a leader, what techniques help you recover quickly and maintain group cohesion?

How can you instil a sense of shared responsibility for tempo across your team so leadership becomes more distributed?

3.7 Voice(s)

Barry

"What do I want to say?"

This is a big question, and the answer can move from the direct and unmediated clarity of a five-year-old to something more refined, constrained, and filtered later in life. Fears can surface around being judged or seen as an imposter, and most of us learn ways to control our behaviour and word choices, even if this contrasts with the things we value.

For a 30-year-old, answering the question "What do I want to say?" is challenging because the truth is likely hidden beneath many layers of self-limiting "mud." This brings up the concept of *Voice*, which directly relates to the question, "Who am I?"

German-born self-help author Eckhardt Tolle (2009) talks of his transformative experience of decoupling the thoughts or voices in his head (doing) from his true being. He uses an X-Y axis to represent this state, with the horizontal axis depicting linear action or doing, and the vertical axis representing the depth of being. Tolle suggests that while both are important, most people only live in the horizontal plane. The *intersection* of X and Y describes the phenomenon of Voice, where actions are rooted in the authenticity of knowing who one is, beyond mere activity.

Discovering one's true voice is a big deal in music. It is a journey I have been on since I was five years old. As a drummer with music and rhythm in my DNA, I have always been drawn to authenticity and messaging in my work. Let me illustrate this with a real-world example. I once observed a drum performance by Efrain Toro in a recording studio directly after another player had recorded a performance in identical conditions using the same instruments. Later that day, when I listened to the playback with the recording engineer, the difference was astonishing. The results were a universe apart. Efrain's take was open, rich, and resonant, while that of the other drummer (same instruments and same microphone configuration) sounded constrained, tight, and airless. This difference is partly due to elevated technique and experience, but more importantly, it reflects the intangible power of intent, soul, or … Voice.

Voice is where you land when technical limitations are overcome. The thousands of hours of "doing" to develop motor skill mastery is a recent popular concept, though I hesitate to jump on board with that because time alone is not enough - one has to invest fully engaged energy and purpose. Without this, more time spent can start to deliver diminishing returns in terms of progress toward mastery, where the focus turns to what needs to be said. In essence, mastery evolves from doing to being.

Voice is a genuine, authentic story shaped by one's worldview, values and passion. This is the difference between a skilled singer on *America's Got Talent*, and an artist like Neil Young, who conveys overwhelming truth in a unique voice, or how Kendrick Lamar's unwavering activism is embedded in music. My late friend Colin

Vearncombe (known as Black), embodied authenticity and had a beautifully resonant voice. He admired Neil Young's songwriting and often referenced Young's powerful messages delivered in a thin, reedy-sounding voice. Similarly, Kendrick Lamar may have a vocal timbre that some find irritating compared to artists like Jay-Z or J. Cole, and his deeply profound messaging, combined with his exceptional rhythmic delivery, truly reflects his Voice. Lamar's work shines a light on and sometimes offers hope and pride for the challenging realities of South Central LA.

In business, managers and leaders rely on performance to translate their ideas to others. Many valuable opportunities, innovations, and solutions have been lost due to a failure to harness the power of words and stories. Matt Abrahams at Stanford Graduate School of Business has developed a course called Strategic Communication, which focuses on cultivating these essential skills. This course is now part of their MBA curriculum and is a strong indicator of the future workplace, where AI-enhanced humans will thrive.

This mix of learned abilities and the confidence of purpose manifests as a Voice which is almost impossible to ignore, and much like a music performance, there are two types:

1. clever words and superficial mastery = low-value voice.
2. simple words, with authenticity and mastery = high-value voice.

For MBA graduates and company executives, this means getting past business jargon and the "growth at all costs" mindset. It involves finding a state of being, a personal set of non-negotiable values described in simple words to oneself, and the courage not to waver from them. Finding your Voice happens when you make decisions that drive actions based on the broadest possible understanding of your existence.

I found my Voice at various points during my music career. It was always when I achieved the sweet spot between mastery, intent, and risk-taking. However, I have also lost my Voice many times, especially when driven by ego, money, or prestige. Without a well-defined internal narrative based on my personal beliefs and intentions, there is no authentic story and, consequently, no authentic voice.

> *My* ***Finding Your Groove Principle:*** *Write your non-negotiable purpose in simple sentences and practice saying it aloud in front of a mirror. Record it on your phone, aiming for clarity, as if explaining it to a six-year-old or grandma. Make listening to the recording a daily practice, and re-record from memory once a week to strengthen your message.*

Chris

In its literal sense, voice refers to vibrations or sound (I'll use a small "v" for this). For musicians, the ability to use their vocal cords as an instrument is a matter of professional importance, much as Barry has reflected on when it comes to playing drums. The same literal weight of voice may be said to be true for those in public life, including in business, management, or leadership. The use of voice is important because it is an intrinsic part of a system of communication and a way to create or carry meaning.

From that, we derive two figurative senses of Voice (using a capital "V" for this). First, for an individual, "Voice" is a mild translation of "voice" as a personal statement of principle applicable, for example, to other parts of life, such as leadership. It is a set of beliefs about how I come across to others and what impression I want to make or leave on them. My Voice, therefore, includes how well I capture and code in my writing. It is important in expressing, fulfilling, influencing, and transferring knowledge or instructions in an effective way. When you think about it, these are all basic management and leadership functions. My individual Voice is how I play my role in the organisation.

Next, and because so much of human life is social, Voice also has a strong translation from small-v voice, and becomes itself a social principle. In this strong sense, there are links to many of the Universal Values we began the book with, such as social justice (being moral) and inclusion (belonging).

It's important to train and maintain your voice, and there are many practical workshops, situations, and coaches to help improve projecting and presenting well in front of others. Within the framework for Groove in this book, however, our focus should be more on the figurative levels of Voice.

Voice as Personal Experience

Barry delves into the importance of finding one's true Voice. This got me thinking. How might we define and improve our individual Voices, whether in personal or professional settings? In business, as in music, Barry suggests that *authenticity, intention, and self-mastery* are key to resonating with others (such as an audience or colleagues) and delivering impactful and genuine messages. Ultimately, individual Voice is about being or becoming an authority by being the one who is clearest and most consistent, and perhaps sometimes just the loudest.

American leadership expert Bill George published a book called *Authentic Leadership* (2004), a management approach where leaders are encouraged to be genuine, self-aware, and transparent. Barry's emphasis on individual Voice aligns well with this concept, as it involves leading with integrity and staying true to one's values. Authority emerges not from position or title but from how well aligned the person remains to their view of core beliefs and values and sense of purpose. This was further expanded in a 2007 book, co-written with Peter Sims, called *True North* (2007), intended as a practical guide to self-reflection and awareness. Authentic leadership is not about perfection but about honesty and alignment between words, actions, and values. The claim is that leaders who find and use their authentic voice are more likely to inspire trust and loyalty among their teams. I have some concerns with this, as I think it may invite you to anchor your sense of self firmly in a past persona or in past conditioning. This can become a fixed lens for a context (self-concept) that is anything but static. Aside from the rigidity this can bring, narratives can reinforce hidden or embedded biases, including cultural norms or family stories, and we end up being authentic (true to) but something quite distorted. Voice must have enough openness to change to balance the strength that a consistent self-image brings.

A second theme in Barry's writing offers a way through the tension by integrating the ideas of Eckhart Tolle, particularly in decoupling the performance of tasks (doing) with personal values and purpose (being).

German-born Tolle is a spiritual teacher and author best known for his books *The Power of Now* (2002) and *A New Earth* (2009). These are grounded in the importance of living in the present moment and transcending the ego to achieve inner peace and clarity. He encourages and embodies mindfulness, presence, and detachment from the conditioned mind. Tolle's personal story may be relevant to understanding both voice and Voice. Plagued by personal anxiety in his youth, he moved to England to study when he was 29 in the late 1970s and experienced further periods of depression that led him to rock bottom and contemplation of suicide. In that extreme existential crisis, he experienced a profound personal awakening, after which he abandoned his academic path and later moved to Vancouver, where he began writing and teaching about his experience. He drew from a number of spiritual traditions, many with Eastern roots in Taoism and Buddhism, and following widespread acclaim for his first book, he has given numerous talks, including to corporate audiences. His voice is small and quiet, but the internal alignment present in his Voice has taken on a magnitude that has influenced many.

Tolle's message is simple yet difficult to distil into cause-and-effect words. I see it as having four aspects:

1. *Emphasis on Presence and Adaptability:* Living in the present moment can counterbalance the risk of being overly anchored in the past, as seen in authentic leadership. Focusing on the "now," leaders can develop a deeper awareness of current circumstances, making them more adaptable and responsive to change, with access to fresh perspectives and creativity, rather than relying solely on past experiences and conditioned responses. Tolle's approach encourages leaders to observe their thoughts and emotions without becoming attached to them, promoting a more flexible and open-minded leadership style.
2. *Detachment from the Ego:* Tolle extensively discusses the dangers of identifying too strongly with the ego, which he defines as a false sense of self rooted in thoughts, memories, and conditioning. Authentic leadership's focus on staying true to one's values and experiences can sometimes reinforce the ego, leading to rigidity or resistance to change. Encouraging inner stillness through practices like meditation and mindfulness can help leaders connect with a deeper sense of purpose that is not necessarily tied to their personal history or conditioned beliefs.

3. *Seeing beyond Personal Narratives:* Tolle invites individuals to transcend their personal stories and identities, recognising that these are just mental constructs. In the context of leadership, this can help prevent overemphasising one's past or conditioning. Stressing compassion and non-attachment can help cultivate inclusivity and minimise potential shortcomings of authentic leadership, where a focus on personal values might lead to a lack of empathy for differing viewpoints. Non-attachment also helps leaders remain open to change, seeing leadership as a service rather than an expression of personal identity.
4. *Balancing Authenticity with Universality:*To ensure authenticity does not become self-serving, a balance needs to be struck between being true to oneself and recognising the interconnectedness of all beings. Unless authenticity is the complete detachment from all connections (as it is for a few), "being" has a dimension of alignment with the broader well-being of a team, organisation, or society.

I rather enjoy Eckhart Tolle, though for many he is an acquired taste. You may find clinical psychologist and professor Dr Shauna Shapiro's (Shapiro and Carlson 2017) approach to mindfulness more accessible, or (like me) find a lot of value in the recordings and writing of the philosopher Alan Watts (2009).

Voice as a Social Construct

Point 4 above provides a bridge between finding one's individual Voice and being in harmony with the collective Voice in society.

If I am aware of my Voice as a leader, but observe that the beliefs and principles of some of those around me are the opposite, or (worse) that my principles are flawed, what should I do? Impose myself, my voice? Some would say yes because as long as I am being true to myself, then I am doing the right thing. This can get very messy and have all sorts of unintended consequences. This happens quite frequently. Many modern organisations still operate with the belief that leadership is all about the leader. The remedy for a lack of or failure in leadership is to find the right person with the qualities that will save the day. They tend to recruit a person who maps to the problem, not the solution. Organisations carry biases, too, even when they recognise that they have an issue of authenticity.

Barry's exploration of Voice as a reflection of identity relates to the broader concept of identity-based leadership. Leaders must understand who they are and what they stand for before they can effectively lead others. On the other hand, they must be ready to accept and include the same rights and responsibilities for other people, who may arrive at different beliefs based on different principles.

We find our Voice in spaces with multiple layers of identities operating in constant and complex relationships with each other.

A second collective view of Voice is the right to be heard. Beyond an individual's struggle to find their Voice, anyone in a leadership or stewardship role must also ensure the ability of all members to have the same opportunity to find and express their beliefs, contribute to the process, and above all, feel secure and valued as individuals in their own right. What happens when people are disillusioned or sidelined in organisations? In 1970, the German economist Albert Hirschman published a foundational paper titled *Exit, Voice, and Loyalty* (2004), which sets out the choices people have when faced with increasingly difficult circumstances (politically, socially, economically, etc.), which are either to leave (Exit) or act to change the situation (Voice). There are obvious links to the concept of Universals that we began the book with. Universal Values deal with power structures where people are given influence in a system, and authority (autonomy in being yourself) and authority (hierarchical control and command) can easily collide. Finding the collective Voice can drive organisational change by uniting members around common goals and amplifying the power of their message.

Questions for Reflection and Groove

What would it sound like if you distilled your core principles and beliefs into a 30-second elevator pitch? How do you know they are truly yours?

What practical steps can you take to ensure your words, decisions, and leadership presence consistently align with those principles?

How can you create an environment where your team members are encouraged to discover and project their authentic voices? Is that even possible?

3.8 Vibes Don't Lie: Find Your People, Find Your Edge

Barry

Throughout my creative journey, I have been fascinated by how certain spaces and people have consistently enhanced my abilities and attitude in positive ways. This isn't just a random occurrence; it's a consistent pattern.

As the drummer for Johnny Clegg's band, when I received the itinerary from our tour manager for our annual North American tour; it initially came in the form of a tour book and, more recently, as a tour app. The first set of show dates I would search for was always in Manhattan, New York City, followed by Los Angeles, Toronto, and so on. Just reading the names of these locations lifted my energy.

A few shows in Manhattan would lift my drumming skills simply by soaking up the city's creative energy. That, and the fact that more world-class musicians either lived or worked on this island than anywhere else on the planet, was inspiring. This collective energy has always been intoxicating for me.

Every year, we would have a short residency at a prestigious venue, either on Times Square or in SoHo, near the Financial District. This allowed me to spend at least four days soaking up the New York City vibe, with friends and musical guests popping into the series of shows. These guests ranged from successful entrepreneurs, members of Paul Simon's and Bonnie Raitt's bands to Hollywood A-list actors and Broadway stars. It was impossible not to feel creatively inspired and experience an elevated personal performance!

I would look forward to getting up early and walking around the city to fully experience this energy. I made a point of appreciating and absorbing the architectural beauty, the blend of old-world village culture with the latest cutting-edge innovations, and the chance to enjoy jazz at the purest and highest level in small clubs that felt no bigger than a large living room.

Similarly, ten days at the National Arts Festival in my home country of South Africa would raise my ceiling of possibility through being immersed in such concentrated creativity in the small festival village, constantly engaging with musicians, dancers, actors, writers and movie makers from across the globe.

Years later, an inspired syndicate session with my MBA cohort would trigger the same experience of flow. I found the "brains trust" and collaborative effort within a highly diverse group incredibly stimulating, as we grappled with new theories, models, and frameworks in the pursuit of solving real-world challenges (or exploiting opportunities) with creativity and innovation.

The MBA's contextual stimulation was similar to that of a musician performing at a high level in Manhattan. This is, of course, a living testament to the power of group culture and collective mindset.

Research has shown that the key differences between hobbyists, semi-professionals, and elite performers are not primarily based on innate talent or the number of hours dedicated to practice. Instead, they hinge on how effectively time is spent on skill development, as well as mindset and attitude. Great performers in sports or music approach their craft differently in terms of skill and technique. This differentiation largely stems from being part of a group that subscribes to and shares a culture of positive attitude and an unwavering belief in what is possible.

This understanding was why I moved from a group of musicians in a small town to a more elite ensemble in a larger city. I frequently made similar geographical moves to epicentres of heightened consciousness and competition. Just as painters during the Renaissance flocked to Florence, Beat novelists gravitated toward Greenwich Village in the 1960s, tech startups congregated in Silicon Valley, and Biotech founders have converged on Cambridge in Massachusetts, I, too, sought environments that triggered growth and excellence.

Working in groups yields the best results, and intentionally placing yourself in a high-quality environment is a key strategy for achieving rapid improvement. This is where you can accomplish far more than you could alone. This concept aligns with what Steve Jobs called the reality distortion field. We can achieve astonishing outcomes when we believe in our capabilities and create a collective narrative that supports this belief.

> *My **Finding Your Groove Principle:** Don't wait for an invite to a group that triggers inspiration for you. Simply identify, move and join.*

Chris

Barry's Note on Tracking Resonance highlights the powerful connection between our surroundings and creativity. He argues that placing myself in the right vibrant, stimulating environments can ignite inspiration and elevate my performance. He invites us all to think about how our surroundings influence creativity, particularly the role of diverse environments and excellence in shaping our potential.

As I read, I gained three key insights in the form of questions.

1. Is There a Ripple Effect in Excellence?

Being in the company of talented, high-performing individuals creates what Barry describes as a "resonance field." When surrounded by excellence, how do we absorb the energy, standards, and innovation of those around us? One explanation could be the principle of social modelling from psychology: we tend to emulate the behaviours, attitudes, and habits of the people we spend time with. By intentionally placing himself in environments where excellence is the norm, Barry elevated his craft, whether drumming at Manhattan residencies or solving business challenges in MBA syndicates.

For leaders and organisations, this suggests that fostering a culture of excellence isn't just about individual talent but creating ecosystems of high standards where everyone uplifts each other. When teams are exposed to outstanding performance and diverse ideas, the collective energy drives creativity and improvement.

His experience reminded me of the concept of a muse. Founded in Greek antiquity, the muses were metaphorical guides for inspiration and creativity. Their function is to put ideas into our minds. In Barry's world, the muses are not mythical goddesses but the vibrant energy of Manhattan, the cultural diversity of a festival, or the collaborative synergy of an MBA syndicate. This Note invites us to reflect on how we can intentionally seek out these muses to inspire us, sharpen our creativity, and expand our horizons.

2. How Important Is Diversity as a Creative Catalyst?

I was struck by the contrasting and diverse environments Barry mentioned. Diversity is a fertile ground for creativity culturally, socially, and intellectually.

Diversity speaks of difference, dissimilarity, and separateness. Throughout human history, diversity has often been viewed as more problematic than desirable. And this constrictive strand of thinking, though very old, still plays a role in contemporary public discourse.

New York City's multicultural energy, however, is firmly rooted in its incredible diversity; a shared narrative of diverse narratives. These differences create a positive friction that sparks innovation, as new ways of thinking emerge from the collision of varied worldviews.

Finding this within an MBA group's interdisciplinary collaboration, where diversity brings together different perspectives, skills, and ideas, is a big clue that there is a deeper pattern at work.

In mainstream management thinking, Diversity, Equity, and Inclusion (DEI) principles are widespread in leadership. Research consistently shows that diverse teams are more innovative because they bring a richer pool of experiences and approaches to problem-solving. By exposing himself to diverse environments and talent, Barry didn't just improve his own performance – he also became part of a creative synergy that amplified everyone's contributions.

3. What Is the Influence of Place on Creativity?

Certain locations evoke a unique energy that can profoundly influence our thoughts and feelings. These environments often offer a mix of novelty, challenge, and stimulation, which are known to boost creative thinking.

Places like Manhattan are hubs of innovation, where the sheer density of talent, ambition, and culture creates a palpable energy. But Barry also reminds us that the essence of these experiences can be replicated locally by finding new corners of our cities or seeking fresh perspectives in everyday spaces. Creativity isn't just about where you are – it's about how you engage with your environment.

Resonance and the Reality of Finding Your Muse

"Don't wait for an invite."

Oh, I like Barry's challenge. It's a call to action, isn't it? Creativity is not always a solitary endeavour. Perhaps it's never that. The people, places, and cultures around us deeply influence us. This processing of "the other" feeds us. Our minds are, arguably, where we invent the muse, which is as good a way as any to capture the idea that inspiration comes from external forces as much as internal effort.

Intentionally seek out your modern muses, whatever form they take. Unlock new levels of creativity and performance. Please don't wait for the muse to find you: seek it out, immerse yourself, and let its resonance transform you.

Here are three practical takeaways:

- Look out for environments that challenge and inspire you. When in them, actively reach out (and lean) into opportunities to learn from those who already excel in their fields. Mentorship, collaboration, or simply being present in spaces where excellence thrives can open things up for you.
- Intentionally curate diverse teams, not just in demographics but also in skills, experiences, and perspectives. Immersing yourself in diverse cultures or industries can help break creative blocks and inspire new ideas. Whether working with people from different fields or exploring new communities, diversity enriches creativity.
- Places can inspire you, whether they're cultural hubs, coworking spaces, or quiet spots in nature. If you are a leader, consider creating spaces that stimulate creativity within your organisation, such as collaborative zones or opportunities for off-site team activities. Encourage your teams to engage with the world beyond their immediate context.

The Muses were believed to create an environment where greatness could become possible. By intentionally placing themselves in resonant environments, managers and leaders can tap into this dynamic, where belief in excellence becomes self-fulfilling.

Questions for Reflection and Groove

Which environments or communities most energise your creativity and ambition? How can you spend more time there?

How might you consciously create similar resonance hubs within your own organisation or team?

What practical steps can you take right now to join (or form) new groups that challenge and amplify your growth?

3.9 The Super Groove

Barry

My lifetime of working with rhythm has largely been based on the binary system of upbeats and downbeats, which define the groove in any piece of music. For example, in a classic rock rhythm, which is typically in a metre of 4, the upbeat would be on beats 2 and 4, and the downbeats on beats 1 and 3. You can experience this by counting out loud to a song like Michael Jackson's *Billie Jean* (i.e., one two three four, one two three four ... etc) and then clapping first on the downbeats (1 and 3), and then the upbeats (2 and 4).

After encountering Efrain Toro's powerful wisdom, first as a student and then as a friend, my perspective broadened to the realisation that musical upbeats and downbeats are replicated in nature and are a tiny slice of a great universal system of wave patterns, containing peaks and troughs (i.e., upbeats and downbeats). In the Billie Jean exercise, the downbeats feel heavy (weighed down by gravity), while the upbeats feel light (free of gravity). Other examples would be when we breathe in (upbeat) and out (downbeat) or in the cycles of summer (upbeat) and winter (downbeat).

I also realised that these explicit rhythms contained implicit rhythms occurring simultaneously, but to "hear" the implicit stuff, one had to develop a form of musical open-mindedness. When experiencing the harmonic richness of a Nigerian drum ensemble performing simultaneous multiple rhythms, the untrained ear would register chaos while the trained ear would enjoy harmonic beauty. This is achieved by practice and a willingness to learn, a form of rhythmical ear training, and a disciplined approach to raising awareness to understand what was initially hidden but was there all along.

The Perspective of 1, 2, 3 (OR +, -, +-)

In the same way that many complex phenomena are understood using the lenses of maths and physics, in music we attach integers to rhythms to keep track of complex scenarios. Using this method, we can understand and learn many complex rhythms that would otherwise take years to learn by simply feeling them. I struggled to truly get inside the complex polyrhythmic concept of "2 against 3," meaning a grouping of 2 and a grouping of 3 occurring harmonically, perfectly aligned, and occupying the same amount of space, where both start and resolve on the same 1. This harmonic system occurs over and over in nature in many ways.

The different rhythmic groups can be substituted for different points of view in groups of people collaborating with a shared purpose and observing the same complex system of opportunities and obstacles. 1 and 2 represent two different perspectives, with 3 representing multiple perspectives. Achieving resonance requires a big-picture approach and an understanding of perspective.

The metaphor of a drone view is useful here, i.e., getting up high enough to view all positions.

Normal perception has blind spots (only seeing one's perceived reality) however, increased consciousness (agreeing to, without the pressure of agreeing with) enables humans to see not only their point of view but also someone else's perspective. Then, we move on to an awareness of the multiple perceptions of reality in a group and how these are interconnected, highly sensitive, and fluid. Developing this systemic approach enables a universal point of view. The learned ability of what I call Super Groove awareness is a powerful tool for resonance in drum ensembles, in teams, and in organisations.

> *My* ***Finding Your Groove Principle:*** *Enabling your Super Groove comes from multi-perspective understanding – getting inside someone else's shoes without the pressure to agree. Build this habit by pausing judgment, truly listening, and noticing both verbal and non-verbal cues.*

Chris

All humans can recognise rhythms. We respond to beats and signals in relation to one or more other beats and can construct sequences of these in a relational web to communicate. We're not alone in this; birds do it, bees do it, and perhaps even the more educated sorts of fleas do. In fact, in the ever-branching tree of life on earth, pattern recognition of rhythm may be one of the oldest evolved features we share with other animal species. Some species, such as whales, octopuses, and primate cousins among the great apes, are able to recognise and signal connections at astonishing levels of sophistication.

Though we are discovering new ways to research these webs of communication, animal systems of communication are direct and more limited than those of humans. We have at least three other layers available to us.

1. We can recognise rhythms of social patterns that need not correspond to actual objects in the world (that is, abstract ideas). We can make connections with concepts that we have made up. In addition, we can bring to mind and communicate about objects that exist but that are not in the present time or space.
2. We are able to transfer and store our thoughts into language, preserving them in a format that may be spread in time and space, and then accessed by others.
3. Because we know we can see patterns, and we also see *patterns* of patterns (that is, meta-patterns). This allows us to speculate about the structure of the world, *and* we can experience that structure using that knowledge. If you can experience Groove and be aware that you are, then you can also experience

the "Super Groove" (something like "the Groove of Groove"). This multi-level perspective can be attained, for example, by seeing yourself as if through another person's eyes.

How does that apply to management?

When we pick up what Barry is pointing to and translate it to the business world, we will eventually find ourselves standing in the field of leadership communication. However, to get there we have first to run a sort of quick thought experiment. Imagine you are looking at your organisation in such a way that you embrace (at least in theory in your mind) its entire set of possibilities at any given moment. Imagine the millions of incomplete details, unfinished threads, unmade and unseen choices, tiny, minute forks in the road.

Imagine the immense and chaotic swirl of potential states that would dance in front of you.

It's not that anything is possible but rather that nothing has been decided. That is also a state, and if you think about it, this is always the situation in the present moment before an answer has been reached, or even a question asked, in business. Leadership is another way of making an organisation's "x" and not "y".

Next, leaders can and should turn that lens and that spotlight back on themselves and ask how (and why) they see the world the way they do. It is a superposition (of a sort) for you to imagine you are someone else looking at you.

Questions for Reflection and Groove

When was the last time you suspended your viewpoint to truly hear someone else's, and what changed because of it?

How can you make multi-perspective listening a systematic part of your team's decision-making process?

What tactics would help you and others notice and honour the diverse rhythms and viewpoints in cross-cultural or cross-functional collaborations?

Making the Transition to Universal Groove

In Chapter 3, you've seen how collective rhythm transforms individual contributions into a vibrant, cohesive team dynamic. As group Groove brings out the best in collective effort, it also lays the groundwork for a broader, more expansive vision. The collaborative practices and shared experiences you've explored now prepare you to step into a wider perspective; one that encompasses universal patterns, natural cycles, and the deeper connections that bind us all. Take a moment to reflect on your team experiences and consider how these collective harmonies mirror the larger, natural patterns at play in our lives.

References

Bandura, Albert. 1977. "Self-efficacy: Toward a Unifying Theory of Behavioral Change." *Psychological Review* 84 (2): 191–215.

Bass, Bernard M., and Ronald E. Riggio. 2006. *Transformational Leadership*. N.p.: Psychology Press.

Boyatzis, Richard E., and Annie McKee. 2005. *Resonant Leadership: Renewing Yourself and Connecting with Others through Mindfulness, Hope, and Compassion*. N.p.: Harvard Business School Press.

Burns, James M. 2004. *Transforming Leadership: A New Pursuit of Happiness*. N.p.: Grove Press.

Csikszentmihalyi, Mihaly. 2002. *Flow: The Classic Work on how to Achieve Happiness*. N.p.: Rider.

Dalio, Ray. 2017. *Principles: Life and Work*. N.p.: Avid Reader Press/Simon & Schuster.

Earley, P.C., and Soon Ang. 2003. *Cultural Intelligence: Individual Interactions Across Cultures*. N.p.: Stanford University Press.

Eisenberger, Naomi I., Matthew Lieberman, and Lipling D. Williams. 2003. "Does Rejection Hurt? An fMRI Study of Social Exclusion." *Science* 302 (5643): 290–2.

Eisenberger, N.I. 2012. "The Neural Bases of Social Pain: Evidence for Shared Representations with Physical Pain." *Psychosom Med.* 74 (2) (Feb.–Mar.): 126–35.

George, Bill, and William W. George. 2004. *Authentic Leadership: Rediscovering the Secrets to Creating Lasting Value*. N.p.: Wiley.

George, William W., and Peter Sims. 2007. *True North: Discover Your Authentic Leadership*. N.p.: Wiley.

Goleman, Daniel. 1996. *Emotional Intelligence*. N.p.: Bloomsbury.

Herbert, Simon A. 1956. "Rational Choice and the Structure of the Environment", *Psychological Review* 63 (2): 129–38.

Hirschman, Albert O. 2004. *Exit, Voice, and Loyalty*. N.p.: Harvard University Press.

Lencioni, Patrick. 2007. *The Five Dysfunctions of a Team: A Leadership Fable*. N.p.: Wiley.

Ries, Eric. 2011. *The Lean Startup: How Today's Entrepreneurs Use Continuous Innovation to Create Radically Successful Businesses*. N.p.: Crown Business.

Shapiro, Shauna L., and Linda E. Carlson. 2017. *The Art and Science of Mindfulness: Integrating Mindfulness Into Psychology and the Helping Professions*. N.p.: American Psychological Association.

Steel, Piers. 2011. *The Procrastination Equation: How to Stop Putting Things Off and Start Getting Things Done*. N.p.: Pearson.

Tolle, Eckhart. 2002. *Practising the Power of Now: Essential Teachings, Meditations and Exercises from the Power of Now*. N.p.: Hodder & Stoughton.

Tolle, Eckhart. 2009. *A New Earth: Create a Better Life*. N.p.: Penguin.

Tuckman, Bruce W. 1965. "Developmental Sequence in Small Groups." *Psychological Bulletin* 63 (6): 384–99.

Watts, Alan. 2009. *The Book: On the Taboo against Knowing Who You Are*. N.p.: Souvenir Press.

Chapter 4

Notes on Universal Groove

DOI: 10.4324/9781003480655-4

In this chapter, the Notes form a constellation of *Finding Your Groove* in the universal rhythms that connect us all. Unlike the previous chapter, which allowed for differences between groups as part of our sense-making, our perspective here tries to reframe ourselves as global. Consequently, it reflects the larger forces of nature, culture as a human idea present in all societies, and the flow of time as experienced by everyone. These shape lives and are the primary source of creativity. It is about recognising and aligning with patterns and cycles beyond the individual, beyond the particular group, and tapping into the broader flow of existence.

Notes included below explore adaptability, interconnectedness, and harmony within complexity. From observing the ebb and flow of nature to understanding cultural dynamics, our questions look at how we can resonate with the universal rhythms that influence us and how we may find our place within them.

Accordingly, the lens zooms out from organisational theories and frameworks to explore the interconnected systems that bind us all. Sometimes, this means our reflections are more abstract, though we hope they are not less useful or practical for that. We invite you to view your actions as part of a greater whole and to embrace the opportunities that arise when you flow with, rather than resist, the Universal Groove. Tuning into these widest patterns gains you clarity, purpose, and a deeper sense of connection.

4.1 Breath and Beat: the Universal Groove

Barry

It is 3 a.m., and I wake up in a panic. My chest feels tight, breathing is difficult, and in the darkness I cry out for help. In a semi-awake state, I am overwhelmed by the cold fear of suffocation. That moment was a recurring event for me at age 12, often happening multiple times a night. My mother would groggily respond by giving me a hand-pumped breathing device, which preceded the Ventolin canisters that we use today for symptomatic relief from asthma. Fast forward four years: I'm 16 and on my daily 10 km running route, starting at a fast pace, determined to break the 40-minute mark and perhaps beat my personal best time of just under 4 minutes per kilometre. It's an exhilarating feeling of freedom and flow.

But wait a minute, what just happened here?

Well, at the age of 13 I developed pleurisy, which is a painful lung infection. Our elderly family doctor, a runner himself, made an unthinkable recommendation for that time. He suggested I start a running programme. Somehow, I decided to trust his advice, as it made intuitive sense to me. I felt I was ready to take control of my response to my asthma, which had been debilitating and uncontrollable. By running, I could put my lungs under some stress and relearn how to breathe properly.

I began by walking and jogging once around a football pitch, gasping for air. It felt right, so I kept at it. Miraculously, my daily attempts began to feel easier, and I will never forget the satisfaction of jogging an entire lap without stopping. Within six months I was running 5 km each day, and within a year I had increased my distance to 10 km, with a long run of 40 km every Sunday. The doctor performed a pleurisy lung X-ray before and after my training, and the results showed that my lungs were robust and healthy. He even used me as a poster child for other asthma sufferers.

I still have an asthmatic condition and use a preventative inhaler twice a day, but I have not had an asthma attack since I started running all those decades ago.

This experience transformed me and changed how I view myself and the world around me. I shifted from a narrative of illness to one of physical confidence. The world, once a cold and fearful place, became warm and full of opportunities.

I have often reflected on how this process has improved both my physical and mental health. I realise that the narratives we tell ourselves can profoundly alter our experiences. Not immediately, but through small, achievable steps taken over time. I had shifted my perspective on my "uncontrollable" asthma condition by focusing on what I *could* control: my mindset and my actions. This is the freedom that comes from finding one's Groove and working in harmony with reality.

Recently, as I have been exploring the concepts of rhythm, frequency, and Groove, I've experienced a significant and connected cognitive breakthrough. I started incorporating complex rhythms into my workshops for corporate executives and teams to highlight the interconnectedness of all things. This approach allowed me to reconnect with what we feel as humans before applying any analytical thinking. I've come to realise that tapping into the root of our experiences, that feeling of form which is so difficult to articulate (actually, is ineffable) represents a way to finding a shared space that connects us universally. In the ensuing complexity, the intellectual calisthenics can follow.

My journey into a new feeling of physical well-being began when I discovered the modern practice of an ancient art known as Breathwork. This introduction came through a recommendation from my old friend Ninja, co-founder of Die Antwoord. During the two years of lockdowns due to Covid-19, we collaborated virtually on music and beat-making. During this time, Ninja mentioned he was practising breathwork followed by cold immersions every morning. Intrigued by his routine, I decided to follow suit, using a practitioner on Insight Timer as my guide. This was incredibly challenging as someone more anxious than most when the oxygen supply was limited. Yet I could feel that taking control of this primary human rhythm was a path to heightened awareness and freedom.

The Global Wellness Institute reports that breathwork, or controlled breathing, is a top trend because of this simplicity and power, supported by neuroscience and research (Bentley 2023). The benefits of breathwork include reduced inflammation, improved mindset, enhanced physical performance, clearer thinking, and increased energy. We take between 15,000 and 20,000 breaths daily, yet how many of us truly understand how to breathe properly or take the time to think about it? Like any natural cycle, the rhythm of breath has two components: action and recovery, which can be described as a peak and a trough or, in musical terms, an upbeat and a downbeat. This brings to mind our primary rhythm – the heartbeat – which also has a two-part structure of action and rest. Like breath, the heartbeat is a rhythm we cannot live without.

Breathing is something we can exert (temporarily, at least) control of. By contrast, our heartbeat tempo, measured in beats per minute (BPM, as in dance music), is not directly controllable. We can, though, influence it through strategic breathing. Research indicates that our brains associate various emotions with different breathing patterns. This is why controlling breath can effectively alter our emotional state. For instance, a happy state is linked to steady and regular breathing, while stress or fear is connected to irregular, shallow, or rapid breaths. By intentionally slowing your breathing during stressful situations, you can trick your brain into believing you are in a calm, safe state. Breathwork teaches us how to manage the nervous system through breath control, promoting a healthier balance between the parasympathetic and sympathetic states and positively influencing our heartbeat.

I have found the breath-to-heart connection to be extremely profound, and I have explored this concept viscerally in my workshop facilitation. My goal is to help attendees experience feelings rather than engage in analytical thinking. One practice I've used involves inviting a group to vocalise their unique heart rhythms using numbers. The results have been astounding; slower heartbeats often synchronise with faster ones, and vice versa. This phenomenon occurs without fail across diverse groups, even without any pre-briefing or set expectations at the start. It is a largely unconscious outcome. Given enough time, space, and stillness, the hearts in the room naturally seek to connect at a fundamental level, beyond conscious thought. This provides a great example of why the heart is often referred to as the second brain.

My learning here is that these rhythms of breath and heart are so primary for us as humans that they represent not only our unique grooves as individuals but also a point of connectivity and common ground with all groups and societies of people and allow us a way in to *feel* the interconnectivity between ourselves and the natural world.

From this experience, I understand that the rhythms of breath and heartbeat are fundamental to our existence as humans. They represent our uniqueness and also serve as common ground that connects us to all groups and societies. These rhythms allow us to *feel* the interconnectedness between ourselves and the natural world.

It is interesting to note that the average resting human heart rate is 60 BPM. This is significant because popular music hits over the decades have typically been produced at approximately 120 BPM beats per minute. This creates an energised state that aligns with our heart rate, allowing us to feel secure and satisfied while at the same time experiencing excitement and joy.

> *My* ***Finding Your Groove Principle:*** *Your heartbeat and breath are powerful tools to regulate your nervous system – calming, balancing, or energising as needed. Use these rhythms to take charge of your energy and mindset – why let your devices decide how you feel?*

Chris

Here is an insight into the rhythms that underpin all human life and creativity. By exploring the interplay of breath, heartbeats, and our interconnectedness with the world, Barry's reflections inspire us to delve into other primary rhythms that tie individuals to the universal, offering a pathway to balance, connection, and vitality.

I have been interested in and intrigued by universals for some time. As you saw in our introductory chapter, I believe that discussing values only in terms of a search for universals is worthwhile because universals are, by definition, social common ground.

To identify a universal is an act of submission. I must surrender to the fact that, for difference or division to exist, behind it must be a common ground of a reality that holds that as a possibility. And if that is true, we can meet each other at that level and make some choices.

Beyond Breath and Heartbeat

Breath and heartbeat are fundamental rhythms. Barry invites us to explore other universal patterns that connect us as individuals to the world around us. These are deeply ingrained in our biology and collective psyche, forming a bridge between our inner selves and the larger ecosystem.

Here are a few complementary rhythms to consider:

Tidal Rhythms as a Metaphor

We experience the tides as the repeating pattern of rising and falling oceans where the combination of the Moon's gravitational mass interacts with the Earth's rotation and topography. The metaphor of ebb and flow is another universal rhythm that maps rises and falls in life, particularly of human emotions and thoughts. This is a natural duality. For centuries, poets and philosophers have considered the ocean a symbol of connection, continuity, and impermanence. Leaning into this can be a metaphorical reminder in management to embrace change and flux. Leaders can think of challenges as low tides that will inevitably shift into opportunities. Similarly, in moments of personal stagnation, reflecting on the constant motion of the tides can inspire resilience and forward momentum.

Here, *Finding Your Groove* aligns with the mutually arising natural flow states of letting go (ebb) and taking action (flow).

Resonance in Collective Movement: Dancing and Synchrony

Barry describes how shared heart rhythms naturally align in group settings, a phenomenon supported by research into entrainment, which is the tendency of organisms to synchronise their rhythms when close. Beyond the physiological, collective activities like dancing, drumming, or even synchronised walking reflect a universal human desire for connection and being in step. This can have powerful applications at work. If you can see and understand how individuals mirror one another's actions, you can evoke this sense of shared rhythm and universal connection. If you model it, others will follow.

Here, as elsewhere, Barry taps into traditional communal activities such as African drumming circles, which have long harnessed collective rhythm to foster connection, healing, and joy. This supports Barry's universal perspective: rhythm is a personal tool **and** a societal glue.

The Paradox of the Universal

In Barry's Groove framework, *universal* refers to those principles, rhythms, and truths that apply to all people and systems, transcending individual and group levels to touch the shared foundation of existence. It is the realm of no exceptions and comprises the patterns underpinning life and nature. Within this universality lies a paradox. While these principles are universal, they only gain meaning through a difference between one human's perception as compared to that of another. The paradox arises because although universals exist independently of their emergent effects, their appreciation and interpretation only appear in **relational dynamics**. In other words, a universal only becomes relevant when perceived, shared, or applied in a specific context.

It stands to reason we first need each other to exist for the idea of common ground to have any meaning. Our differences are necessary for either or both of us to recognise the idea of a universal. The general and the particular are mutually arising. It takes at least two people – or entities – to appreciate and interpret the universal, create meaning, and explore its nuances. Science, philosophy, and systems thinking can illuminate this paradoxical relationship between the universal and the relational. This is what makes life so rich and interesting.

At its core, a universal concept represents (or attempts to represent, as this is quite challenging) a consistent and unchanging phenomenon. Some examples include:

1. *Laws of Nature:* Scientific principles such as gravity, thermodynamics, and the speed of light are universal in their applicability. They exist independently of individual or collective perception, although their meaning and impact are revealed through observation and interaction.
2. *Cyclic Universals:* All humans and many other species share rhythms, such as breathing, heartbeat, and circadian cycles. These patterns form the physiological basis of life.
3. *Cognitive Universals:* German philosopher Immanuel Kant argued that human cognition must contain certain categories of thought, such as space, time, quantity, and causality, that exist as *a priori* and serve as universal frameworks through which humans interpret and then synthesise a meaning for reality via sense data. That's a complicated way of saying that although humans interpret the world into existence for *them* (i.e. you see the world not as it is, but as you are), the world must be such that this variety of views is the result. Separate from your interpretation, some underlying patterns are true, whatever we think.

Barry brings a universal to life by getting everyone involved in this process of their universal rhythm. It also explains how a group acting together in a shared universal pattern can create harmony and joy.

Concepts like the Golden Ratio (φ), Fibonacci sequences, and other mathematical structures consistently appear in nature, art, and architecture. These universal patterns are independent of human perception and become meaningful through observation and application.

Barry's Note touches on this paradox through breath and heartbeat as examples of universal rhythms. These rhythms exist independently and only gain meaning through conscious practice, group synchronisation, or connection to the natural world. Similarly, the universality of rhythm in music creates a shared experience, and it takes two (performer and listener) to bring that experience to life.

This paradox becomes a practical framework for leadership and teamwork. Important organising principles such as fairness, trust, and respect apply to all teams and organisations. However, their exact construction, limits, meaning, and application are only brought to life through the dynamics between individuals and groups. Leaders must navigate the universal (what principles must apply to *everyone*) and the relational (how everyone experiences and interprets those principles).

For personal development, we still need relational dynamics. We can only understand how a universal is acting on us by interacting with others. This interplay invites us to engage with universal rhythms while appreciating the relational contexts in which they manifest.

Questions for Reflection and Groove

Where can you learn to actively use breath or other natural rhythms to regulate your emotional state and improve decision-making during stressful moments?

How can synchronising with others' rhythms (physical or metaphorical) enhance collaboration and connection in your workplace or community?

How might technology influence or disrupt you in connection to these natural rhythms, and what strategies could you adopt to reclaim balance?

4.2 Finding and Feeling Groove

Barry

I remember it like yesterday – Joey Heredia, a fiery drumming legend in LA, sitting down at the same generic drum set we used daily at music school. He wasn't world-famous by choice, but revered as one of the greatest on the planet. A purist who turned down global pop tours to stay true to his Latin jazz roots, Joey's groove was overwhelming. In that instant, I knew – I didn't just want to play drums, I wanted to *feel* them the way he did. It wasn't just virtuosity; it was the sheer power of groove that reframed ordinary into extraordinary.

How Do You Choose to Feel?

I have a visceral understanding of the concept of *reframing*, even though I have never really articulated it or thought about it deeply until now. I am a self-taught street musician who has always relied on emotion and only pursued formal music education long after mastering my instrument.

Let me elaborate …

As a drummer, I use emotion to delve deeper into accessing soul or groove, which essentially means total commitment and flow. For instance, I may visualise a specific image or memory while playing a drum part to create a completely different sound. While the technical performance – the craft – remains the same, the *emotional* nuances alter the listener's experience. It's a magical process whereby identical notes played on a set of drums by two different musicians can sound completely different. It's all about the intangible feeling conveyed through wood and skin.

This is the essence of reframing.

Reframing can help translate and expand mutual resonance among a group of musicians playing as an ensemble. Find a unifying emotion, and it can make this music sound sadder, richer, happier, bolder, or all of the above.

Another important aspect is that emotion is more powerful than technique. For example, consider a great songwriter with something powerful to express, such as Bob Dylan, and compare them to a singer, like many finalists in talent shows such as *The Voice* or *Idols*, with technical talent but no authenticity and nothing meaningful to say. My favourite drummers are those who deeply move me with their expression, where core emotion is an integral part of their performance rather than just technical showing off. However, the ultimate sweet spot is when virtuosity, emotion, and purpose converge, as artists like Mozart, Prince, or John Coltrane exemplify.

In education, this is the distinction between rote learning patterns without understanding, and without the bigger picture, and truly appreciating complex systems and your place within them. There is a huge difference between effortlessly reciting memorised data and effortlessly making sense of complex stuff in simple ways

I recently watched YouTube videos of two orchestras performing the same musical piece, *Mambo*, from Leonard Bernstein's *West Side Story*. The first was the Berlin Philharmonic (Philharmoniker 2014), widely recognised as one of the top ensembles in the world, and the second was the Venezuelan Youth Orchestra in Caracas (Dudamel 2012), which, as the name implies, is a group of enthusiastic young amateurs. To illustrate my point, please watch each and see which version moves you!

How Do You Choose to Tell Your Story?

Another factor at play here around achieving flow and intent is being able to surrender to emotion. I have had some sublime performance experiences under the most challenging conditions. For instance, during South Africa's National Arts Festival, 9 a.m. on a freezing Grahamstown (officially renamed as Makhanda) morning. Our venue, a hotel function room, was almost empty, and we had very few people through the door. I was feeling tired from too little sleep and too much frivolity the night before. Yet within seconds of the first note being played, all this was replaced for a full 90 minutes by focus, energy, and euphoria.

Of course, two people could see the same situation in opposite ways. For example, one might see the lack of sleep, overindulgence, small audience, and zero income as bleak scarcity and a barren, energyless landscape for creativity. Another, holding a different frame, might see this as a wonderful chance to conjure up incredible energy for a magical performance, view the small audience as an opportunity to gain advocacy, and the gig as the chance to attract a bigger business down the line. The facts of the day don't change, the frame is what provides a powerful sense of abundance.

> *My **Finding Your Groove Principle:** Trust what moves you. Your perception shapes your rhythm. Choose your frame, choose your Groove.*

Chris

When Barry compared the two orchestras' renditions of *Mambo*, I had to go and see for myself what he meant. I know which concert I would rather have been in the audience for! Neither orchestra was short on technique or talent, but these were two different experiences. So, yes, what *was* the difference?

Emotion vs Technique

Barry's exploration of emotion versus technique in performance speaks to a broader debate in the arts and, for that matter, in leadership theory-building about the balance between emotional expression and technical mastery. When authentically expressed, emotion can be more compelling than technical precision alone. This idea resonates with Transformational Leadership Theory, where leaders inspire and motivate by connecting with their followers emotionally, not just through skill, competence, or authority.

In leadership, conveying genuine emotion can enhance a leader's impact, fostering trust and deeper engagement. However, as Barry notes, the ultimate sweet spot is when emotion and technique converge. This balance is also seen in the concept of flow in positive psychology, where a person's skill level matches the challenge at hand, creating an optimal state of performance characterised by both focus and joy.

By integrating emotional intelligence with technical competence, leaders can deliver more impactful performances, whether on stage or in a boardroom. Barry's emphasis on the emotional dimensions of music performance can be translated into leadership practice, suggesting that leaders should master the technical aspects of their roles and also remain emotionally present and responsive to their teams and contexts.

Reframing in Leadership and Management

Reframing is a powerful leadership and management technique involving changing how a situation is viewed to find more constructive or empowering perspectives. This is an approach that American academics Lee Bolman and Terry Deal (2021) have used for their Four Frames Model; effective leaders use multiple frames or perspectives to interpret and tackle challenges, enhancing their ability to lead dynamically and adaptively. The four frames are:

- *Structural Frame:* This is about the organisation of the pieces of a business and focuses on rules, roles, goals, and policies to organise and structure groups effectively. This is the most traditional and rational framing.
- *Human Resources Frame:* Emphasising the fit between individual and organisation, fostering engagement and development, this reframe grew in importance in management from the mid-20th century.
- *Political Frame:* More recently, about 50 years ago, a reframing of organisational management acknowledged the importance of power dynamics and relationships in navigating complex organisational landscapes where resources are scarce, and conflict arises from differing opinions on how those resources should be allocated or used.
- *Symbolic Frame:* This is a philosophical reframing that holds that meaning is not inherent in organisational life; meaning is uncertain, ambiguous, and ascribed by us as social actors. We use symbols, rituals, and stories to build culture and convey meaning, reinforcing a shared vision and purpose.

By understanding and applying these frames, leaders can reframe challenges and situations to align with their strategic goals and values.

A frame is a category. We use them to make judgments, and frames contain their own (often hidden) judgments and biases about their boundaries. For example, the Bolman and Deal frames are a tool you can apply to your organisation. Equally, the authors must have used a formative reframing of their own to get to these. One hopes they used critical thinking, just as you will need to do as a manager applying them to your organisation.

On the other hand, Barry suggests we go to a place where reframing finds deeper roots for individuals in their development and practice. He uses reframing to channel different emotions and energies into his performances, affecting both his experience and that of his audience. This inner world of changing perspectives, a complement to the competence of musical technique, is also a technique.

Around the middle of the last century, several notable counsellors and therapists pioneered radically new approaches to showing how communication can challenge our self-limiting beliefs or conditioned worldviews. Letting go of those frames can open the way for different, healthier outcomes. These sources were introduced to a much wider audience during the rise in popularity of Neuro-Linguistic Programming (NLP) (Grinder and Bandler 1989), an attempt to train oneself and others in the tools and techniques of communication. NLP has (correctly, in my view) fallen out of fashion. With reframing, though, it was definitely onto something significant. Stoicism, a philosophical movement dating back 2,000 years, used reframing by asking us to question everything negative to see how it might be reframed as something useful.

Deliberately changing the context or meaning assigned to a situation can alter its emotional impact. Something like this is a core component of CBT, or Cognitive Behaviour Therapy, a therapeutic technique for reshaping emotions and feelings about oneself. Leaders, for instance, might shift from viewing a challenge as a problem to seeing it as an opportunity, thereby fostering a more positive and proactive mindset among their teams.

Control over Personal Narrative

Reframing can be direct or indirect. Barry gives us access to the conscious, direct experience of reframing, exercised through a deliberate decision to stop one way of looking and choose another.

Control over personal narrative involves consciously shaping your story to align with your values, purpose, or desired outcomes. This concept is crucial in leadership, as a leader's personal narrative can significantly influence their authenticity, credibility, and impact on others.

Barry's practice of asking, "How do you choose to tell your story?" reflects the importance of narrative control in leadership. By choosing how to frame experiences and setbacks, leaders can inspire resilience and a growth mindset in themselves and their teams. This aligns with Bolman and Deal's *Symbolic* Frame, where leaders act as storytellers, using their personal narratives to shape culture and drive engagement. Developing a strong personal narrative helps leaders navigate complex situations by maintaining clarity of purpose and consistency in their messaging.

Many leadership theories, such as Transformational Leadership (Bass and Riggio 2006), include aspects of direct, emotional reframing. In this theory, leaders are encouraged to inspire and motivate their teams by connecting on an emotional level, not just through skill or authority. They balance emotional intelligence with technical competence to achieve outstanding performance.

Finally, because we can frame, we are framing all the time. Social identity is a complex web of interrelationships, categories, norms, and (of course, because nothing stays still) reframes. Social Identity Theory (Tajfel 1978) is a framework for mapping the delicate relationship between an individual, the groups they are in (or groups they are not in), and their beliefs about their identity. The group you are part of will always be more favourably viewed than the group you are not. You will unconsciously look for things to reinforce that.

In groups where we feel at home, most behaviours are about changing status inside the frame but not the frame itself. Anyone or any group outside our in-group is viewed (quite unconsciously) less favourably. Every now and again, we get the chance to challenge that status quo. One small event at the Paris 2024 Olympic Games (Eurosport 2024) illustrates this quite nicely. In the women's beach volleyball, during a fiercely contested gold medal match between Canada and Brazil, the four players got into a bad-tempered argument at the net. The umpire placed themself between the two sides to try and calm things down, with little effect. Then, as the players were seething and staring at each other for the next point, the venue's DJ broke the rules and started to play some music very loudly. It was John Lennon's *Imagine*. Within 5 seconds, the point was made, tension diffused, and boundaries expanded to place both teams inside a unifying whole. A wonderful, emotional reframe.

Personal Development may challenge you to face up to a few things you've always taken for granted.

Questions for Reflection and Groove

What personal narratives or stories are you telling yourself that might limit your ability to achieve your purpose right now?

How can you maintain balance while remaining adaptable to challenges and opportunities along the way?

In your organisation, how can leaders better encourage teams to reframe obstacles as opportunities for growth and innovation?

4.3 Change Pain

Barry

As a teenager, I was deeply committed to music and excelled at playing the drum set. I noticed that whenever things became too comfortable for me, I subconsciously developed a strategy that sought out painful changes. This meant that after achieving certain musical milestones, I felt compelled aggressively to pursue new opportunities, often leading to me moving to new geographical places, facing new fears of the unknown, and putting important and meaningful relationships on hold or ending them altogether.

Throughout my life I've felt a stronger push to move forward than a pull to stay put, which has led me on a cyclical journey. I started in my hometown on the southeast coast of South Africa, then moved to the bustling city of Johannesburg, followed by London, and then Los Angeles. All by age 22. These relocations weren't planned in detail and were accomplished without a financial safety net or a definite place to stay upon arrival, aside from a few nights on the sofa of an acquaintance.

During these periods I found my authentic voice. I learned with a ferocious inspiration and experienced significant shifts in my journey from unconscious incompetence to mastery of my craft. This wouldn't have been possible without embracing the vision, confronting fears, and feeling excitement.

My life experience justifies this repeated disruption of complacency and stress-free living as a principle of pushing myself into periods of discomfort in pursuit of knowledge. These experiences often involved overwhelming situations. Moving from a small town to a huge city and dealing with scarcity, for example: I still recall arriving in London with enough money for only one week! Or, facing fear head-on when I first attended music school in LA and was surrounded by 300 drummers, all competing for a spot in the top intake streams.

These were visceral sink-or-swim moments where failure was not an option, and I developed resilience and confidence in what I could bring to the world. As I grew as a musician through a steep learning curve, I expanded my worldview, welcomed cultural diversity, and became a passionate advocate for global citizenship.

Later, during my years as a long-time member of Johnny Clegg's group, I once heard him mention a Zulu proverb: *utshani obulele buvuswa omlilo*, which translates as:

> *The old dry grass needs to be removed by fire for the new green shoots to appear.*

This proverb has become my guiding principle in life. It's not perfect, but it has been effective for me in a blunt instrument manner.

At some point in my life, I started feeling more serene and began exploring new activities and learning opportunities instead of solely focusing on mastering one area. I realised that constantly reassessing my situation every few years out of habit was neither healthy nor sustainable. This is still a struggle for me, and I use techniques such as journaling, long-distance running, and mindfulness to counter irrational behaviours. Would I have sustained a 30-year international career as a drummer in bands without experiencing recurring self-inflicted change pain? I would say not.

The lesson here is to develop a more sophisticated and mindful approach based on my philosophy of change. This approach is empowering and avoids the negative impact of a blunt-force method. It is natural to avoid changing our behaviours and environments, and this can lead to complacency and dullness. I find that pushing myself to learn new things in new places with inspiring people is invigorating and sharpens my thinking processes. This is the same follow the fear approach I use when I don't feel like going for a run on a cold morning. By simply showing up and doing it, the benefits far outweigh the investment of time, exponentially more than if I had stayed in bed!

> *My* ***Finding Your Groove Principle:*** *Fear signals growth. Lean into discomfort; your next breakthrough is just beyond it.*

Chris

The themes suggested in Barry's narrative are numerous. Self-reflection, mindfulness, and self-awareness are present, of course, and are woven throughout this book. Restlessness, determination, renewals, and new starts are also present. There is also a theme closely tied to exploring and using cultural diversity and a global perspective (global citizenship), which I'll return to at the end of this reflection.

For him, Barry's cycles of repeatedly leaving a comfort zone and the cosy, familiar searching for the next unknown have resulted in corresponding cycles of continuous learning and adaptation. The rewards are new opportunities and new skills. This reflects a mindset of lifelong learning, which is crucial in personal development and management. Barry's experiences suggest that learning is not a finite process but an ongoing journey that requires adaptability and openness to new experiences, and this is reminiscent of the effort and persistence implied by Carol Dweck's *Growth Mindset* (2012) mentioned earlier.

As I read, the shadow side of learning and change jumped out at me: the pain of loss. You may not have considered that all learning involves loss, which is painful almost by tradition.

Learning something new often involves letting go of the old. This can be easy or difficult, depending on our attachment to the emotions and unresolved issues we carry with us. If we haven't dealt with these, our new learning and development can be distorted, preventing us from experiencing true freedom. The same is true in business and organisational life, too.

Embracing Discomfort for Growth

Change is generally a signal that a person or a group of people, such as an organisation, is moving through a liminal space. *Liminal* means being on a boundary or threshold, a crossover point between one thing and another, such as an intermediate state of development or a rite of passage. It is one of my favourite words because it is a characteristic of personal development and growth. We are often at the threshold; a probationary period in a new role is a liminal space, as is a bar mitzvah, job loss, relationship breakup, or graduation.

Between one comfort and another, there is a discomfort (otherwise, you wouldn't sense a change). Between stagnation and growth, for example, there is often fear of the potential failure that a risk implies. Barry emphasises the importance of intentionally seeking out discomfort and change as a means of personal and professional growth. By moving to new locations and immersing himself in unfamiliar environments, Barry learned to confront fears and developed resilience. With the right thinking, that discomfort can be a catalyst for learning and improvement.

Overcoming Fear

Resilience is a theme here. Barry frequently places himself in situations where failure is not an option. By pushing himself into situations that demanded resilience – like moving to new cities without a safety net – he cultivated the ability to thrive under pressure. This resonates with the message that many people have taken up from Positive Psychology, and from self-help books such as *Feel the Fear and Do It Anyway,* by Susan Jeffers (2017), which advocates the practice of confronting your perspective by replacing one set of thinking habits with another, to understand the nature of fear itself. This fits a cultural view of fear, and pain, as a thing somewhat outside yourself that is there to be resisted, fought, and overcome.

This is a bit like trying to fight fire with fire because you will be extinguishing one fear from the perspective of another fear. Barry is getting at something else, something more profoundly useful. By acknowledging the need for a sustainable balance in his approach to change and learning, he recognises that periods of intense learning and change are balanced with stability and reflection.

Barry hints at a philosophy of "Change Pain," where deliberately provoking a pattern change is seen as a way to avoid complacency and maintain vitality in both personal and professional life. His use of a Zulu proverb about burning old grass to make way for new growth is a metaphor for this approach, and this is relevant to management learning, suggesting that leaders should periodically reassess and redefine goals to foster innovation and prevent stagnation.

Leaders in many organisations try to harness their fears about change and use them to motivate growth. One thing that might be useful to understand this is *Approach-Avoidance Conflict Theory,* developed in 1935 by social psychologist Kurt Lewin (2007). This tension appears when facing a decision that has both appealing and unappealing aspects, and they become torn (which is a painful emotion) between moving forward and avoiding the challenge. If the negative outcomes are given greater weight, their perception will follow, and they may suppress their ambition. That can be the decisive factor if they embrace the excitement of change. The point is to see and understand that this is happening and that *both* aspects are desirable and acceptable. They then carry their awareness with them.

If individuals interpret follow the fear as a rule that stops them from truly understanding the fear they experience, they may discover that nothing has changed. They might realise that they haven't given anything up and, as a result, have not learned anything.

Constant disruption is unsustainable. Reraming is *not* facing up to fear with a brave face but (eventually) closely examining it. That is why self-reflection, the kind Barry finds he can now do, is vital. *Wherever You Go, There You Are* is a wonderfully succinct book title by the American psychiatrist and pioneer of the study of the benefits of mindfulness meditation in clinical settings, John Kabat-Zinn (2004). Mindfulness-based stress Reduction (MBSR) can help managers and individuals develop greater self-awareness and a more balanced approach to personal and professional challenges.

Global Perspective and Cultural Diversity

Barry's journey across different cities and cultures expanded his worldview and promoted a sense of global citizenship. This theme highlights the value of cultural diversity and exposure in personal and professional development, suggesting that engaging with varied perspectives can enhance creativity and empathy, vital traits in effective management.

Sonder

The word *sonder* is a recently invented addition to English. It comes from John Koenig's online project and book, *The Dictionary of Obscure Sorrows* (Koenig 2021), a project to fill gaps in the English language with new words to describe complex, often fleeting emotions. *Sonder*, says Koenig, is "the profound realization that each random passerby is living a life as vivid and complex as your own."

It captures a moment of awareness and reminds us that everyone is the main character in their own story, with a unique perspective shaped by their personal history, relationships, and experiences. Sonder is useful in discussions about empathy, human connection, and awareness. It is a powerful word to describe a moment of realisation about learning by putting yourself in novel and challenging situations, places, or roles where part of the unknown is the contact with strangers around you.

Barry's newfound reflective path encourages empathy and perspective-taking. Poignantly, he and I are also part of your sonder, of course.

The *Cultural Intelligence (CQ) Framework* (Earley and Ang 2003) might be useful for contextualising these ideas within an organisation. This outlines the capability to function effectively across various cultural contexts. This framework is relevant to

Barry's development as a global citizen and his appreciation of cultural diversity. CQ contains four capacities: motivation (drive), cognition (knowledge), meta-cognition (strategy), and behaviour (action). The intention is that these can help managers understand and adapt to different cultural norms and practices, which is essential in today's globalised business environment.

Questions for Reflection and Groove

Reflect on a recent moment of fear, confusion, or discomfort: what can you learn from it, and how might that guide you toward growth and well-being?

How can you create work environments where individuals feel supported in taking risks and exploring beyond what is already within their reach?

How do you differentiate between productive discomfort that drives growth and burnout caused by excessive strain?

4.4 The Frequency of Resonance

Barry

In 2020, I heard Matthew McConaughey respond to the usual question, "So, how's it going?" on Dax Shepard's podcast (*Armchair Expert*, EP258, 2020) with, "Well, I'm tuning in, finding my frequency." This is a profound statement and something I have also been exploring for decades as I play with musical rhythm. Frequency and rhythm are interchangeable terms that describe discernible cycles of ebb and flow. There can be no rhythm without space and no melody without rhythm. These are fundamental, ontological patterns. Ontology means any statement about the nature of reality, independent of what we think or know about it. Epistemology refers to how we come to know, and what we can know.

The epistemology of frequency, or rhythm, is quite fascinating. Do we all hear the same thing? On one level, yes. We perceive rhythm by encountering a repeated pattern. Depending on our way of knowing and our sense-making, we may interpret those patterns as either comfortable or unsettling. For instance, the fast, intense beat of a speed metal band may be enjoyable for some people and disturbing for others. Similarly, the unpredictability of free-form jazz can either please or annoy different listeners.

Our judgment of rhythm is based on how we interpret the relationship between the beats map and the silence that makes up a particular rhythm.

Musicians use a process called ear training to identify the intervals, or steps, between tones. For example, they learn to distinguish between a root note and a major 3rd in a scale, a distance of 3 whole steps or tones. They dedicate hours to this process to differentiate between frequencies (tones are rhythms vibrating faster or slower than one another) and to extract specific frequencies from a complex mess of layered rhythmic events. Each note contains all tones in the spectrum, with an overarching root note to which we assign a letter, such as C, A, or G, and so on.

In good music schools, drummers and percussionists are taught rhythmic ear training. I remember an instructor tapping out a rhythm (starting simple and getting longer and more complex), which we would repeat by first singing the rhythm and then singing while tapping it out. The goal is to improve the ability to truly hear, remember, and understand the intricate connections between tones and beats.

The lesson here for me is this: as humans enhance their ability to sense and identify multiple frequencies and the relationships between them, they better understand what would previously have seemed merely like chaos or randomness. I remember the day at music school in Los Angeles when I broke through months of frustration to finally grab hold of a pattern of three connected rhythms and hear them all simultaneously. I initially recognised something powerful within what my brain perceived as chaos. After months of persistent practice, I was able to distinguish the individual frequencies and the emergent "super frequency" that was greater than the sum of its parts!

In our daily lives, a simple example of this concept would be taking the time to consider the different, layered rhythms and cycles we go through when we are active and then when we are resting. We all have an intuitive sense of whether we are morning or evening people, and we may not often pause to think about this within the context of a 24-hour cycle. Map this as a graph with dots on the X-axis in two-hour intervals, measuring energy levels as low, medium, or high on the Y-axis. By connecting the dots, you can visualise your unique daily rhythm. It's not an exact science, it's something we can all do quickly and with some accuracy.

Then, think about and list the activities you need to accomplish on an average day. Categorise each activity based on how much cognitive energy needs to be available and expended on each. Again, measure this as high, medium, or low. The result will be three energy categories of activities.

Finally, link the highest creative bandwidth activities with the times in the day that you have identified as those where you naturally feel the most energised.

This is a practical example of joining dots, recognising patterns, and making sense of multiple frequencies that were previously blurry and, at times, overwhelming and exhausting.

Of course, like all economic models, this diagnostic tool assumes a perfect and rational world. In reality, there will be many days when activities and energy cannot be perfectly matched. However, the difference now lies in a raised awareness. Understanding that as a morning person, you may battle to generate creative options at 4 p.m. can save you and your team from much frustration and time wasting. I believe that the development of this sensing ability translates to all aspects of life. The better we get at it, the better we fit into our groups, societies, cultures, and the natural world. This is not possible without dedicated and sustainable practice.

For over two decades of international touring as a musician, I relied on biohacks to generate energy when needed. As a morning person, my natural rhythm didn't align with a 9 p.m. showtime, so I used techniques like meditation, running, multiple small high-protein meals, supplements, power napping, and visualisation to shift my energy levels. These methods helped me sustain the intensity required for a two-hour performance late at night.

> *My* ***Finding Your Groove Principle:*** *Leading a healthy life means tuning into the frequencies that bring balance, from basic things like sleep patterns to higher awareness, such as sensing the neural activity of others. Whether connecting with an inspiring speaker or creating the right environment for a presentation, it's about tuning into yourself, others, and your surroundings.*

Chris

The Frequency of Resonance tapped into something I have been exploring for well over a decade in Management Learning, namely the question of identifying and understanding complex patterns of relationships.

Because of its ephemeral nature, explaining complexity is quite difficult. Academics employ precise and formal language to communicate what is essential to understand. This can make it feel too abstract and remote from everyday life. However, as Barry notes, complexities are part of everyday life. We have a lived understanding of them without first needing to know the theory.

So, does this matter to you?

If you want to live fully as a person (or use a persona, such as the roles of leader or manager), then yes, you must begin to educate yourself a little more about your life and practice and the nature of the world in which you live and practise. The strongest theories are those that are aligned on three levels, and it might help to employ the metaphor of maps for this:

1. *Using the Map:* Deciding where to go, and why. The wisdom and value of the choices and decisions (better actions).
2. *Making the Map:* Deciding what should be represented from the territory on the map. *What* you know and *how* you know about the world (better knowledge).
3. *The Territory:* What is actually "out there" (a better understanding of fundamental reality).

Most people and, it follows, most managers live life at the first level, looking for help choosing the right next move. Philosophers call that level *axiology*, a fancy term for theories of value, ethics, and judgments, and there is no shortage of supply of ideas, opinions, frameworks, tips, and shortcuts on offer. They call the second one *epistemology*, or theories of knowledge. All judgments embedded in the first level were based on assumptions about knowledge, even if they have hidden what those assumptions were. Hidden assumptions can be quite dangerous when making big decisions. Choices should be informed by robust knowledge. Robust knowledge is that which is in tune with reality. Finally, philosophical enquiry into reality on the third level is called *ontology*, or fundamental theories. This is deep into the mine (of the mind) and a difficult place to get to without a reason to go there. But, and this is crucial, ignorance of theories of reality can indeed be very costly. An awareness of reality (even if necessarily cramped, dark, or limited) can pay dividends.

Therefore, Barry's education in rhythm and frequency provides insight that applies not just to music but also works as a broader metaphor for life and leadership. It suggests a wider, connecting pattern. And this book's main argument is that *Finding Your Groove* involves awareness of all three levels.

Ontological Understanding of Rhythm and Frequency

It doesn't get more fundamental than reality. And yet, we do not have a way of accessing it. We can only infer it from events and our experience. There have been many attempts by different schools of philosophy to bridge this gap. Broadly, these divide between the *realists*, who assume there is a reality out there, generating patterns we experience as events (my preferred view), and the *idealists*, who assume our experience is as far as we can investigate or say anything about. Reality, they say, is a mental phenomenon.

Philosopher Roy Bhaskar (2015), the founder of **Critical Realism** (CR), presents a framework emphasising that our experience (which he calls the empirical) and the observable events (which he calls the actual) are only the surface manifestations of deeper, often hidden, processes in nature (which he calls the real). Barry hints at the idea that energy, effort, and rest cycles are embedded in reality. Bhaskar's **stratified ontology** (the real, the actual, and the empirical, or observable events), says that while we perceive rhythm at the empirical level, there are deeper structures (psychological, physiological, and social) that govern how we experience and interpret it.

Phenomena are not what they appear to be on the surface because they involve deeper, unseen mechanisms and structures. It can be hard to get your head around this. In leadership, it means that the events we see in our organisations (such as declining morale or stalled innovation) also contain information about underlying patterns and structures. In leadership, information is always a plus, so recognising these deeper layers can help managers get beyond just reacting to surface issues and addressing their root causes.

Just as musicians learn to hear beyond the chaos, leaders and individuals must train themselves to perceive the deeper structures that influence personal and organisational behaviour. For example, consider a situation where an organisation is experiencing declining market share despite implementing numerous marketing campaigns and product innovations. At the empirical level, it might appear that the company's strategies are ineffective or that competitors outperform them. On the other hand, a Critical Realist approach views the organisation as an open system interacting with its broader environment. This means delving deeper to uncover internal factors, such as misaligned organisational culture, inadequate leadership communication, or flawed incentive structures, and external systemic factors, like changes in market regulations, shifts in consumer behaviour, technological advancements, or economic conditions. These deeper structures and mechanisms can significantly hinder the effective execution of strategic initiatives.

Leaders can develop a deeper understanding of personal and organisational cycles and human behaviour by recognising the unseen systemic forces (economic pressures or psychological tendencies) that shape the rhythms of daily work life. Barry tuned into complex rhythms in music, which led to more grounded decision-making. This perspective aligns with **process philosophy**, a tradition in which reality is dynamic change and relational processes rather than static entities.

Epistemology and Perception

When Barry reflects on how we perceive rhythm, as structured or chaotic, he is relating to how we make sense of the world around us. His breaking through the perceived chaos of layered rhythms is a form of knowing and illustrates an embodied, **epistemological** step.

Tuning in to one's personal rhythm, such as energy levels throughout the day, and linking that to decisions on where best to be productive reflects principles of **embodied cognition**, which argues that our physical experiences deeply influence our mental processes. By being attuned to our bodies and environments, we can optimise performance and decision-making. This could be part of a wider self-awareness process for a manager or leader. Understanding one's physical and emotional rhythms improves personal productivity, team performance, and even the timing of critical decisions. There is a concept called **social entrainment** (Phililips-Silver, Aktipis, and Bryant 2010) that says individuals in a group align and synchronise their rhythms (physical, emotional, or cognitive) to achieve a collective goal. This kind of synchronisation with others is well-studied in music and dance. It is not too big a stretch to see it at work as a principle in organisations and teams.

In leadership, fostering team alignment or getting everyone on the same frequency can improve group cohesion and productivity. Leaders can promote this through activities that enhance communication, create shared goals, and synchronise the team's effort in response to collective energy patterns. How you present to and resonate with other people may be more important than the message you are trying to get across to achieve success. Donna Ladkin illustrates this in her paper on embodied leadership (2008) using the musician Bobby McFerrin as a case study.

A leader can foster this emergence of frequency synchronisation in many ways. These include mindfulness sessions and breathwork, which remain effective in team building, personal communication skill development, coaching, and anything that requires resonance in communication. In practical terms, you may start by developing empathy and deep listening skills, becoming more sensitive to others' emotional and cognitive states. This can enhance communication, improve decision-making, and create more meaningful team connections.

Ilya Prigogine's Dissipative Structures and Creative Destruction

Nobel laureate Ilya Prigogine's theory of **dissipative structures** (Prigogine and Stengers 1984) explains how systems can evolve through periods of instability and chaos. Rather than disintegrating, these systems reorganise into higher levels of complexity.

Barry's breakthrough in recognising rhythms after a period of chaos reflects Prigogine's idea of **creative destruction**, where disorder leads to the emergence of new, more sophisticated structures. Just as musicians break through moments of confusion to find harmony, leaders, and teams must navigate periods of uncertainty and change to reach higher levels of performance and innovation. In organisations, this could involve promoting a culture where experimentation and failure are seen as essential parts of the creative process, allowing for the emergence of innovative ideas and solutions during periods of uncertainty.

Ecologies of Mind and Pattern Recognition

British scientist and anthropologist Gregory Bateson's work on **cybernetics** and the **ecology of mind** (Bateson 1972) emphasises the interconnectedness of systems and the importance of pattern recognition. Bateson saw all living systems – individuals, societies, ecosystems – as interrelated through feedback loops of communication patterns. His ideas have influenced many fields, including psychiatry, zoology, systems thinking and complexity theory, anthropology, and communication studies. Barry's process of discerning complex patterns of rhythm aligns with Bateson's emphasis on recognising patterns in systems. Barry moves from chaos to understanding, much like Bateson's concept of epistemology, where knowledge is derived from recognising regularities in the world, such as rhythms or cyclical processes in nature and social systems, something we've returned to several times in this book. In fact, we are working with deeper patterns across the Notes, of course. As Bateson famously said:

> Information is a difference that makes a difference.
>
> (Bateson 1972, p. 459)

He adds that the question is already implicit in the complex and recursive pathways of relationships in a system. Whenever you foster environments where teams recognise the natural rhythms of work and rest, better synchronising individual energy patterns with organisational needs, you are operating using these principles because you are relying on the *relationship* between elements that influences the rest of the system.

Finding the Frequency of Wicked Problems

One of Bateson's legacies is a contribution to our understanding of open systems. This is proving extremely important as we face multiple crises and "Wicked Problems," which are:

> A class of social problems which are ill-formulated, where the information is confusing, where there are many clients and decision makers with conflicting values, and where the ramifications in the whole system are thoroughly confusing.
>
> (Rittel, in Buchanan 1992, p. 15)

A wicked problem is one with no clear definition, multiple stakeholders operating with differing priorities and aims, and no one right answer. There is just the tension between what can be determined and what is indeterminate (which turns out to be almost everything). The Covid-19 pandemic and the global climate emergency are examples of wicked problems. Organisations are affected by and are sometimes part of large, complex issues, and tuning in to find *that* frequency takes immense resources, wisdom, and courage.

Questions for Reflection and Groove

How well do you understand your personal energy rhythms, and how can you align your most demanding tasks with your natural peaks of productivity?

How might you use the "frequency" concept to better tune into your team's needs and foster a harmonious work environment?

In what ways can your paying attention to wider collective rhythms (e.g., meeting cycles, group energy) enhance team performance and cohesion?

4.5 Cultural Authenticity

Barry

When I was a kid in 1970s Port Elizabeth, at the southeastern tip of Africa, my mentor, the late Taliep Petersen, instilled in me a sense of pride in the music of my region. I later expanded this appreciation to encompass the whole sub-Saharan region.

Taliep championed Cape Malay culture and music, which is his authentic birthright as a descendant of the Malaysian slave trade. As a child, I resonated instantly with those rhythms and melodies, in the same way that I fell in love with the rhythms of Brazil. I've often reflected on this, and the best explanation I have for why a kid in the southeast of Africa would experience these emotions, is a universal feeling of form that connects us as humans at the deepest level.

Taliep later achieved global fame and fortune in the world of musical theatre with productions based on this Cape Malay *Goema* tradition alongside his partner David Kramer. This music was formed from a mix of Indonesian, Dutch, and African traditions, as the Dutch East India Company established a halfway stop on the Spice Route in present-day Cape Town. *Goema* is the name of the drums that the newly purchased Malay slaves made out of empty Dutch brandy barrels from the ships. It also describes the intoxicating rhythms and music styles unique to this part of our planet.

This story had a massive impact on me and guided my music career. Do your stuff authentically, with pride and even some playful bravado (the Cubans and the Nigerians do this beautifully). Taliep and David created a new genre for global consumption, with timeless stories packaged in a world-class delivery that audiences from the West End to Broadway could understand.

There is rich learning here, and it can be transferred to any industry. Instead of trying to mimic films from Hollywood, designs from Copenhagen, jazz from Manhattan, or startups from Silicon Valley, a more effective and powerful strategy is to package your ideas authentically and creatively regarding who *you* are and where *you* come from. Global markets (whether Hollywood or Wall Street) are more interested in fresh approaches from Johannesburg or Lagos than impersonations or inauthentic versions of what has already been done really well elsewhere.

A great example of this in music would be Amy Winehouse. Learning from American culture, mainly jazz and early R&B, she created her own unique "Camden Soul" style of writing and performance. This is very different from doing cover versions of works by Billie Holliday or Mavis Staples and perfectly copying their performance style.

I remember Amy vividly from Nelson Mandela's 90th birthday celebration concert in London's Hyde Park on a beautiful summer evening on the 27th of June 2008. I had performed twice, with Sipho Hotstix Mabuse and then Johnny Clegg, and headed to the hospitality marquee for a well-deserved pint of English beer. As I was about to order, I was gently nudged aside and, on turning to confront the queue-jumper, found myself up close to Amy Winehouse, who was far more beautiful up close than in the tabloids! She gave me a playful smile, and I stepped aside for her to grab two drinks before going on stage for a blistering set of hits that brought the proverbial house down. I had watched her rehearse the house band earlier that afternoon, and her leadership, intentionality, and control were masterful. I was mesmerised by her authenticity, as was Quincy Jones, who was her guest at the concert and the recipient of one of the drinks mentioned above.

Throughout my years as the drummer in the Johnny Clegg Band, I experienced firsthand and in a pragmatic way the significance of showcasing one's uniqueness and mastery. We would be performing at various festivals in North America alongside the biggest names in the business. I noticed that when the pressure to perform was dialled up, Johnny's approach to handling pressure was instinctive. Before performances, he would often engage in traditional Zulu dancing and singing in the communal backstage area, making the band's distinctiveness highly visible to the other acts. This served, in a very nice way, to assert our unique identity and expertise and to emphasise that we were not trying to mimic American culture. I particularly cherish the memories of Peter Gabriel and Robert Plant eagerly participating in these Clegg warm-ups at a festival in Norway with all the excitement and enthusiasm of children!

The point? The Clegg band didn't try to outperform the best in the business in America at their own game. Instead, our show was more interesting than most because it was 100% rooted in cultural authenticity and then delivered with excellence and professionalism in composition, arrangement, performance, and technical staging. This strategy helped us maintain a strong brand for over 30 years at the highest level.

> *My* ***Finding Your Groove Principle:*** *Once you've found your ideal environment, stay true to yourself and your beliefs. This may require stepping outside the norm and embracing bold, playful behaviour to stay aligned with your core principles and goals.*

Chris

Humans are intriguing. On the one hand, we are formed in the image of complex patterns in our cultures and surroundings, family upbringings, and even our local geography. We also observe, recognise, and absorb patterns from other cultures and influences. On the other hand, we then form patterns and influence others. Done well, this constant give-and-take keeps human societies vibrant and resilient. It is a delicate and sometimes fragile balance of patterns.

Barry's reflections here suggest to me rich themes of eclectic roots, authenticity, and retaining distinctive identity, which can be explored philosophically and practically in the realms of creativity, leadership, and personal development.

Eclectic Roots and Early Influences

Barry's musically and culturally diverse upbringing, rooted in the rhythms of Cape Malay Goema and influenced by the diverse cultural mix of sub-Saharan Africa, demonstrates a musical *syncretism*, where distinct cultural elements merge and are reconciled into something new. This resonates with a cultural theory coined by anthropologist Claude Lévi-Strauss, **Bricolage**, where seemingly disparate influences are drawn together to form a unique, hybrid identity. Taliep Petersen's mentorship, grounded in the music of the Cape Malay, serves as the foundation for Barry's appreciation of diverse influences that shaped his musical identity. Bricolage gets us busy playing and rearranging the found pieces in a situation. It is an iterative and open investigation technique suitable for explorers, musicians, academic researchers, and leaders.

In leadership, embracing eclectic roots can encourage innovation and originality. Leaders can draw on diverse influences, whether cultural, historical, or experiential, to create unique approaches to solving problems or developing strategies. Instead of attempting to replicate Silicon Valley startup culture, for example, leaders in emerging markets can integrate local values and practices to craft unique, sustainable models of success that resonate with their specific context.

Barry's experiences mirror the African philosophical concept of **Ubuntu**, which emphasises interconnectedness and shared human experience. His connection to southern African rhythms is an aesthetic choice and an expression of identity and community. This eclecticism isn't about imitation but the creation of something new and authentic by merging global and local influences. After global commerce was boosted by the rise of multinationals and the reduction of time and distance through technology, *glocalisation* represents an attempt to blend global practices with local culture to create something distinct. The problem with this has been the question of authenticity.

Finding One's Authentic Take in Practice

As Barry describes it, authenticity transcends mere self-expression and creates a unique cultural narrative. I think the transcendent next step is the key one here.

The search for the authentic self is famously ancient (just search for the dictum "know thyself" online). The additional call to live aligned with this self-awareness is famously captured by Shakespeare in Hamlet. Here, he has Polonius dishing out life advice to his son Laertes:

> This above all: to thine own self be true,
> And it must follow, as the night the day,
> Thou canst not then be false to any man.
> (*Hamlet*, Act 1, Scene 3)

This idea aligns with *existentialist philosophy*, for example in the works of Jean-Paul Sartre or Albert Camus, who advocated for individuals to create their essence through choices and actions. Barry's decision to embrace his roots, rather than reproducing the American or European traditions those roots once absorbed, reflects this existentialist notion of authenticity, where everyone takes responsibility for shaping their identity in a way that is true to themselves. A willingness to stand out, even if perceived as bold or disruptive, resonates in art and culture, where breaking norms and challenging traditional aesthetics are often celebrated.

This makes it an interesting topic in business, management, and leadership. It may help create a space for authenticity in a sphere of life (commerce, trade, business, etc.) where simple imitation often thrives. How can an organisation truly be itself? What does that even mean? It has become increasingly difficult not to simply follow other industries' latest trends or strategies. Our expectations as consumers are now also global, and it follows that our education systems are becoming increasingly standardised.

The good news is that if you *do* practice authenticity well, you can escape the imitation game and craft a narrative rooted in personal values, experiences, and cultural heritage. This can translate into business practices that are innovative, distinctive, and ultimately more engaging for stakeholders, as seen in Barry's discussion of Amy Winehouse's *Camden Soul* style.

The bad news is that success like this will encounter increasing external pressure to conform to expectations and norms, many imitators, and an internal temptation to play to the gallery and create according to what you think are others' images and expectations of you.

Retaining a Distinctive Identity in Weaving Patterns

What is the self? You have two choices in how you deal with this question.

- Seek and entirely accept an outside authority's answer.
- Ask and answer it entirely on your terms.

For the first option, a bewildering variety of viewpoints and opinions are available. Many sources influence us in the early development of self, and we may continue with this as a tactic to explain what self is. This is not problematic as long as you appreciate that.

Ultimately, no one person can dictate to you which one is true.

And here is the problem: we are seeing the term Authentic Leadership everywhere. Modern interpretations of authenticity in leadership development risk becoming formulaic and performative. You may feel pressure to conform to a particular style of authenticity expected in your organisation rather than exploring your genuine self-expression. This creates a paradox. Authenticity, by definition, should be unique and self-determined. In practice, it is often shaped by external expectations and pressures. Are leaders truly encouraged to be themselves, or are they being shaped only to align with corporate goals and outcomes? If so, standing out and not conforming may be penalised.

Is there a middle identity ground for leaders in organisational life?

We can't avoid the influence of the outside for something that is by its nature a definition experienced by the inside. The notion of *interweaving* different influences, such as Cape Malay Goema, Zulu culture, and rock and roll, is undoubtedly the tinder needed for the creative spark to get that fire of a distinctive version of self going. Success does not come from outperforming others at their own game but by creating a distinctive, woven tapestry of influences others cannot replicate. Proper thought leadership is a cultural brand that is impossible to mimic because it's deeply personal and unique.

Retaining your identity while integrating external influences can be viewed through the lens of French philosopher Gilles Deleuze's philosophy of **difference** and **repetition** (2014). Rather than repeating established patterns or imitating existing models, Deleuze suggests that true creativity comes from constantly reinterpreting and reconfiguring familiar elements to create something genuinely new. Barry's approach to authenticity, where cultural uniqueness is preserved even in international contexts, reflects Deleuze's concept of difference and is an example of resistance to homogenisation and embrace of continuous evolution.

For leaders, this means crafting a leadership approach (finding a groove) that retains a distinctive identity while navigating different environments. In business, maintaining a company's core values and cultural authenticity in global markets is often more powerful than attempting to conform to global norms.

Staying human is just as intriguing and complex as being human.

Questions for Reflection and Groove

How can you celebrate your unique identity and principles in professional settings without compromising professionalism or effectiveness?

For you, does meaning come from outside and before (handed down to you by others) or from inside and in the present (handmade by you)?

How can bold, playful behaviour be used strategically to challenge norms and drive innovation within your field?

4.6 The Beatles, Bieber, and a Tree

Barry

I find the term "overnight success" in the music industry quite amusing. It seems to suggest that the Beatles achieved sudden success after their first hit song, *Love Me Do*, in 1962, without acknowledging the years they spent honing their songwriting and performance skills. In reality, as a group, the Beatles had already accumulated thousands of hours of practice during their 8-hour shifts, seven days a week, while performing as a covers band in Hamburg, long before they achieved their seemingly sudden success.

Consider, too, Justin Bieber, the child star who exploded "overnight" in 2009 with *One Time*. Strip away the media attention, both positive and negative, and how many people grasp the incredible effort and focus that preceded this? As a young child, he mastered multiple instruments and spent hours honing his craft by (very successfully) busking in Toronto and embarking on his legendary North America road trip with manager Scooter Braun. During this journey of several months, they visited small regional radio stations. Bieber would do multiple interviews daily and then play a song in the studio with his guitar, gradually converting America's media gatekeepers state by state by age 14.

Our world is measured in numbers. An act is successful when revenue exceeds *x*, *y* tickets are sold, or *z* number of streams logged. It is important to establish benchmark metrics to assess progress, and rhythms and cycles are measured and understood by using numbers, from musical beats and frequencies to a company's financial statements. However, growth is organic. In nature, a tree is not assembled part-algorithmically and linearly. Bieber and the Beatles grew their creative output organically and universally, very much influenced by their specific environment, not by following an explicit series of steps like a recipe for a cake.

I do see the value and importance of numbers. Humans generally do not like change, and to measure our performance, we require some metrics to gauge movement to compare against. For example, how many units were sold, how much cash we generated, how many people showed up to our concerts … and so on. By comparing these numbers with previous years or with competitors over the same period, we can determine whether our relative movement has been progression or regression.

What is missing is the backstory, which is about human resonance with one another and the world. We are in the economy of the algorithm. If x happens, then do y. Binary, unemotional stuff, and when used to assess creativity it is mostly way off the mark. Is anyone else dismayed by the choices Spotify or Netflix offer to make for you next?

Whether in their education or their career, someone is deemed talented or not, a success or a failure, smart or dumb, up or down, creative or uncreative. And so forth. This blinkered perspective makes the Beatles or Bieber an overnight success without deeper understanding or curiosity.

Our growth is not binary. This is not how nature works. Nature is ebb and flow, and we are part of nature. This universal order behind our journey in life is best described in terms of waves, which have peaks and troughs, not by linear "yes" or "no" reactions. The Beatles' success in 1962 was the peak of a wave, preceded by continuous effort, talent, and luck. This was followed by a trough, and then more peaks. The ebb and flow of the ocean is not constructed using 1's and 0's.

Following this continuous and non-binary perspective in nature, a tree is not constructed by research and development, supply chain, and assembly activities. It grows out of nature, imperfectly and uniquely influenced by its surroundings – the opposite process of a new BMW.

The Beatles and Bieber grew in similar ways to the tree: harmonic growth, with multiple areas growing at varying speeds, all at the same time. Our creativity and power are unique to each of us, and particular talents are distributed unevenly, which is why the Beatles were a vocal, guitar, bass, and drum team (and not four guitars or four bassists).

I remember moments in my career where I experienced sudden breakthroughs, marked by recognition from others, from peers, media attention, and so forth. For example, I was at a music festival in the Drakensberg Mountains, South Africa, where the Hothouse Flowers were headlining, and the word went out that they needed a drummer urgently for the following night's performance. I was at the festival performing with my friend Colin Vearncombe (aka Black) and was called to the Flowers guest accommodation. We met, talked about the show, and it was decided that I would join them onstage, with no physical rehearsal, for their set. The next night, I played the Hothouse Flowers setlist for 90 minutes, using only experience, intuition, deep listening, and cues from these amazingly gifted guys with the biggest debut album sales in Irish rock history!

The show went beautifully, and a live album was planned from the rough recording (until the South African Broadcasting Company admitted to re-recording a club rugby match over 50% of the 2-inch master tape). I was lauded as the "man of the match" at the festival for a pretty good drumming performance and for being a good example of channelling stress in a healthy direction … Flow! My association with the Flowers continued from there, and I count Fiachna Ó Braonáin as a good friend and collaborator, though we have yet to release our *Africa* project to the world.

Was this an overnight success as a session musician and drummer? Perhaps to the audience and media, but not for me. My reality was playing drums every day for as long as I could remember, watching, listening, practising, failing, being humiliated, starting again, and inching my way forward for years, for decades. So, the Flowers show was one of many lovely moments where passion, technique, experience, and luck intersected.

We can learn from the natural order around us and try out a simple perspective shift.

> *My* ***Finding Your Groove Principle:*** *Success is a rhythm, not a straight line. Trust the flow, and stay adaptable. Work fiercely toward your vision while remaining open to change and flowing with the natural current of power, much as a tree grows.*

*Try this **Zooming Out** exercise:*

Individual: Identify a personal challenge.
Organisational: How does this challenge relate to your organisation's patterns?
Systemic: What larger trends influence it?

Finally, the actionable step: What one thing can you shift today?

Chris

In *The Beatles, Bieber, and a Tree,* Barry contrasts our perception that people's experiences of success are instant (or overnight) triumphs with the slow, organic processes behind real achievement. That a threshold is crossed when someone moves from obscurity to widespread fame is not in doubt. Nor is that the real question. I see two powerful thematic opportunities for management reflection here. The first concerns the roots of success, and the other is the distinction between digital (binary) and analogue (relational) modes of growth.

Success and Its Roots: an Organic Process

Barry challenges the notion of overnight success by illustrating that true success results from long-term, persistent effort, as seen in the stories of the Beatles and Justin Bieber. The idea that excellence requires habitual dedication and preparation over a long time is not new. In his teachings on ethics, Greek philosopher Aristotle singled out the concept of *arete* (excellence) as achieved through habitual action over time, rather than instant recognition or isolated achievements. More recently, and covered elsewhere in this book, Malcolm Gladwell's depiction of the 10,000-hour rule in his book *Outliers* suggests that mastery in any field requires extensive practice and sustained effort. Excellence can have and does have markers and metrics to quantify it. The path to excellence is not linear or instantaneous but layered and gradual, often requiring a deep connection to one's craft and environment.

The concept of success is complex, and it's important to consider it more deeply. I agree with Barry's critique of the current shortcut, numbers-focused view of success. He finds this view in the creative industries, and it would be logical to believe that it is happening across all kinds of businesses.

Success has become a loaded word. It is now most often measured using external, measurable outcomes such as money or social status. Our metrics for success are comparisons outside ourselves. By association, we can easily start thinking of excellence in the same way. The measures of success are arbitrary; they are what we decide or agree they are. A more naturalistic or organic model of success has significant implications for leadership and organisational growth. Instead of focusing on short-term metrics or singular milestones, companies should prioritise long-term development, sustained innovation, and continuous learning. This would align with sustainable leadership models emphasising long-term growth over quick wins. Regenerative business models, such as the *Circular Economy model* proposed by the Ellen Macarthur Foundation (2013), are growing in popularity. These call for a rethink on how we define and measure success by keeping products and materials in circulation, thereby separating consumption of raw materials from economic activity and value.

Binary (Digital) vs Analogue (Relational) Growth

Are we over-using reductionist thinking when we break complex phenomena down into metrics or algorithms? I support Barry's position on binary thinking (yes/no, success/failure, etc.). It is far more useful to see success as an analogue process. In arguing for a more holistic approach, he uses the imagery of flow and nature, using the example of how a tree appears as an object in the world.

On some occasions, success is seemingly binary. The absence of success may be how we can define failure (or vice versa). In that case, they operate together. However, in the spirit of the *Finding Your Groove* framework, success needs a **holistic view**. Success describes a person's relationship to a context, situation, or set of other relationships. It is dynamic, evolving, and influenced by many factors.

Success is a *pattern*.

This perspective aligns quite well with an ecological outlook, which says that systems (whether natural, social, or personal) are interconnected and cannot be understood merely through linear cause-and-effect logic. Soil quality, sunlight, weather, and so on determine a tree's growth. We interpret this rather purposively – that the tree is successful by using all those things to grow.

A holistic view doesn't separate a tree from its environment. A healthy environment is indistinguishable from a healthy tree (or any element). Translating this into business is no easy matter. I rely on the systemic view of Gregory Bateson as my guide for rethinking how we define success. Here are some ideas that might be useful:

1. *Systemic Harmony and Balance:* Success involves maintaining harmonious relationships between different parts of a system and avoiding overexploitation or disruption. A successful system (including a person) can adapt to changing circumstances without losing its essential integrity.
2. *Adaptation and Learning:* Bateson emphasised the importance of feedback and learning in any system. Success, in his terms, might be measured by how well an individual or organisation is learning from the loops of information over time and adjusting behaviour accordingly. Success may be seen as a higher level of learning to learn, a category that includes binaries such as win/lose or yes/no).
3. *Integration:* Success would likely be defined as fitting into and sustaining (stewarding, in leadership terms) broader ecological and social systems. Exploiting resources or focusing on short-term gains that harm the environment or social fabric would not constitute success.

4. *Valuing Flexibility over Control:* Success is not about dominating or controlling the environment but being flexible enough to change in response to it. Bateson would critique the notion of success as mastery or control as a form of hubris that leads to systemic breakdown.
5. *Recognition of Interconnectedness:* Success *requires* recognition and respect for the interconnected nature of all things. Our ignorance of this reality can lead to errors that result in negative consequences, such as ecological degradation or social conflict.

This calls for a shift from data-driven, purely numerical assessments to more qualitative, relationship-based metrics in leadership and management. Leaders should focus on building healthy ecosystems within organisations, where collaboration, creativity, and adaptability are valued over rigid control mechanisms. This is especially true in creative industries, where success measured as hitting targets contrasts with a view of producing meaningful, impactful work that resonates with people on a deeper level.

From a personal growth perspective, understanding oneself as part of a relational, evolving system encourages adaptability and resilience. Instead of viewing setbacks or failures in binary terms, individuals can see them as part of a larger cycle of growth and learning. Success is always in the eye of the beholder. Barry sees value in incremental progress, reflection, and persistent effort as ends in themselves. I agree.

Success, whether in a personal career or business, should be measured holistically, including outcomes, the journey, experiences, and adaptability. Overnight or not, we should aim for a holistic and organic definition of success that mirrors the natural world's ebb and flow.

Questions for Reflection and Groove

Reflect on a personal or organisational achievement: what unseen or gradual efforts led to its success, and how can these lessons inform future goals?

How can you, as a leader, access adaptability within your teams or staff while maintaining a strong sense of direction?

What practices can your organisation adopt to encourage organic, sustainable growth rather than rigid, step-by-step approaches?

4.7 Shaking Things Up

Barry

10 a.m., a dark hotel room with the phone ringing. Somebody wakes up after two long flights, with a 7-hour time change, and answers the phone to hear an indecipherable voice speaking in what turns out to be heavily accented English.

Total confusion.

The person is me, and the place is the Grand Hyatt Hotel in Seoul, South Korea. I had arrived the previous night with the Johnny Clegg band to perform at a festival at the Olympic Stadium and had indulged a bit too much at a media event with members of the German metal band, the Scorpions. 48 hours later, I came within 30 minutes of playing drums for the Scorpions set after their drummer's flight was delayed. I had done the afternoon sound check with Rudolph Schenker, singing me the drum parts on stage and signalling the song sections like an air traffic controller!

The morning wake-up call was at my request, as I wanted to maximise my free day by exploring a strange and overwhelmingly enormous city versus the easy route of a day at the pool with menus in English. This was typical of my touring days as an international musician, always leaning into being slightly uncomfortable and exploring the unknown.

Ever since I can remember, the idea of travelling has filled me with hope and energy, from simple things like going on a night away with my parents to longer road trips to the thrill of train travel and finally experiencing flying to different places. I've always loved the process, especially trains, planes, and hotels, as a way of engaging with my environment. The feeling of stepping into the unknown, with no turning back, being curious about what's waiting along the way, and learning about how other people experience life.

My career as a drummer touring internationally was the perfect manifestation of this. Throughout, I have spent months on the road each year in North America, Europe, and Australasia.

I have always made a point to experience and immerse myself in the local culture wherever I go. Even with just a few hours of free time, I have become adept at quickly taking in my surroundings. I am good at taking mental snapshots. I would get up earlier or find time between soundcheck and showtime to go running in the vineyards of Provence, explore the architecture of Chicago, or observe the plains of Wyoming from the tour bus window at 5 a.m. These brief moments have had a lasting impact on me. I've stored these experiences as a collection of inspiring, multi-sensory snapshots that continue to motivate me to this day.

Immersing myself in a different cultural order is incredibly invigorating and powerful. It allows me to break free from my usual routine, stop being so self-absorbed, and see beyond the limitations imposed by my surroundings. In short, it's a way of "getting out of my own way."

Our minds are wired to filter out or cancel mundane details that don't pose any immediate threat, focusing instead on potential new dangers. While this was beneficial for our ancestors hunting in the savannah, it is more limited in modern city life, where it can lead to the side effects of boredom and complacency.

The strategy is one of deliberately imposing new things as a way to refresh and resharpen the senses, and to learn about oneself. Of course, this means changing things up and breaking the patterns you feel are normal. This kind of change is uncomfortable. However, the discomfort is usually felt only in the *prospect* of impending change, and it disappears soon after starting to do it!

Expanding my experience expands my perspective. This is often about absorbing new parts of the world, and it is possible to do so without moving far geographically. Simply exploring a new part of the city I live in, even for a few hours, can refresh my view of the world. For example, choosing a supermarket other than my normal destination when popping out of groceries, talking to someone in the checkout line (if, like me, you don't normally do this), or having a coffee in the newly opened roastery that I haven't yet tried because I usually gravitate to my regular coffee shop. These three simple and slightly uncomfortable actions can do wonders for inspiration, energy and raising awareness.

Everything I've described involves deliberately doing things slightly differently as a strategy for refreshing one's outlook, establishing a wider perspective for a while, and regaining enthusiasm, which will always wane when repeating the same familiar cycles and patterns.

> *My **Finding Your Groove Principle:** When feeling stuck and uninspired, commit to doing at least three things differently for a day. And then another day, and another day, to make a week. This means catching yourself when on autopilot and becoming conscious of choices and actions.*

Chris

This Note addresses a topic I have often contemplated. Barry's emphasis on shaking things up to refresh how we see the world relates closely to my concept of personal development, which I will elaborate on below. My experience during a sabbatical year spent in Tokyo, Japan, several years ago exemplifies this idea. Coming from the UK, my immersion in the Tokyo suburb of Hachioji represented a significant pattern change.

I explored the city's western edge, where there were few tourists and a wealth of unfamiliar local culture to experience. With free time on my hands, I adopted the motto "Just start walking." I set off without a fixed destination or plan, simply observing everything around me. At first, I needed to translate my impressions into words, and soon I began to rely solely on photographs. Initially, I sought answers to questions I had brought with me from my cultural background. I wrote a blog and posted on LinkedIn, and I still found that I could not make much headway. Eventually, I shifted my focus to framing new questions with my phone's camera. The result was a book of images and a small exhibition when I returned to the UK.

In the arts, many creative breakthroughs occur when patterns are disrupted. Artists often find inspiration by shifting mediums, environments, or techniques. In business or management, having the cognitive flexibility or the ability to shift between thinking about different concepts is essential for creative insight. Breakthroughs are often found outside established norms.

By breaking patterns, Barry encourages *lateral thinking*, a term coined by Maltese author and physician Edward de Bono (2016). In lateral thinking, one breaks free from logical, linear thinking to approach problems from novel or unexpected angles. The origins of IKEA's iconic flat-pack furniture lie in a piece of lateral thinking by the company's founder, Ingvar Kamprad. He did not invent the idea of furniture that could be assembled or disassembled. He had the problem of slow and difficult distribution of bulky items to customers, and for his business to grow, he had to break many patterns (e.g. consumers would not be willing to do some of the work).

Some leadership and management theories touch upon routine, breaking patterns, and fostering creativity through disruption. Routines are often beneficial for efficiency and can equally lead to complacency and inhibit innovation. In organisations, breaking patterns is essential for fostering a culture of *innovation*. Managers can implement small changes to workplace routines, such as how meetings are conducted or feedback is delivered, to challenge employees to think differently. By disrupting the familiar, leaders create space for new ideas and perspectives to emerge.

Adaptive Leadership Theory, developed at Harvard by Ronald Heifetz and Marty Linsky (2009), focuses on a leader's ability to encourage their teams to break out of established patterns to tackle complex challenges. The theory uses five principles, which I paraphrase as:

1. Perceive and handle your emotions and your perception of the emotions of others.
2. Have transparency and equity in all your dealings and communication.
3. Be open to continuous learning, change, and development – and encourage this in others.
4. Have the character to change a belief, a practice, a principle when it isn't working, and be open to feedback from a diverse set of people and contexts.
5. Seek solutions where no one loses.

Disruptive Innovation

Much pattern change is about innovation. In business, a special class of innovation was coined by a Harvard Business School professor, Clayton Christensen (2013). Christensen identified two types of innovation. The first type *is high-level* refinement, which occurs when an organisation seeks to maintain its traditional definition of competitive advantage. To outperform its competitors, a company will work hard to introduce new and additional features that customers may perceive as valuable and be willing to pay more for. Christensen refers to this type of innovation as sustaining innovations. Successful companies always strive to provide their best customers with what they desire. It is difficult to outperform an established company in their own game because they will always be more profitable than you at the top end.

Low-level disruption refers to the introduction of a simpler and often more affordable alternative technology, product, or service. Market leaders tend to focus on high-profit customers, which leaves an opening for new entrants at the lower end of the market. This shift is often overlooked initially because existing players are focused on refining high-level products and services. However, new entrants can be game-changers and even threaten established players by introducing disruptive innovations that can potentially put them out of business.

Breaking out of established routines allows companies to discover new, disruptive ways to serve their markets, fostering innovation. The Japanese approach, known as kaizen, is another application of this method of interrupting a process.

Kaizen and Continuous Improvement

Observers tend mainly to see the routine side of Kaizen (カイゼン), or continuous improvement, which encourages small, incremental changes over time. However, Kaizen also advocates breaking patterns by regularly evaluating processes to eliminate inefficiencies. This continuous feedback loop is a form of deliberate, small-scale disruption in which habitual practices are continuously reassessed to ensure they remain effective. Barry's idea of changing three small things daily reflects Kaizen's philosophy of breaking patterns into small, manageable ways to foster constant improvement and prevent complacency.

This is part of a general field of study into Complex Adaptive Systems (CAS), which argues that previous leadership theories have tended to be hierarchical and top-down. It explores how leaders can facilitate adaptive, emergent change by disrupting the routines that can lead to organisational inertia. Drawing from complexity science, it emphasises that systems must remain dynamic. In harmony with this view, Barry points out that if leaders are to act more as catalysts for change, they *must* know how to introduce disruptions that break existing patterns of behaviour if those patterns have become static and problematic.

Whether figuratively or (if you can) literally, your task is to just start walking. My task, only figuratively, as an educator is to stand in your way just enough to get you to stop and think.

Questions for Reflection and Groove

When was the last time you consciously disrupted a personal or professional routine? What impact did it have on your perspective?

How can you design team processes that regularly challenge assumptions and encourage fresh thinking?

What small, deliberate changes could you implement this week to explore new opportunities or overcome stagnation?

4.8 What Moves You (On)?

Barry

I asked a young salesman at B&H, an independent electronics store in Manhattan, for tech advice while I was buying a Bluetooth speaker. This sparked a conversation about music, and it turned out he was a songwriter. He inquired about my accent, and when I mentioned I was South African, he immediately referenced Die Antwoord as one of his favourite acts. He was astonished to hear that I had worked with them over the years. I then asked him what kind of music he liked the most, and his answer was profound and insightful: "I like music that surprises me." I realised that this sentiment perfectly sums up my relationship with all styles of music.

I have always been interested in exploring a variety of musical styles instead of sticking to just one genre. As a ten-year-old, my musical tastes were much broader than those of my peers, ranging from folk and country to rock, jazz, and pop. On reflection, my "musical thermometer" was whether the music moved me. This could happen if a melody or groove resonated deeply with me or if the lyrics painted a vivid picture that evoked a similar response. To this day, I enjoy the excitement of being surprised by different musical styles, compositions, or performances. However, I tend to get bored quickly and soon feel the need to seek out my next surprise.

Throughout my career as an international performer and producer, I have often experienced these impatient impulses, which can be misinterpreted as a lack of focus or follow-through. In reality, these reflect my extreme curiosity as I continuously seek out new work that delights and surprises me. The central question I always ask is: Does it move me? My playlist on any given day can range widely, featuring both new and old music, agnostic of genre. From Nick Cave's *Jubilee Street* to John Coltrane's *Naima*, or from Kendrick Lamar's *Alright* to Bach's *Cello Suites 1–6* …

One universal to note is that people often use pieces of music as anchors that transport them back to specific experiences. For example, a song might remind you of a summer holiday, or an anthem may bring back memories of a particular sports match. While I see the powerful tweak of nostalgia at play here, that is not the kind of resonance I am referring to.

My excitement is for music, new or old, to resonate in the moment, as opposed to being a trusted vehicle for revisiting cherished memories. In this case, I believe the contextual experience is what affects people, not the music itself.

For decades, one thing that has frequently stopped me in my tracks has been the search for the primary source behind music. I'm fascinated by the code underlying our resonance with music. Why have humans been obsessed with experiencing melodies, beats, and vocal narratives for thousands of years? This is a deeply universal topic, and the code is embedded in frequencies that resonate with each of us in unique ways. Certain rhythms and specific combinations of notes have a visceral appeal to certain people, evoking emotions such as happiness, sadness, nostalgia, and excitement. Of course, this varies across cultures; for example, the Flamenco of

Seville may not elicit quite the same response in Liverpool, just as the urban beats of Brooklyn might not have the same effect in Vienna.

Even then, however, it depends. I have had amazing experiences connecting across cultures when the only filter is simply, "Does this move me?"

During my 2007 tour in France with the Johnny Clegg Band, we rehearsed a dance section that combined traditional Zulu dancers with Parisian breakdancers. This fusion beautifully illustrated timeless connectivity and was launched at the Fête de L'Humanité festival in Paris, where it received thunderous applause. In 2005, I performed traditional percussion with an unexpected ensemble, the London Chamber Orchestra and Ladysmith Black Mambazo, the South African Isicathamiya group that gained global fame from their contribution to the choral elements of Paul Simon's Graceland album. We blended traditional African rhythms with classical music and vice versa. This collaborative mix was so successful that the recording, *No Boundaries*, was nominated for a Grammy.

I have observed that when art is authentic, and mastery is achieved, it transcends cultural boundaries. A great example is a video clip of Paul McCartney and Dave Grohl composing a song together during a performance in the documentary series *Sound City*. Grohl expresses his amazement by saying, "That was so easy!" to which McCartney replies "That's how it's supposed to be."[1]

I believe this relates to a universal order of things. Whether it is the Tao, David Bohm's Implicate Order, or Richard Feynman's Glorious Mess, this primary code manifests in various ways, influenced by different cultures and geographical regions. For example, the core harmonic rhythm of Africa transforms into the fluidity of Flamenco, the complexity of Indian Tala, the second line beat of New Orleans, the Rock and Roll of Liverpool, the machismo of Guaguancó in Havana, the Blues of Chicago and Timbuktu, and the Neo-Bop of New York City.

The core elements of rhythm are consistent and best understood by assigning integers to frequencies; 1, 2, and 3 (and their multiples). This basic rhythmic structure can vary slightly depending on regional influences, culture, accents, and trends. However, to the listener, the resulting innovation sounds fresh and new. When executed authentically, it creates music that resonates deeply with people. I never tire of exploring this topic; it has been my lifelong passion.

This universal principle also applies to the business world. A good example is the multitude of opportunities available at any given time for leaders and entrepreneurs looking to expand and increase company value. From my perspective, a multi-faceted and curious approach is more effective than a narrow, blinkered one. It's about being wide-ranging and fast-moving rather than limited and slow, though neither approach is inherently right or wrong. Better decisions align with the fundamental reasons for being in business, which must include considerations for both people and the planet.

My ***Finding Your Groove Principle:*** *What drives an organisation can (and should) be captured in a single word. For example, "Safety" comes to mind for Volvo, and "Sustainability" for Patagonia. My friend Pepe Marais,* *founder of Joe Public, has built a multinational advertising business around this concept. His approach is authentic, competitive, and people-centred, as outlined in his book* Growing Greatness *(Marais 2018). Distilling core ideas into one word unifies efforts, creating a cohesive and unmistakable guiding groove.*

Chris

Barry's Note juxtaposes two ideas, "being surprised" and "being moved." I think there's a lovely synergy between them, and it's part of a universal groove in that novelty and feeling are immediate and unmediated. If we can tap into that, we know we are close to what it must feel to *Find Our Groove*.

On Being Surprised

We all love the idea of surprise. Etymologically, its roots lead to the word "prehend", or grasp, and so it's a distant cousin of comprehend, apprehend, enterprise, and even prison.

Logically, surprise must be an indicator of learning. We can't be surprised by what we already know. Psychologists such as Daniel Kahneman have noted that humans are hard-wired to pay attention to unexpected events, as these disrupt our cognitive patterns and demand focus. In neuroscience, this is tied to the **prediction error**, where deviations from expected outcomes activate dopamine release, fostering curiosity and motivation. Prediction Error Theory starts by saying surprise arises when there is a discrepancy between expected and actual outcomes. It suggests this leads individuals to adjust their mental models to better align with reality. Self-reflection also requires another capacity. Without critical thinking, we will attempt to fit reality with our perspective, not vice versa.

There's a relationship between surprise and expectation. Surprise often emerges from deviations from familiar patterns, such as unexpected harmonies or rhythms in art and music. Leonard Meyer explored this principle in *Emotion and Meaning in Music* (1957). It suggests that surprise in creative forms triggers emotional responses because it balances novelty with familiarity. This kind of surprise offers just enough difference to excite but not overwhelm.

Surprise plays a powerful role in leadership by disrupting complacency and sparking innovation. Leaders who create environments where teams encounter unexpected ideas or challenges can inspire creativity and foster resilience. This doesn't mean chaos. It means deliberately introducing novel perspectives or methods to keep people engaged.

For example, at Pixar's Braintrust Meetings, surprise fosters creativity. In regular feedback sessions, directors receive candid, unexpected peer critiques, challenging their assumptions and pushing their storytelling to new heights.

You can use this understanding by creating environments that encourage innovation and adaptability. By introducing novel challenges or perspectives, you can stimulate employees' cognitive flexibility and create a culture that embraces change and continuous learning.

All other things being equal, humans will always be attracted to surprises. If we already knew the result, what would the point of the game be?

On Being Moved

To be moved is to experience a deep emotional resonance. This ties to the universal emotion of empathy, where humans connect to stories, music, or art that resonate with their lived or imagined experiences. Philosopher Martha Nussbaum argues in *Upheavals of Thought* (2003) that emotions are personal reactions and judgments about what matters most to us. To be moved is to encounter something that aligns with, challenges, or deepens our values. As Barry reminds us, emotional resonance transcends cultural boundaries. He finds this universal when there is authenticity in music, and neuroscientific research supports this observation. Listening to music activates brain regions involved in emotion, memory, and reward. The effect is magnified when the music aligns with the listener's cultural or personal context.

Limbic resonance is a term introduced by the authors of *A General Theory of Love* (Lewis, Amini, and Lannon 2001). It describes how humans establish deep emotional connections with one another, allowing for the nonverbal sharing of emotional states. The authors argue that this ability is the foundation for all social relationships and individual and societal health and well-being. The nervous system, particularly the limbic system in the brain, is naturally and universally attuned to recognise and synchronise with the nervous systems of others. For instance, if you have ever been around someone yawning and felt the urge to yawn, or if you've been in a room full of laughter and found it impossible not to smile and laugh along, you have experienced limbic resonance. Conversely, lacking this empathic connection with others can lead to suffering for everyone involved.

A leader can tap into this by communicating authentically and connecting initiatives to shared values or emotional anchors. Storytelling, for example, can convey the significance of a company's mission in a way that moves employees and stakeholders. Companies like Patagonia succeed because they are innovative, *and* their mission moves employees and customers.

The ability to move others emotionally is a key aspect of effective communication and influence in leadership. Leaders who craft compelling narratives or create shared emotional experiences can inspire their teams to align with a common vision or mission. For example, Nelson Mandela's decision to wear a Springbok jersey during the 1995 Rugby World Cup Final in South Africa was a bold move, as the jersey had previously been a divisive symbol in the country. This surprising and profoundly meaningful gesture signified unity and reconciliation, transcending cultural divides and inspiring a nation.

Integrating Surprise and Being Moved in Practice

Just how far what is sometimes called *mood contagion* can be treated as another management tool is debatable. Without a deeper understanding of relational principles, it can easily be manipulated. Many leaders and organisations devote resources to training managers to assess and respond to employees' emotions in the hope that this will build a more supportive and responsive workplace culture. This approach ignores the essential nature of the connection between being surprised and being moved. Being surprised opens the mind to the unexpected, while being moved opens the heart to authenticity, and together, they foster a profound sense of engagement and meaning.

Questions for Reflection and Groove

What single core word or phrase captures your current purpose?

How can you, as a leader, create opportunities for your teams to explore what inspires and moves them, fostering deeper engagement and innovation?

Reflect on a time when a piece of art, music, or storytelling moved you. What elements contributed to that resonance, and how might similar principles apply to your work?

4.9 Disconnected Leadership in a Resonant World?

Chris

Barry and I agreed to turn the writing tables for this final Note. I get the first word, and he will respond. I chose to revisit the subtitle of our book, *Resonant Leadership in a Disconnected World.*

The words Leadership and World are screens for projecting management ideas and opinions onto. We have given each a qualifier adjective, and all such attributes contain perspectives and assumptions. Critical thinking and reflective practice require us to surface those or remain a prisoner to them. Because I do not have a lifetime or career of making music to draw upon, I must instead ransack my formative experiences for a way in. To begin with, here is my take on why we chose those words.

> **"Resonant"** Leadership (that jack-of-all-trades term) is our call to action. We want leadership that reverberates, is in tune with, is vibrant, and meets and greets the world's complexities with joy and charisma. All that. It's what we suspect is absent.
>
> The action we call you to is to Find (and practise) Your Groove. Why?
>
> A "**Disconnected**" World is the context for that resonant leadership. It's why we need a different view of leadership. We never had as much potential to connect with each other as we do now if we want, instantly and in any part of the world. And still, we are isolated from each other, never closer to equilibrium, and never properly nourished. We sit at a feast of data and connectivity, but all within a famine of meaning and connection. Worse, our technology and hubris are tipping us over several points of no return in our ecology that threaten to silence us completely. And permanently.

I'm curious to see whether Barry has a different take on this. He and I are very similar in age, and during his formative years – the liminal period during which an individual may discover aspects of themselves that are not derived from others – he spent time playing and learning music. Although I listened to and was influenced by a lot of music, my contact with it has been vicarious. I had a brief and forgettable spell as lead singer in a punk band in 1980, and a brief and cherished moment as a team member organising a free rock concert in a London park in 1983. And that's about it. I found *my* rhythm – my "freedom in" – through words and language.

Adolescence is a synonym for the Dunning-Kruger effect, whereby people overestimate what they know, usually in inverse proportion to what they think everyone else knows. Socially, this can be disastrous because psychological maturity develops later in life. Intellectually, this arrogance can be useful because it can foster creativity and a love of learning (just at a time when most formal school systems are trying to stifle it). During this phase, I found an outlet and use for my over-confident curiosity. One way was by creating mock-ups of newspapers and magazines that no one else would read. No doubt the creation of small, inner worlds reflected my limited knowledge of the big outer world around me. Time and some talented educators and guides have broadened my horizons since, and I now see that language can be used to cover up an idea just as much as it can to reveal one.

Throughout my life, my work experiences have varied. When I was younger, I volunteered for an NGO in London that campaigned for a political issue. I also helped organise a free rock concert, worked in a bar, spent time on a kibbutz, and took on roles as a cycle courier, language teacher, DJ, outdoor experiential learning trainer, coach, administrator, and (now) academic. The common thread that connects these is that each provided me with an opportunity to shape my thoughts and engagement with the world, primarily through the sense-making that language affords.

If I want to mould a new form, I can begin by playing around with the language used in the current version. To understand our subtitle better, I feel the urge first to rearrange the word order and see what we get. By swapping the qualifiers, I get:

> "Disconnected Leadership in a Resonant World"

This new phrasing provides a clearer angle on the real issue that *Finding Your Groove* addresses. We now have a broad context that is not fundamentally flawed; the world is assumed *already* to be resonant, reverberating, in tune, vibrant, and its complexities joyful and charismatic. *It* doesn't need fixing. Therefore, if we perceive something as broken or out of balance, the problem lies with our relationship to that world, not with the world itself.

A common response, especially among middle management or leadership, is to dismiss this idea, often saying, "Yes, but if only it were that simple."

If that is you, I would first suggest changing the word "but" to "and." This adjustment significantly changes our perspective on it. We start from where we currently are, right inside the problem. While "Yes, and ..." still leaves much work ahead of us, the core question is clearer because now we accept that this. How should we relate to each other? To ourselves? To the environment and ecology?

It is essential for us to find ways to connect with each other. You are already connected with the world as it is, though you may not see it. Establishing that connection isn't difficult to communicate; it's a sentiment present in many areas of life, including music and art.

William Blake (1757–1827) was a visionary British poet and artist known for works that combine vivid imagery with profound emotional depth and moral questioning. His poetry often explores themes of empathy, compassion, and the dualities of human nature, encouraging us to confront the emotional and spiritual aspects of life. In his poem "On Another's Sorrow," he reflects on this connection:

> Can I see another's woe,
> And not be in sorrow too?
> Can I see another's grief,

And not seek for kind relief?
(William Blake, *Songs of Innocence* 1789)

That is a fitting place to start.

Chris's (one and only) ***Finding Your Groove principle:*** *Know where to look,* ***and*** *how to see. This can be learned.*

Barry

I agreed with Chris to flip things around for this final note. I then immediately felt the anxiety of "what if I have nothing intelligent to say?" knowing that his reflections on our title would be provocative and profound. My imposter's voice vanished on reading, leaving a feeling of stillness and flow. This is how I have made sense of challenging moments in music performance for as long as I can remember: by following the fear, the cool stuff often emerges beyond this edge.

I realised two things: (i) what we have created through our Notes is a rhythm in a groovy metre of two, and (ii) while Chris intuitively foregrounded the words Leadership and World, I did the opposite by backgrounding these words and intuitively leaning into the adjectives.

On Rhythm

Rhythm is another way of describing universal punctuation, and here I'm borrowing from Chris to describe the order of things and Gregory Bateson (1979) when finding a word to describe the pattern and the relationship with context. Rhythm requires action and energy interspersed with space, silence, and recovery to perceive the pattern. Nature shows up in the meta rhythms of the seasons, the smaller calibrations of awakeness and sleep, or breakfast, lunch, and dinner, and down to the tiny frequencies of rippling water and the pulse of a baby mammal. Humans also punctuate with action and recovery or space if we consider phenomena such as coordinated time (hours, minutes, seconds), players in a tennis match, or co-writers in a call-and-response style conversation.

Foreground/Background

Because of different contextual settings, both current and retrospective, Chris and I viewed the title differently. I perceived resonance/rigidity and connection/disconnection as meta rhythms, or upbeats and downbeats if music is used as a metaphor. Then, when Chris describes Resonance and Connection as our call to action, we are in perfect harmony because this is where Groove lives. Resonance, after all, means different elements working well with one another, and human beings do this very well face-to-face. Virtually, not so well.

My take on how we have entered the most networked era in human history is that this massive network lacks the resonance of personal connection, from teenagers not knowing how to engage with each other beyond the perfect world of a flashing screen to cultures losing the ability to sense the universal connection with the natural world, while simultaneously taking game-changing strides in biotech, physical health, and space exploration. Could we extend the lifespan and travel span of humanity while diminishing the feeling of being human and the sensation of groove at multiple levels?

What's Your Story?

I was interested in Chris's notes on his earlier years, especially the shared influence of popular music. Interestingly, throughout my career, I have found the most meaning in playing drums in support of great songwriters, where the lyrics tell a story that makes you feel something. I found that I could easily construct interesting rhythm parts to support a singer's words, while instrumental music felt too self-absorbed and emotionless. Although I enjoyed many great concerts as a soloist in the improvised music context of jazz, this did not feel as fulfilling as playing a simple verse/verse/chorus/bridge/chorus arrangement behind a very average vocalist singing beautiful words. So Chris and I resonated about finding rhythm or freedom in words and language.

I, too, was an overconfident early years musician, depending largely on the positive feedback I received when performing with older musicians and then from teachers when I attended music college in the USA. On reflection, my career path was defined by successively putting my hand up for opportunities I was not yet ready to seize. I would have to strain and stretch to get through a situation where I was consciously incompetent and then learn fast from my mistakes to close knowledge and performance gaps. I managed to do this successfully, more than not, and I estimate a ratio of 70/30. This was, and is, a good metric for musicians, entrepreneurs, and leaders.

Syncopation

I love the flipped adjectives. This delivers profound insight and is mirrored in music as syncopation, which is accenting the notes that would not usually be accented, normally on the upbeat of the rhythm, and is what great improvisers do for us, the listener. The musical universe of rhythms, tones, overtones, and microtones simply exists. It's just there and not within our control. Musicians who are serious and have something to say work within this context to create sonic shapes and patterns that are aimed to resonate with certain listeners. Listeners then have the opportunity to choose to resonate or not, sometimes needing more understanding and knowledge to feel the resonance. When these shapes and patterns truly align, we find a musical fundamental that is felt universally. Think about the Beatles' "Hey Jude" or "I Feel Good" by James Brown.

From my perspective, the closing paragraphs of Chris's note wrap things up beautifully. Managers and leaders are faced with the dilemma of change at a rate never before experienced, driven by Science, Technology, Engineering, and Math, whereby new industries and job descriptions are being invented at an astounding frequency. With STEM-driven change in the foreground, the background is made up of individuals and groups losing touch on how to connect at a human level.

William Blake's poem is a timeless lens into knowing oneself and truly seeing and knowing others. Surely, the starting point is with the individual (which is our position with MBA candidates at Henley Business School) to raise awareness and build acceptance. Individual grooves can and will influence group grooves, which will influence environmental grooves. This is the same process as *Hey Jude* flowing from Paul McCartney to create universal resonance. At that point, you cannot ask why.

Question for Reflection and Groove

As you move forward now, note where you feel most "in groove" and where you feel disconnected. What patterns do you see? What small shifts will you make?

Note

1. "Cut Me Some Slack" is a rock song by Paul McCartney and former members of Nirvana. Released in 2012 on YouTube and the following year on the soundtrack to Dave Grohl's documentary film Sound City, the song won the Grammy Award for Best Rock Song in 2014.

References

Bass, Bernard M., and Ronald E. Riggio. 2006. *Transformational Leadership*. N.p.: Psychology Press.

Bateson, Gregory. 1972. *Steps to an Ecology of Mind.* N.p.: Chicago University Press.

Bateson, Gregory. 1979. *Mind and Nature: A Necessary Unity*. N.p.: Wildwood House.

Bentley, Tanya G. 2023. "Breathing Practices for Stress and Anxiety Reduction: Conceptual Framework of Implementation Guidelines Based on a Systematic Review of the Published Literature." *Brain Sciences* 13 (12): 1612. https://doi.org/10.3390/brainsci13121612.

Bhaskar, Roy. 2015. *The Possibility of Naturalism: A Philosophical Critique of the Contemporary Human Sciences*. N.p.: Routledge.

Bolman, Lee G., and Terrence E. Deal. 2021. *Reframing Organizations: Artistry, Choice, and Leadership*. N.p.: Wiley.

Buchanan, Richard. 1992. "Wicked Problems in Design Thinking." *Design Issues* 8 (2): 5–21.

Christensen, Clayton M. 2013. *The Innovator's Dilemma: When New Technologies Cause Great Firms to Fail.* N.p.: Harvard Business Review Press.
De Bono, Edward. 2016. *Lateral Thinking: A Textbook of Creativity*. N.p.: Penguin UK.
Deleuze, Gilles. 2014. *Difference and Repetition.* Translated by Paul Patton. N.p.: Bloomsbury Academic.
Dudamel, Gustavo. 2012. "Gustavo Dudamel & Simon Bolivar Symphony Orchestra – Bernstein: West Side Story: Mambo." YouTube. https://www.youtube.com/watch?v=NYvEvP2cmdk.
Dweck, Carol S. 2012. *Mindset*. N.p.: Robinson.
Earley, P. C., and Soon Ang. 2003. *Cultural Intelligence: Individual Interactions Across Cultures*. N.p.: Stanford University Press.
Ellen MacArthur Foundation. 2013. *Towards the circular economy Vol. 1: an economic and business rationale for an accelerated transition.*
Eurosport. 2024. "Tensions Are High! Defused by DJ (Paris Olympics 2024)." YouTube. https://www.youtube.com/watch?v=1UPtlT6_FOA.
Grinder, John, and Richard Bandler. 1989. *The Structure of Magic I: A Book About Language and Therapy*. N.p.: Science and Behavior Books.
Heifetz, Ronald A., Alexander Grashow, and Martin Linsky. 2009. *The Practice of Adaptive Leadership: Tools and Tactics for Changing Your Organization and the World.* N.p.: Harvard Business Press.
Jeffers, Susan J. 2017. *Feel the Fear & Do it Anyway*. N.p.: Vermilion.
Kabat-Zinn, Jon. 2004. *Wherever You Go, There You are: Mindfulness Meditation for Everyday Life*. N.p.: Piatkus.
Koenig, John. 2021. *The Dictionary of Obscure Sorrows*. N.p.: Simon & Schuster.
Ladkin, Donna. 2008. "Leading beautifully: How mastery, congruence and purpose create the aesthetic of embodied leadership practice." *The Leadership Quarterly* 19, no. 1 (February): 31–41. 10.1016/j.leaqua.2007.12.003.
Lewin, Kurt. 2007. *A Dynamic Theory of Personality – Selected Papers*. N.p.: Read Books.
Lewis, Thomas, Fari Amini, and Richard Lannon. 2001. *A General Theory of Love*. N.p.: Knopf Doubleday Publishing Group.
Marais, Pepe. 2018. *Growing Greatness: A Journey Towards Personal and Business Mastery*. N.p.: Tracey McDonald Publishers.
Meyer, Leonard B. 1957. *Emotion and Meaning in Music*. N.p.: University of Chicago Press.
Nussbaum, Martha C. 2003. *Upheavals of Thought: The Intelligence of Emotions*. N.p.: Cambridge University Press.
Philharmoniker, Berliner. 2014. "Bernstein: Mambo/Metzmacher · Berliner Philharmoniker." YouTube. https://www.youtube.com/watch?v=Bp33WX9xIGs.
Phililips-Silver, Jessica, Athena C. Aktipis, and Gregory A. Bryant. 2010. "The Ecology of Entrainment: Foundations of Coordinated Rhythmic Movement." *Music Perception* 28, no. 1 (September): 3–14. 10.1525/mp.2010.28.1.3.
Prigogine, Ilya, and Isabelle Stengers. 1984. *Order Out of Chaos: Man's New Dialogue with Nature*. N.p.: Verso Books.
Tajfel, Henri. 1978. *Differentiation Between Social Groups: Studies in the Social Psychology of Intergroup Relations*. Edited by Henri Tajfel. N.p.: European Association of Experimental Social Psychology by Academic Press.

Epilogue – the Coda

Barry

In 2020, I found myself in conversation with my Henley Business School colleague and fellow creative thinker, Louise Claassen. Our discussions revolved around an idea that had been brewing in my mind for years: rhythm, resonance, and flow not just as musical concepts but as a toolkit for navigating leadership and life. We talked about how to turn this into something practical for business executives, perhaps a workshop opportunity waiting to be exploited.

After one of our brainstorming sessions, Louise looked at me and asked, "May I offer you some advice?" I immediately said yes. She paused, smiled, and said, "Write, have fun!"

I asked her to tell me more, and she explained that focusing solely on workshops was too limited. There were so many ways to bring these ideas to life. "There's a book here, Barry."

The journey began informally. I started jotting down short pieces, thoughts that felt as if they needed to be transferred from my mind to paper. It was a way to make sense of my experiences. Over 8–10 months, as these fragments accumulated, patterns began to emerge. I wasn't embarking on a master narrative, I was simply responding to moments in my life that felt important. Themes that had been circulating in my mind for years, ideas about connection, cycles, and the underlying rhythm of life began to align into a coherent thread.

Chris Dalton graciously joined me on this path, decoding Groove in a business education setting as something unique and deeply relevant. He saw the relevance and potential of these ideas and helped me see how they could bridge the creative and the professional. Together, we began shaping *Groove* into something bigger than either of us imagined at the start.

This journey has been about bringing my life as a creative – a drummer, a collaborator, an innovator – into my work with leaders, educators, and businesses. These two worlds, which once felt so separate, now feel like home.

And this is just the beginning.

To you, the reader, I extend an invitation. I hope you've found something within these pages that resonates, something that you can carry forward into your personal life, your teams, your communities, and your broader world. Test the principles of *Groove.* Take them for a spin. Reflect on Chris's questions. And, as Louise urged me, write.

When I started this journey, my understanding of *Groove* was intuitive – a sense, a feeling, a connection. Now, with time and reflection, I can feel it *and* articulate it. Stay with me as we keep asking questions, raising awareness, and building the theory.

Groove is a thing.

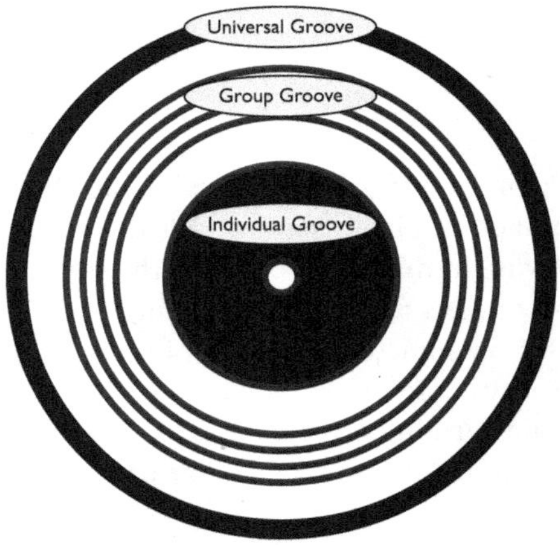

Appendix

Universal Values Questionnaire

Prepared by Dr Chris Dalton
Associate Professor of Management Learning
Henley Business School, University of Reading

To cite this document use:
Dalton, C. (2023) Universal Values Questionnaire, Henley Business School, University of Reading.

Universal values, collective principles, individual beliefs and actions

Universal values are the common ground that define and connect us all as humans. They are concerned with life's fundamental questions of survival and meaning. Universal values give rise to our beliefs and give meaning to our actions (Figure A1). This questionnaire allows you to explore how.

Values are the best expression and representation of our deepest and most fundamental need to ask and answer certain 'why' questions that we assume underpin every human civilisation in every era. **Universal values** are what all societies have in common. From that common ground, each society constructs its own set of answers, which over time and space evolve into locally appropriate social **systems** of **beliefs** and **principles**.

Every community relies on such principles for its survival and well-being, though they can also evolve and change over time. For example, the principles that form the basis of our systems of politics, law and commerce, and that inform our systems of education, all find their roots in just a few core 'why' questions. Values are also part

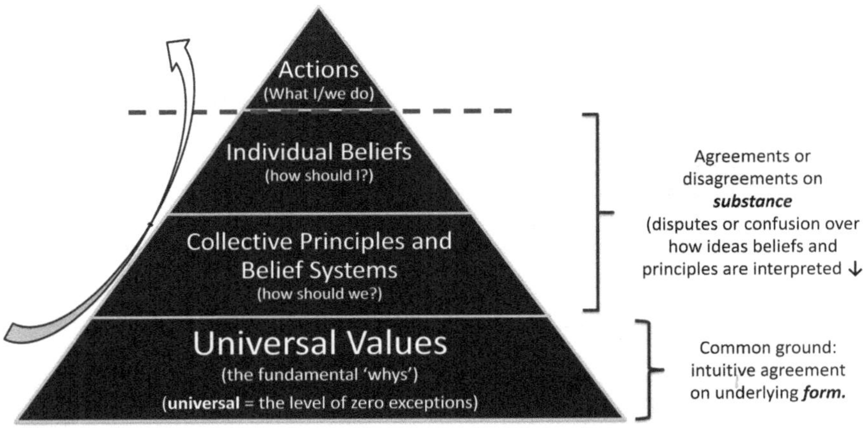

Figure A1 Universal values, collective principles, individual beliefs and actions

of the grammar of our conditioning – of how we see the world. These socially constructed rules and boundaries appear as the principles communities use to negotiate, uphold and preserve norms of behaviours among members. These principles, however, also form the boundaries and limits of understanding between different social groups when there is conflict. The bigger the issue or conflict, the deeper the parties need to dig to find common ground.

Without common ground, **collective belief systems** are what **individuals** rely on to form appropriate **beliefs**. Beliefs are the guidelines used in the decisions that become our actions. Our personal **actions** are the product of social norms and principles. They carry the deep code of the fundamental 'whys' of universal values. We may not see this without reflection and self-awareness. This is important for any situation where our actions are not aligned with the health and well-being of a wider context.

This questionnaire will help you identify your individual beliefs and principles. It will give you a better vocabulary to find out about the beliefs and principles of others. More importantly, it will be the first step in finding out what needs to change to be more effective and have a wider range of actions available. It will help you become unstuck. Changing a personal belief can gain new possibilities and more choices in decision-making. Understanding the bigger principles used to justify an existing individual belief can reveal new ways of understanding what makes you (and everyone else) human.

When we come across a difference in belief or principle between ourselves and someone else, we must start an enquiry to find the deeper common ground that we share. Then we can start a dialogue, and perhaps each adjust and expand our principles, or create new beliefs. If we can do this, then we will have more choices available for us to act.

We rarely think about our beliefs or principles; in fact, we rarely need to. Most of the time, we can take them for granted. *However, in times of stress, trauma or rapid change – or in intense adult education and career development – the understanding of our values needs examining at the deepest level. We need to see our values.* This is not because we need to change or reject them (we cannot do that), but to liberate our beliefs and free up more choice in our actions.

Four universal values

Over the years, researchers have developed and proposed many models and frameworks to define and categorise **values**. The word is, arguably, now overused in corporate life and even in personal development.

Universal values don't change and are not a matter of choice; beliefs can and do change and are what inform our actions. Beliefs can and do change. Different beliefs allow for different actions but values are what all humans share.

This questionnaire uses four such universal values (see Figure A2), which are elemental ideas that operate at a level even deeper than any one particular society or culture. In fact, they are what enable societies and cultures to exist in so many forms. All four are therefore essential for a healthy human society. Each universal value has an almost limitless power to generate choices and guidelines for how to behave, what to strive for, or what to seek.

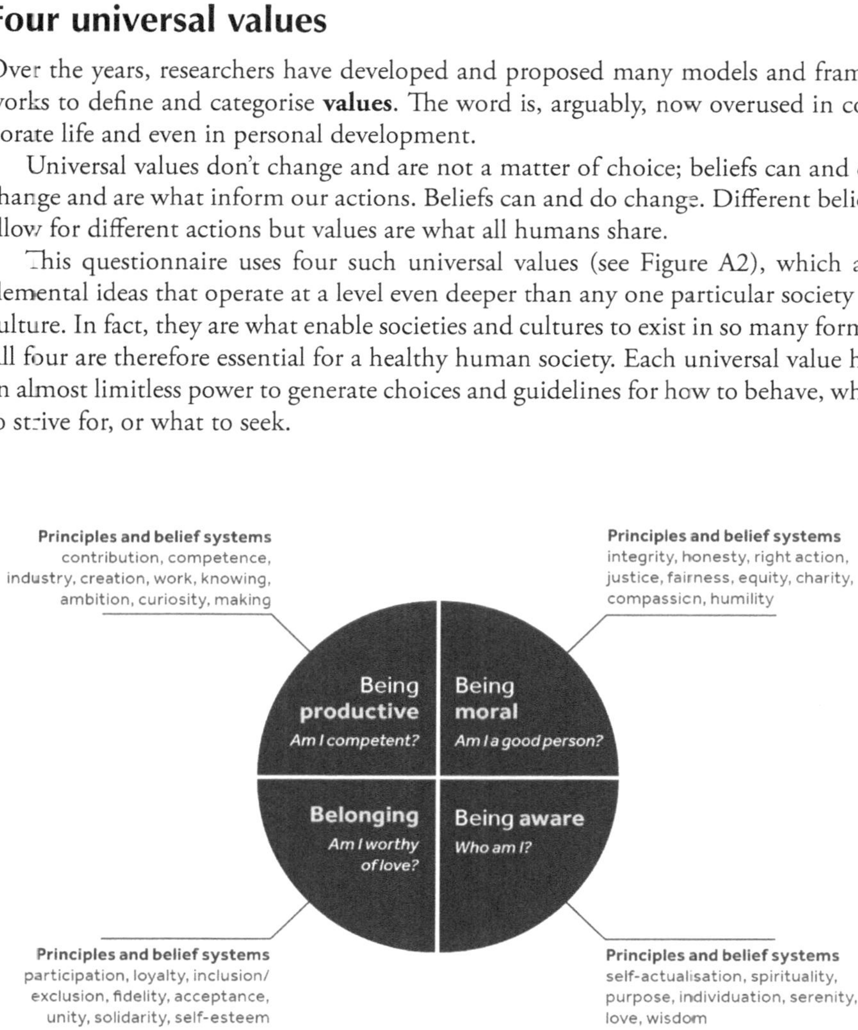

Figure A2 Universal values

Instructions

Please note that this is not a standardised test; it is a self-assessment, designed to help you think about what is important for you in your personal development.

The questionnaire contains three parts:

Part 1

Four open-ended questions to get you thinking about what is important for you in your life and where your beliefs come from. Try to write the first thoughts that come to your mind; you can always revise your answers later on.

Part 2

Reflect on four universal value areas (being productive, being moral, belonging and being aware) and then identify the meaning and relative importance to you of eight different core principles or beliefs arising from each.

Part 3

Pull this information together and review the most important principles in each category and also reflect on your answers from Part 1.

Part 1 – Values: getting down to your 'why?'

1. What are the three most important words or phrases in your life? For each, make a short note on why it is important to you.

What	*Why this matters to me*
1.	
2.	
3.	

2. Where did you grow up? How did that place and society shape the kind of person you have become? In just a few words, summarise the key points below.

3. What have been the most important lessons passed on to you by significant people in your life? Think of parents, grandparents or other family members, as well as friends, teachers or colleagues.

4. What would you say are the three most important words or phrases in the organisation where you work? Again, for each, make some short notes on why.

What	*Why this matters to us*
1.	
2.	
3.	

Part 2 – Principles and belief systems

Identifying, naming and coming to terms with our principles and beliefs is an essential part of long-term thinking in leadership. Our beliefs are usually seen in our behaviours.

Unwanted behaviours can indicate self-limiting beliefs and need to be examined. Sometimes you may also need to change or amend your beliefs or principles.

In this Part, you can start to understand the connection between deep values and actions.

5. Over the following pages you will find four tables. Each contains (in no particular order) eight suggestions of principles and beliefs associated with:

   (A) being a **productive** member of society
   (B) being a **moral or ethical** member of society
   (C) **belonging** to society, the collective or a group
   (D) being **self-aware**

A short description of each principle/belief is provided, and you are free to make your own interpretations if you wish.

The task is to indicate how important each principle is for you on a scale of 1 to 5 (where 1 = not at all important; 3 = neutral; 5 = extremely important).

Put a cross under the relevant heading in the table to indicate your choice.

If you have a strong feeling **against** a principle or belief, then indicate this by marking it as –1 (by putting a cross under –1).

There is a space after each entry for you to type any notes, thoughts, reflections or memories that come to mind. Contextual observations are very important here.

(A) Some common principles and beliefs associated with the universal value of being a productive member of society

Being productive	*–1*	*1*	*2*	*3*	*4*	*5*	*Notes/thoughts/ reflections/memories about this*
1. **Competence** (ability to perform tasks well, recognition of skills by significant others)							
2. **Legacy** (concern for the future, respect for the past, a long-lasting effect, transfer of responsibility or assets to another)							
3. **Authority** (obedience to and from others, influence over others, power)							
4. **Logic** (intelligence, reasoned and rational thinking, problem solving from conclusions based on inference)							
5. **Material wealth** (possessions, assets, money, absence of debt)							
6. **Ambition** (desire to be seen to achieve success, work toward goals and objectives)							
7. **Industry** (drive to work hard, personal effort, pleasure from executing a task, application of skill and ingenuity)							
8. **Curiosity** (interest in new things, innovation, delight in discovery, desire to know or learn)							

(B) Some common principles and beliefs associated with the universal value of being a moral member of society

Being moral	*−1*	*1*	*2*	*3*	*4*	*5*	*Notes/thoughts/ reflections/memories about this*
1. **Equality** (same opportunity or status for all, without prejudice or discrimination)							
2. **Humility** (modesty, self-effacing, absence of pride, without pretension)							
3. **Honesty** (integrity, keeping of promises, sincerity, not deceiving others)							
4. **Social order** (stability of a group, predictability in rituals and norms of behaviour, clarity in how power is defined)							
5. **Hope** (belief, faith or trust in others, the expectation of something)							
6. **Safety** (sense of security, freedom from danger or threat)							
7. **Peace** (absence of conflict, unrest or disorder, amity, accord, freedom from external disturbance)							
8. **Charity** (care or concern with the welfare of others, natural goodness in acts of generosity (e.g. to the poor))							

(C) Some common principles and beliefs associated with the universal value of belonging to society

Belonging	*–1*	*1*	*2*	*3*	*4*	*5*	*Notes/thoughts/ reflections/memories about this*
1. **Solidarity** (united in a community with others by interests, opinions, or aspirations and goals)							
2. **Esteem** (have favourable opinion of, respect for, place a high value or worth on, high reputation among others)							
3. **Family** (social unit related by blood, marriage or adoption, any group sharing descendent traits)							
4. **Participation** (taking part, contributing to a group, having a place, acceptance by others, having things in common)							
5. **Status** (recognition and importance of rank or position in the eyes of others, being respected, social relation to others)							
6. **Harmony** (balance and accord between different parts, agreement between yourself and others)							
7. **Tradition** (unwritten practices, customs or beliefs handed down and preserved from one generation to the next)							
8. **Fidelity** (loyalty, faithfulness, keeping your word, allegiance)							

(D) Some common principles and beliefs associated with the universal value of being aware of self

Being aware	*–1*	*1*	*2*	*3*	*4*	*5*	*Notes/thoughts/ reflections/memories about this*
1. **Reflection** (contemplation, process of enquiry into the basis of – and assumptions behind – actions and opinions)							
2. **Freedom** (without constraint, independence of thought and action, control over what you choose to do)							
3. **Spirituality** (concern with the nature of existence, seeking answers from the non-material)							
4. **Aesthetics** (the principles for appreciating beauty in art or in nature, pleasure from visual appearance)							
5. **Wisdom** (good judgement through accumulated knowledge, the knowledge of what to do and what not to do)							
6. **Religion** (practices based on belief in, or acknowledgement of, a deity, acting according to written or spoken dogma)							
7. **Joy** (strong, positive feeling of pleasure, emotion of gratification or delight, bliss, good wishes)							
8. **Self** (one and the same, referencing a specific person and their thoughts, ego)							

Part 3 – Consolidation

6. Now look back over your responses and, for each of the universal values, identify the **two** principles or beliefs that are the most **important** or **influential** for you.

Universal value	*My two most important principles or beliefs are*	*This principle is reflected in what I do when I*
A. Being productive	1.	
	2.	
B. Being moral	1.	
	2.	
C. Belonging	1.	
	2.	
D. Being aware	1.	
	2.	

7. Revisit your answer to Question 1 (three most important words) and reflect on the similarities, differences or connections. Do you notice any pattern? Do any themes seem to occur, or recur? Are there conflicts?

8. Think about your own personal development as a manager or leader, and also your ideas on career direction and outcomes you wish to have. Revisit your answer to Question 4. How does this fit with your answers to Questions 6 and 7? Write down any reflections or thoughts that strike you.

Index

2-against-3 rhythm game 58
3M 40
10,000-hours rule 24–26, 35, 147
15% culture 40
20% time policy 40–41

Abrahams, Matt 102
Adaptive Leadership Theory 152
agile project management 41
Agile Thinking 66, 89–91
algorithmic processing 38
allergies 2
analogue growth 148–149
Approach-Avoidance Conflict Theory 130–131
artificial intelligence 67, 102
axiology 135

balance 64–68
Bass, Bernard 76
Bateson, Gregory 138, 148–149, 161
the Beatles 61, 79, 145–147, 162–163
Berlin, Jeff 84–85
Bhaskar, Roy 136
Bieber, Justin 145–147
Big Band culture 43–44, 46, 73–74, 76, 96–97
binary growth 148–149
Blake, William 160–161, 163
Blakely, Art 43, 97
Blood, Sweat & Tears 37
body language 53
Bohm, David 6, 58, 155
Bolman, Lee 125–126
Bowie, David 61
Boyatzis, Richard 56
Branson, Richard 29
breathwork 118–119
Bricolage 142
Build-Measure-Learn feedback loop 91
Burroughs, William 61
busking 27–28

Camus, Albert 142
Cassidy, Bruce 37
Castle, Roy 25
Chambliss, Daniel 32
Christensen, Clayton 152
chronobiology 5, 14, 16, 18
circadian rhythm 16, 18
circaseptan rhythm 16
Circular Economy model 148
Claassen, Louise 165–166
Clegg, Johnny 78, 96, 107, 128, 140–141, 155
Cognitive Behaviour Therapy 126
Cognitive Load Theory 45
Cognitive Theory of Multimedia Learning 45
cognitive universals 121
Combinatorial Creativity 60
Commentary Driving 45
commonplace books 62
competence (conscious vs. unconscious) 35–36
Complex Adaptive Systems 153
complexity theory 66, 135
consciousness 55
constructs 51–52
consumerism 3
continuous improvement 153
coordination in medium-sized groups 99–100
coordination of the self 55
Covid-19 pandemic 118, 139
creative destruction 137–138
Critical Realism 136
critical thinking 50, 126
Csikszentmihalyi, Mihaly 6, 82
cultural adaptation 75–76
cultural authenticity 95, 140–144
cultural intelligence 76, 131–132

cybernetics 138
cyclic universals 121
cyclical rhythms 38–40, 42

Dalio, Ray 44, 46, 83, 85–86, 92
Darwin, Charles 62
de Bono, Edward 152
Deal, Terry 125–126
Deleuze, Gilles 144
deliberate practice 25–26, 33–34
Design Thinking 66
Dewey, John 50
Die Antwoord 59–60, 118, 154
differentiation through authenticity 77
discomfort 130, 151
disruptive innovation 152–153
dissipative structures 137–138
dissonance 53, 56–57
Diversity, Equity, and Inclusion (DEI) 109
Donjeany, Trevor 78
Dual Coding Theory 46
dual-process theory 39–40
Dunning-Kruger effect 159
Dweck, Carol 26, 51, 129
Dylan, Bob 123

ear training 133
ecology of mind 138
edge of chaos 66
embodied cognition 137
emergence 14, 17–18
emotional intelligence 56, 76, 78–79, 81
environmental problems 3
epistemology 133, 135, 138; and perception 136–137
EQ *see* emotional intelligence
Ericcson, Anders K. 25–26, 35
European Union 93
existentialist philosophy 142–143
Experiential Learning Cycle 50

failure 83–84
fear 76, 130–131
Ferguson, Kirby 61
Feynman, Richard 6, 37, 42, 83, 155
Fibonacci sequences 121
Fig, Anton 96
first principles thinking 43–44, 46–47
fixed mindset 51
Flow 5–6, 9; characteristics of 82; and optimal experience 82; as a state of energy and focus 56, 146
Four Frames Model 125–126
freelancing 93–95
Fry, Art 40

Gabriel, Peter 141
Gadd, Steve 43
Gallwey, Timothy 66
Geary, David 45
George, Bill 103
Gladwell, Malcolm 25; 10,000-hours rule 24–26, 35, 147
Global Wellness Institute 118
glocalisation 142
Goema 23–24, 140, 142, 144
Golden Ratio 121
Goleman, Daniel 81
Google 40–41
Grohl, Dave 155
Groove: definition of 1–2, 4–5; essentials for finding 13–18; finding and feeling 123–127; foundations of 1–18; group 5, 68, 72–113; individual 5, 22–68; multi-level 37–42; universal 5, 114, 116–163
group development 80–81
group groove 5, 68, 72–113
growth mindset 26, 51, 95, 129

heartbeat 118–119
Heifetz, Ronald 152
Henley Business School 7, 10, 28, 30, 163, 165
Herbert, Simon 90
Heredia, Joey 123
Hirschman, Albert 106
Hoffman, Reid 87
Hotfoot Symphony Orchestra 37
Houghton, Steve 73–74, 76

Ibarra, Herminia 29–30
illusion of knowledge 66–67
Implicate Order 6, 155
incremental improvement 33–35
individual groove 5, 22–68
Innes, Andy 78
Insight Timer 118

Jackson, Michael 31, 111
Jeffers, Susan 130
Jobs, Steve 61, 108
Johnny Clegg Band 96, 141, 150, 155
Johnson, Steven 60
Jones, Quincey 141
Just-In-Time (JIT) manufacturing principle 41

Kabat-Zinn, John 131
Kahneman, Daniel 38–39, 42, 64, 66, 156
kaizen 153
Kamprad, Ingvar 152
Kelly, George 51
Koenig, John 131
Kolb, David A. 50
Kramer, David 23, 140

Ladkin, Donna 137
Lamar, Kendrick 101–102
law of nature 121
Lawson, Ricky 31–32
Lean Startup methodology 91
Lencioni, Patrick 81
Lennox, Annie 64–65
Lévi-Straus, Claude 142
Lewin, Kurt 130
life chapters 9–11
life expectancy 2
limbic resonance 157
Linsky, Marty 152
Locke, John 62
Lukather, Steve 43

Mandela, Nelson 157
Marais, Pepe 155–156
mastery 24–26, 66–67
materialism 3
Mayer, Richard E. 45
McCartney, Paul 155, 163
McConaughey, Matthew 133
McFerrin, Bobby 137
McKee, Annie 56
meaning-making 65
mentoring 37, 43, 110
meta-patterns 112–113
metaphors 42, 59, 64–65, 93, 120, 130
metric rhythms 38–40, 42
Meyer, Leonard 156
Milton, John 62
mindfulness 129, 131
mood contagion 157
multi-level groove 37–42
muses 108–110
Musk, Elon 44, 46

Narrative Inquiry 50
natural world 15
Neuro-Linguistic Programming 126
neuroplasticity 51
Nussbaum, Martha 157

obesity 2
Ó Braonáin, Fiachna 146
ontology 133, 135–136
order 14–15, 18
organisational dynamics 55–56
overconsumption 3
overnight success 145, 147

Paivio, Allan 46
paradox of the universal 120–122
pattern: definition of 14; looking for 62; meta-patterns 112–113; and order 14–15; recognition 138; retaining identity in weaving 143–144; social 15, 17–18, 112; understanding and leveraging 60
Perazzo, Karl 78
perfectionism 25, 89–90
personal branding 77
Personal Construct Theory 51–52
perturbation 100
Peterson, Taliep 23–24, 140, 142
physicality 53–56
Plant, Robert 141
play 35–36
Player, Gary 24
polyrhythm 4, 58
Porcaro, Jeff 43
Porcaro, Joe 43
Post-it Notes 40
power imbalances 3
power of words 48–53
Pozzi, Dave 73, 96
practice 24–26, 31–36; integrating content with 62–63; vs play 35–36
Pragmatism 90
Prediction Error Theory 156
Prigogine, Ilya 137–138
problem-based learning 46–47
process philosophy 136
procrastination 89–90
professionalism 24, 31, 141

quality of life 2
Queen 38

reality distortion field 108
reassembly 57–63
reflective practice 50
reframing 123, 125–126
rehearsal trap 87–91
relational dynamics 120–121
resonance 53, 56–57, 79, 108–110, 120, 133–140, 159–161

return on invested hours (ROIH) 31–32, 34
Rich, Buddy 43, 97
Ricoeur, Paul 50
Ries, Eric 91
ripple effect 108–109
Rolling Stones 79

Santana, Carlos 78, 82
Sartre, Jean-Paul 142
satisficing 90
Schenker, Rudolph 150
Schön, Donald 50, 67
Scientific Management 50
screen time 2
seasonal rhythms 16
self-employment 93
self-narrative 49–50
Senge, Peter M. 60
sense-making 13–14, 65
sensorimotor coupling 99
SGC model 33–35
Shaffer, Paul 96
Shapiro, Shauna 105
Shepard, Dax 133
shout chorus 44
Silver, Spencer 40
Sims, Peter 103
situational awareness 45–46
Six Horn Band 84
sleep patterns 2
Slow, Gradient, and Context approach 33–35
social entrainment 137
Social Identity Theory 127
social intelligence 56, 79, 81
social patterns 15, 17–18, 112
social self-efficacy 81
social world 15
sonder 131–132
Space X 46–47
Steel, Piers 89
Stiegler, Bernard 67
stratified ontology 136
Super Groove 111–114
suprachiasmatic nucleus 15
Sweller, John 45
systems mapping 62
Systems Thinking 60, 64, 66

tala (drum) 43–44, 46, 155
talent 31–32, 92
Tao 6, 104, 155
technology 2–3, 163
Tedesco, Tommy 27
tempo of leadership 96–100
terroir 93, 95
three important words 9, 11–13
tidal rhythms 120
Tolle, Eckhardt 101, 104–105
Toro, Efrain 5, 10, 54, 101, 111
Toto 43
Toyota Way 26, 41
Transformational Leadership 76–77, 124, 126–127
Tuckman, Bruce 80

Ubuntu 142
universal groove 5, 114, 116–163
Universal Values 9, 103, 106, 167–177

Vearncombe, Colin 101–102, 146
Venezuelan Youth Orchestra 124
verbalisation in learning 43–47, 54
visualisation techniques 37–38, 42
Voice(s) 101–103; as personal experience 103–105; as social construct 105–106
Vygotsky, Lev 35

walking 53–54, 56–57
Watts, Alan 6, 83, 105
wicked problems 138–139
Winehouse, Amy 140–141, 143
Wood, Phil 38
Woolf, Virginia 62
words: power of 48–53; verbalisation in learning 43–47, 54; and Voice 102
Working Identity 29–30
World Bank 2, 93

"yes, and…" 13, 160
Young, Neil 101–102

Zen philosophy 66
Zone of Proximal Development 35

Kolibri 360 GmbH
Ferdinand-Jühlke-Straße 7
99095 Erfurt, Deutschland
produktsicherheit@kolibri360.de